97 ✓

Contemporary German Fiction

The German Library: Volume 99

Volkmar Sander, General Editor

CONTEMPORARY
GERMAN FICTION

Edited by A. Leslie Willson

CONTINUUM · NEW YORK

1996
The Continuum Publishing Company
370 Lexington Avenue
New York, NY 10017

The German Library is published in cooperation
with Deutsches Haus, New York University.
This volume has been supported by Inter Nationes, and
a grant from Stifterverband für die Deutsche Wissenschaft.

Printed in the United States of America

Library of Congress Cataloging-in-Publication Data

Contemporary German fiction / edited by A. Leslie Willson
    p.   cm. — (The German library ; v. 99)
    ISBN 0-8264-0740-4 (alk. paper). — ISBN 0-8264-0741-2 (pbk. :
alk. paper)
    1. German fiction—20th century—Translations into English.
I. Willson, A. Leslie (Amos Leslie), 1923–   . II. Series.
PT1327.C66   1996
833'.91408—dc20   96-3601
                                                                CIP

Acknowledgments will be found on page 243,
which constitutes an extension of the copyright page.

Contents

Introduction

Short narrative as a literary genre has flourished for millennia and has proved to be a viable and enduring form, in recent centuries steadily the favorite of authors and celebrated by readers. The development of the novel, long narrative fiction, followed its shorter sibling and has occupied a large niche in literature. But short narrative endures. Short narrative—from the fable, to folk tale and fairy tale, to idealistic and realistic forms, to the novella (in modern times referred to as short novel or *Erzählung,* long story)—has adapted to changes in literary fashion, has demonstrated its malleability and vitality at the hands of myriad authors, and continues to offer readers a richness and multiplicity of form and content that delight, amuse, awe, and challenge the most intrepid among them.

In a "Perspective" in the second issue of volume 18 of *Dimension* (1989), entitled "Making Corners Visible," Hans Bender, writing as an acknowledged master practitioner of the short story, offers a retrospective of the development of the story in Germany following 1945. Faced with the Nazi despoliation of their language and weary of abhorrent, politically propagandistic themes, German writers took contemporary American short story authors as their models—in thematics, vocabulary choice, and grammatical terseness—and embarked immediately upon a revivification of the story form in German.

The literary Group 47—founded in 1947 by Hans Werner Richter—opened its first meeting with a story by Wolfdietrich Schnurre, "The Burial," which epitomized the new and revived German story: stark, unadorned, shocking, unsentimental. In 1949, a collection of thirty stories in an anthology edited by Wolfgang Weyrauch, *A Thousand Grams,* became a model for authors. Weyrauch demanded "a new start in language, substance, and conception." At the same time, Wolfgang Borchert, with quiet and fascinating short narratives, succeeded in highlighting dread, suffering, and humanistic endurance. The leftover forms of the past were supplanted by radical new trends, as in Heinrich Böll's first novel—in reality a long short narrative—*The Train Was on Time* (1949), which was followed by his many short stories that served as the foundation for his popularity.

The efforts to cleanse and obliterate Nazi disfigurements of short narratives were soon decried in favor of experimental writing (Friederike Mayröcker) and surrealistic prose as in stories by Ilse Aichinger and Marie Luise Kaschnitz. Themes were increased to include criticism of social mores, an element that has flourished with changes in society, including feminism, environmental dangers, and the encroachment of technology that has transformed everyday life. Narrative models were cast aside, and authors finetuned stories in form and content to suit their personalities and their own interests, including fantasy (Christoph Meckel), science fiction (Günter Kunert's "Letter in a Bottle"), a new subjectivity, and interpersonal relationships.

New models of short forms in international literature (Italy and France) were discovered and "multilayered reality" was included. Helmut Heißenbüttel's *Text* became a new model where the familiar "characteristics of the 'story' or 'tale' were negated: theme, event, anecdote, identification were [supplanted by] montage, collage, [and] 'language developed from language.'" Change was in the air. As Walter Höllerer described it in an issue of *Akzente* in 1964, "Description has reached its limits. . . . Description has erected something new, a landscape of consciousness, which is indeed based on perceptivity but which, in addition to the facticity of what can be perceived, also brings the presentation of its uncertainty, changeability, producibility, and fantasy into the picture." Peter Handke's notorious attack on "descriptive literature" at the Group 47 meeting at Princeton University in 1966 injected the demand for change with a sense of desperation, a plea that young writers endorsed and put into practice.

The fact that short narrative form has not been the topic of critical debate in the past decade or two indicates that it has become familiar to authors and readers alike, both of whom are comfortable with the form and approve its variations. Short fiction has become an accepted and welcomed province of writers principally of drama (Peter Weiss) and the long novel (Günter Grass,

Uwe Johnson, Gerhard Köpf, Siegfried Lenz), even of poets (Marie Luise Kaschnitz, Christa Reinig). Stories are not just written on the side; rather, they are an inherent and essential part of the literary life and work of a great number of writers who "make the corners and edges visible," twenty-two of whom are found in the present volume.

Short fiction is something infinite, uncircumscribed, and uninhibited. Even in its finite form as published pages, it contains in itself boundless variety and possibility. It is microscopic and macroscopic, realistic and fantastic, relentlessly honest and deliriously fabulous, bitterly ironic and hilariously ridiculous. It can amuse, horrify, bemuse, and furnish food for thought. It can adjure and caution, demonstrate and suggest, transport and transfix. It entertains and it liberates.

The author of short fiction treads, and the reader follows, on what Gerhard Köpf describes as "the blue path of the possible."

Just a word on the translators represented in this volume: they range from the professional to the apprentice, and in each instance their efforts to transmit the essence of the authors they have translated should be acknowledged and applauded. They are the best of their kind and, I hope, will accept the gratitude this editor has for them.

A. L. W.

Ilse Aichinger

The Bound Man

Sunlight on his face woke him, but made him shut his eyes again;
it streamed unhindered down the slope, collected itself into rivulets,
attracted swarms of flies, which flew low over his forehead, circled,
sought to land, and were overtaken by fresh swarms. When he
tried to whisk them away, he discovered that he was bound. A thin
rope cut into his arms. He dropped them, opened his eyes again,
and looked down at himself. His legs were tied all the way up
to his thighs; a single length of rope was tied around his ankles,
crisscrossed up his legs, and encircled his hips, his chest, and his
arms. He could not see where it was knotted. He showed no sign
of fear or hurry, though he thought he was unable to move, until
he discovered that the rope allowed his legs some free play and
that around his body it was almost loose. His arms were tied to
each other, but not to his body, and had some free play too. This
made him smile, and it occurred to him that perhaps children had
been playing a practical joke on him.

He tried to feel for his knife, but again the rope cut softly into
his flesh. He tried again, more cautiously this time, but his pocket
was empty. Not only his knife, but the little money that he had on
him, as well as his coat, were missing. His shoes had been pulled
from his feet and taken too. When he moistened his lips he tasted
blood, which had flowed from his temples down his cheeks, his
chin, his neck, and under his shirt. His eyes ached; if he kept them
open for long he saw reddish stripes in the *sky*.

He decided to stand up. He drew his knees up as far as he could,
rested his hands on the fresh grass, and jerked himself to his feet.

An elder branch in bloom stroked his cheeks, the sun dazzled him, and the rope cut into his flesh. He collapsed to the ground again, half out of his mind with pain, and then tried again. He went on trying until the blood started flowing from his hidden weals. Then he lay still again for a long while and let the sun and the flies do what they liked.

When he awoke for the second time the elder bush had cast its shadow over him, and the coolness stored in it was pouring from between its branches. He must have been hit on the head. Then they must have laid him down, just as mothers lay their babies behind bushes carefully when they go to work in the fields.

His chances all lay in the amount of free play allowed him by the rope. He dug his elbows into the ground and tested it. As soon as the rope tautened he stopped and tried again more cautiously. If he had been able to reach the branches over his head, he could have used them to drag himself to his feet, but he could not reach them. He laid his head back on the grass, rolled over, and struggled to his knees. He tested the ground with his toes, and then managed to stand up almost without effort.

A few paces away lay the path across the plateau, and in the grass were wild pinks and thistles in bloom. He tried to lift his foot to avoid trampling on them, but the rope around his ankles prevented him. He looked down at himself.

The rope was knotted at his ankles and ran from one to the other in a kind of playful pattern. He carefully bent and tried to loosen it, but, loose though it seemed to be, he could not make it any looser. To avoid treading on the thistles with his bare feet he hopped over them like a bird.

The cracking of a twig made him stop. Someone in the vicinity was suppressing laughter with difficulty. He was alarmed by the thought that he was—as always—in no position to defend himself. He hopped on until he reached the path. Bright fields stretched far below. He could see no sign of the nearest village, and if he could move no faster than this, night would fall before he reached it.

He tried walking, and discovered that he could put one foot before another if he lifted each foot a definite distance from the ground and then put it down again before the rope tautened. In the same way he could actually swing his arms.

After the first steps he fell. He fell right across the path and made the dust fly. He expected this to be a sign for the long-suppressed laughter to break out, but all remained quiet. He was alone. As soon as the dust had settled he got up and went on. He looked down and watched the rope slacken, grow taut, and then slacken again.

When the first fireflies rose up, he managed to look up. He felt in control of himself again, and his impatience to reach the nearest village faded.

Hunger made him lightheaded, and he seemed to be going so fast that not even a motorcycle could have overtaken him; alternatively, he felt as if he were standing still and that the earth was rushing at him like a river flowing at a man swimming against the stream. The stream carried branches, that had been bent southward by the north wind, stunted young trees, and patches of grass with bright, long-stalked flowers. It ended by submerging the bushes and the young trees, leaving only the sky and the man above water level. The moon had risen and illuminated the bare, curved summit of the plateau, the path, which was overgrown with young grass, the bound man making his way along it with quick, measured-steps, and two hares, which ran across the hill just in front of him and vanished down the slope. Though the nights were still cool at this time of the year, before midnight the bound man lay down at the edge of the escarpment and went to sleep.

In the light of morning the animal tamer who was camping with his circus on the meadow outside the village saw the bound man coming down the path, gazing thoughtfully at the ground. The bound man stopped and bent down. He held out one arm to help keep his balance and with the other picked up an empty wine bottle. Then he straightened himself and stood erect again. He moved slowly, to avoid being cut by the rope, but to the circus proprietor what he did suggested the voluntary limitations of an enormous swiftness of movement. He was enchanted by his extraordinary gracefulness, and while the bound man looked about for a stone on which to break the bottle, so that he could use the splintered neck to cut the rope, the animal tamer approached him across the meadow. Not even the first leaps of a young panther had filled him with such delight.

"Ladies and gentlemen, the bound man!" His very first movements let loose a storm of applause, which out of sheer excitement caused the blood to rush to the cheeks of the animal tamer standing at the edge of the arena. The bound man rose to his feet. His surprise whenever he did this was like that of a four-footed animal that has managed to stand on its hind legs. He knelt, stood up, jumped, and turned cartwheels. The spectators found it as astonishing as if they had seen a bird that voluntarily remained earthbound and confined itself to hopping.

The bound man became an enormous draw. His absurd steps and little jumps, his elementary exercises in movement, made the rope dancer superfluous. His fame grew from village to village, but the motions he went through were few and always the same; they were really quite ordinary motions, which he had continually to practice in the daytime in the half-dark tent in order to maintain his shackled agility. In that he remained entirely within the limits set by his rope he was free of it, it did not confine him but gave him wings and endowed his leaps and jumps with purpose; just as the flights of birds of passage have purpose when they take wing in the warmth of summer and hesitantly make small circles in the sky.

All the children of the neighborhood started playing the game of "bound man." They tied one another up, and one day the circus people found a little girl lying in a ditch with a cord tied around her neck so that she could hardly breathe. They released her, and at the end of the performance that night the bound man spoke to the spectators. He declared briefly that there was no sense in being tied up in such a way that you could not jump. After that he was regarded as a comedian.

Grass and sunlight, tent pegs driven into the ground and then pulled up again, and on to the next village. "Ladies and gentlemen, the bound man!" The summer mounted toward its climax. It bent its face deeper over the fish ponds in the hollows, taking delight in its dark reflection, skimmed the surface of the rivers, and made the plain into what it was. Everyone who could walk went to see the bound man.

Many wanted a close-up view of how he was bound. So the circus proprietor announced after each performance that anyone who wanted to satisfy himself that the knots were real and the rope not made of rubber was at liberty to do so. The bound man generally waited for the crowd in the area outside the tent. He laughed or remained serious and held out his arms for inspection. Many took the opportunity to look him in the face, others gravely tested the rope, tried the knots on his ankles, and wanted to know exactly how the lengths compared with the length of his limbs. They asked him how he had come to be tied up like that, and he answered patiently, always saying the same thing. Yes, he had been tied up, he said, and when he awoke he found that he had been robbed as well. Those who had done it must have been pressed for time, because they had tied him up somewhat too loosely for someone who was not supposed to be able to move and somewhat too tightly for someone who was expected to be able to move. But he did move, people pointed out. Yes, he replied, what else could he do?

Before he went to bed he always sat for a time in front of the fire. When the circus proprietor asked him why he didn't make up a better story he always answered that he hadn't made up that one, and blushed. He preferred staying in the shade.

The difference between him and the other performers was that when the show was over he did not take off his rope. The result was that every movement that he made was worth seeing, and the villagers used to hang about the camp for hours, just for the sake of seeing him get up from in front of the fire and roll himself in his blanket. Sometimes the sky was beginning to lighten when he saw their shadows disappear.

The circus proprietor often remarked that there was no reason why he should not be untied after the evening performance and tied up again next day. He pointed out that the rope dancers, for instance, did not stay on their rope overnight. But no one took the idea of untying him seriously.

For the bound man's fame rested on the fact that he was always bound, that whenever he washed himself he had to wash his clothes too and vice versa, and that his only way of doing so was to jump in the river just as he was every morning when the sun came out, and that he had to be careful not to go too far out for fear of being carried away by the stream.

The proprietor was well aware that, when it came down to it, what protected the bound man from the jealousy of the other performers was his helplessness; perhaps he deliberately left them the pleasure of watching him groping painfully from stone to stone on the river bank with his wet clothing clinging to him. When the proprietor's wife pointed out that even the best clothes would not stand up indefinitely to such treatment (and the bound man's clothes were by no means the best), he replied curtly that it was not going to last forever. That was his answer to all objections—it was for the summer season only. But when he said this he was not being serious; he was talking like a gambler who has no intention of giving up his vice. In reality he would have been prepared cheerfully to sacrifice his lions and his rope dancers for the bound man.

He proved this on the night when the rope dancers jumped over the fire. Afterward he was convinced that they did it not because it was midsummer's day but because of the bound man, who as usual was lying and watching them with that peculiar smile that might have been real or might have been only the effect of the glow on his face. In any case no one knew anything about him because he never talked about anything that had happened to him before the day he emerged from the wood.

But that evening two of the performers suddenly picked him up by the arms and legs, carried him to the edge of the fire, and started playfully swinging him to and fro, while two others held out their arms to catch him on the other side. In the end they tossed him, but too short. The two men on the other side drew back—they explained afterward that they did so the better to take the shock. The result was that the bound man landed at the very edge of the flames and would have caught fire if the circus proprietor had not seized his arms and quickly dragged him away to save the rope, which was starting to get singed. He was certain that the object had been to burn the rope. He sacked the four men on the spot.

A few nights later the proprietor's wife was awakened by the sound of footsteps on the grass and went outside just in time to prevent the clown from playing his last practical joke. He was carrying a pair of scissors. When he was asked for an explanation he insisted that he had had no intention of taking the bound man's life but only wanted to cut his rope because he felt sorry for him. He was sacked too.

These antics amused the bound man because he could have freed himself it he had wanted to whenever he liked, but perhaps he wanted to learn a few new jumps first. The children's rhyme: "We travel with the circus, we travel with the circus" sometimes occurred to him while he lay awake at night. He could hear the voices of spectators on the opposite bank who had been driven too far downstream on the way home. He could see the river gleaming in the moonlight, and the young shoots growing out of the thick tops of the willow trees, and did not think about autumn yet.

The circus proprietor dreaded the danger that sleep involved for the bound man. Not so much because attempts were continually made to release him while he slept. The chief culprits were sacked rope dancers, or children who were bribed for the purpose. Measures could be taken to safeguard against these. A much bigger danger was the bound man himself. In his dreams he forgot his rope and was surprised by it when he woke in the darkness of morning. He would angrily try to get up but lose his balance and fall back again. The previous evening's applause was forgotten, sleep was still too near, his head and neck too free. He was just the opposite of a hanged man—his neck was the only part of him that was free. You had to make sure that at such moments no knife was within his reach. In the early hours of the morning the circus proprietor sometimes sent his wife to see whether the bound man was all right. If he was asleep she would bend over him and feel the rope. It had grown stiff from dirt and damp. She would test the amount of free play it allowed him and touch his tender wrists and ankles.

The most varied rumors soon circulated about the bound man. Some said he had tied himself up and invented the story of having been robbed, and toward the end of the summer that was the general opinion. Others maintained that he had been tied up at his own request, perhaps in league with the circus proprietor. The hesitant way in which he told his story, his habit of breaking off when the talk got around to the attack on him, contributed greatly to these rumors. Those who still believed in the robbery-with-violence story were laughed at. Nobody knew what difficulties the circus proprietor had in keeping the bound man, and how often he said he had had enough and wanted to clear out, for too much of the summer had passed.

Later, however, he stopped talking about clearing out. When the proprietor's wife brought him his food by the river and asked him how long he proposed to remain with them, he did not answer. She thought he had got used not to being tied up, but to remembering every moment that he was tied up—the only thing that anyone in his position could get used to. She asked him whether he did not think it ridiculous to be tied up all the time, but he answered that he did not. Such a variety of people—clowns, freaks, and comics, to say nothing of elephants and tigers—traveled with circuses that he did not see why a bound man should not travel with a circus too. He told her about the movements he was practicing, the new ones he had discovered, and about a new trick that had occurred to him while he was whisking flies from the animals' eyes. He described to her how he always anticipated the effect of the rope and always restrained his movements in such a way as to prevent it from ever tautening; and she knew that there were days when he was hardly aware of the rope, when he jumped down from the wagon and slapped the flanks of the horses in the morning as if he were moving in a dream. She watched him vault over the bars almost without touching them, and saw the sun on his face, and he told her that sometimes he felt as if he were not tied up at all. She answered that if he were prepared to be untied, there would never be any need for him to feel tied up. He agreed that he could be untied whenever he felt like it.

The woman ended by not knowing whether she was more concerned with the man or with the rope that tied him. She told him that he could go on traveling with the circus without his rope, but she did not believe it. For what would be the point of his antics without his rope, and what would he amount to without it? Without his rope he would leave them, and the happy days would be over. She would no longer be able to sit beside him on the stones by the river without arousing suspicion, and she knew that his continued presence, and her conversations with him on bright evenings when the rope was the only subject, depended on it. Whenever she agreed that the rope had its advantages, he would start talking about how troublesome it was, and whenever he started talking about its advantages, she would urge him to get rid of it. All this seemed as endless as the summer itself.

At other times she was worried at the thought that she was herself hastening the end by her talk. Sometimes she would get up in the middle of the night and run across the grass to where he slept. She wanted to shake him, wake him up, and ask him to keep the rope. But then she would see him lying there; he had thrown off his blanket, and there he lay like a corpse, with his legs outstretched and his arms close together, with the rope tied around them. His clothes had suffered from the heat and the water, but the rope had grown no thinner. She felt that he would go on traveling with the circus until the flesh fell from him and exposed the joints. Next morning she would plead with him more ardently than ever to get rid of his rope.

The increasing coolness of the weather gave her hope.

Autumn was coming, and he would not be able to go·on jumping into the river with his clothes on much longer. But the thought of losing his rope, about which he had felt indifferent earlier in the season, now depressed him.

The songs of the harvesters filled him with foreboding. "Summer has gone, summer has gone." But he realized that soon he would have to change his clothes, and he was certain that when he had been untied it would be impossible to tie him up again in exactly the same way. About this time the proprietor started talking about traveling south that year.

The heat changed without transition into still, dry cold, and the fire was kept going all day long. When the bound man jumped down from the wagon he felt the coldness of the grass under his feet. The tips of the blades were covered with frost. The horses dreamed on their feet and the wild animals, crouching to leap even in their sleep, seemed to be collecting gloom under their skins which would break out later.

On one of these days a young wolf escaped. The circus proprietor kept quiet about it, to avoid spreading alarm, but the wolf soon started raiding cattle in the neighborhood. People at first believed that the wolf had been driven to these parts by the prospect of a severe winter, but the circus soon became suspect. The proprietor could not conceal the loss of the animal from his own employees, so the truth was bound to come out before long. The circus people offered the burgomasters of the neighboring villages their aid in tracking down the beast, but all their efforts were in vain. Eventually the circus was openly blamed for the damage and the danger, and spectators stayed away.

The bound man went on performing before half-empty seats without losing anything of his amazing freedom of movement. During the day he wandered among the surrounding hills under the thin-beaten silver of the autumn sky, and, whenever he could, lay down where the sun shone longest. Soon he found a place which the twilight reached last of all, and when at last it reached him he got up most unwillingly from the withered grass. In coming down the hill he had to pass through a little wood on its southern slope, and one evening he saw the gleam of two little green lights. He knew that they came from no church window, and was not for a moment under any illusion about what they were.

He stopped. The animal came toward him through the thinning foliage. He could make out its shape, the slant of its neck, its tail which swept the ground, and its lowered head. If he had not been bound, perhaps he would have tried to run away, but as it was he did not even feel fear. He stood calmly with dangling arms and looked down at the wolf's bristling coat under which the muscles played like his own underneath the rope. He thought the evening wind was still between him and the wolf when the beast sprang. The man took care to obey his rope.

Moving with the deliberate care that he had so often put to the test, he seized the wolf by the throat. Tenderness for a fellow creature arose in him, tenderness for the upright being concealed in the four-footed. In a movement that resembled the dive of a great bird (he felt a sudden awareness that flying would be possible only if one were tied up in a special way) he flung himself at the animal and brought it to the ground. He felt a slight elation at having lost the fatal advantage of free limbs which causes men to be worsted.

The freedom he enjoyed in this struggle was having to adapt every movement of his limbs to the rope that tied him—the freedom of panthers, wolves, and the wild flowers that sway in the evening breeze. He ended up lying obliquely down the slope, clasping the animal's hind legs between his own bare feet and its head between his hands. He felt the gentleness of the faded foliage stroking the backs of his hands, and he felt his own grip almost effortlessly reaching its maximum, and he felt too how he was in no way hampered by the rope.

As he left the wood light rain began to fall and obscured the setting sun. He stopped for a while under the trees at the edge of the wood. Behind the thin veil, which was thickened from moment to moment by gusts of wind, down below he saw the camp and the river, the fields and meadows where the cattle grazed, and the places where they crossed. Perhaps he would travel south with the circus after all. He laughed softly. It was against all reason. Even if he continued to put up with the sores that covered his joints and opened and bled when he made certain movements, his clothes would not stand up much longer to the friction of the rope.

The circus proprietor's wife tried to persuade her husband to announce the death of the wolf without mentioning that it had been killed by the bound man. She said that even at the time of his greatest popularity people would have refused to believe him capable of it, and in their present angry mood, with the nights getting cooler, they would be more incredulous than ever. The wolf had attacked a group of children at play that day, and nobody would believe that it had really been killed; for the circus proprietor had many wolves and it was easy enough for him to hang a skin on the rail and give a free show. But he was not to be dissuaded. He thought that the announcement of the bound man's act would revive the triumphs of the summer.

That evening the bound man's movements were uncertain. He stumbled in one of his jumps and fell. Before he managed to get up he heard some low whistles and catcalls, rather like birds calling at dawn. He tried to get up too quickly, as he had done once or twice on awakening during the summer, with the result that he tautened the rope and fell back again. He lay still to regain his calm and listened to the boos and catcalls growing into an uproar. "Well, bound man, and how did you kill the wolf?" they shouted, and: "Are you the man who killed the wolf?" If he had been one of them, he would not have believed it himself. He thought they had a perfect right to be angry: a circus at this time of year, a bound man, an escaped wolf, and all ending up with this. Some groups of spectators started arguing with others, but the greater part of the audience thought the whole thing a bad joke. By the time he had got to his feet there was such a hubbub that he was barely able to make out individual words.

He saw people surging up all around him, like faded leaves raised by a whirlwind in a circular valley at the center of which all was yet still. He thought of the golden sunsets of the last few days; and the sepulchral light which lay over the blight of all that he had built up during many nights, the gold frame which the pious hang around dark, old pictures, this sudden collapse of everything, filled him with anger.

They wanted him to repeat his battle with the wolf. He said that such a thing had no place in a circus performance, and the proprietor declared that he did not keep animals to have them slaughtered in front of an audience. But the mob stormed the ring and pressed toward the cages. The proprietor's wife made her way between the seats to the exit and managed to get around to the cages from the other side. She pushed aside the attendant whom the crowd had forced to open a cage door, but the spectators dragged her back and prevented the door from being shut.

"Aren't you the woman who used to lie with him by the river all summer?" they called out. "How does he hold you in his arms?" She shouted back at them that they needn't believe in the bound man if they didn't want to, they had never deserved him. Painted clowns were good enough for them.

The bound man felt as if the bursts of laughter were what he had been expecting ever since early May. What had smelled so sweet all through the summer now stank. But, if they insisted, he was ready to take on all the animals in the circus this very night. He had never felt so much at one with his rope.

Gently he pushed the woman in his way aside. Perhaps he would travel south with them after all. He stood in the open doorway of the cage, and he saw the wolf, a strong young animal, rise to its feet, and he heard the proprietor grumbling again about the loss of his exhibit. He clapped his hands to attract the animal's attention, and when it was near enough he turned to slam the cage door. He looked the woman in the face. Suddenly he remembered the proprietor's warning to suspect of murderous intentions anyone near him who had a sharp instrument in his hand. At the same moment he felt the blade at his wrists, as cool as the water of the river in autumn, which during the last few weeks he had barely been able to stand. The rope curled up in a tangle beside him while he struggled free. He pushed the woman back, but there was no point in anything he did now. Had he been insufficiently on his guard against those who wanted to release him, against the sympathy in which they wanted to lull him? Had he lain too long on the river bank? If she had cut the cord at any other moment, it would have been better than this.

He stood in the middle of the cage and rid himself of the rope like a snake discarding its skin. It amused him to see the spectators shrinking back. Did they realize that he had no choice now? Or that fighting the wolf now would prove nothing whatever? At the same time he felt all his blood rush to his feet. He felt suddenly weak.

The rope, which fell at its feet like a snare, angered the wolf more than the entry of a stranger into its cage. It crouched to spring. The man reeled and grabbed the pistol that hung ready at the side of the cage. Then, before anyone could stop him, he shot the wolf between the eyes. The animal reared and touched him in falling.

On the way to the river he heard the footsteps of his pursuers—spectators, the rope dancers, the circus proprietor, and the proprietor's wife, who persisted in the chase longer than anyone else. He hid in a clump of bushes and watched them hurrying past, and later on streaming in the opposite direction back to the camp. The moon shone on the meadow; in that light its color was both of growth and of death.

When he came to the river his anger died away. In the morning twilight it seemed to him as if lumps of ice were floating in the water, and as if snow had fallen yonder in the meadows, obliterating memory.

Translated by Eric Mosbacher

Jurek Becker

End of the Line

Man, yesterday I really liked her. I wish I understood myself. All of this agonizing, and I still can't make sense of it. Not that I would have suddenly lost interest in her, that's out of the question; but something is basically different. And it can't possibly be because she came over to my place last night, even though we have known each other only a couple of days. That's what I wanted, more than anything else. At first she did put on a little show of modesty.

The blue lamp is still on, and here it is, the middle of the day. Fine, so they all put on airs, nothing more needs to be said about that. But she went about it in a very unusual way. I don't even know if you could really call her behavior an act. She merely had to overcome some doubts, which she did, without a big fuss.

I won't make a long story of it, but it is true that I had convinced myself that this time was going to be something special. Maybe it is something unique; but even if it is, I'll still need a good long while to figure it out. I had told myself a thousand times that it wouldn't happen again, that sooner or later you have to grow up and settle down a little, and such things people always say. And so, as best I could, I indulged in what I call waiting it out. It's better you don't ask me exactly what I was waiting for, I could only come up with hazy notions. But something had to happen, this extraordinary event just had to take place, I mean, a girl showing up who was so much different from all the others. How, nobody knows, just different. She was bound to be as good-looking as my brother's wife, and she'd have to be as understanding as my mother has been on five or six occasions, and her way of handling people could be compared to Doris Day's, right now I've forgotten the title of the movie. And that would be it, the end of the line, so I thought.

And now, here I am, seeing myself almost like a sailboat that has got a good wind at the start, but hits a lull half-way out, and is just drifting around. Nobody can expect me to fool myself, make myself believe that I've ended up exactly where I always wanted to be. I'd give anything, if right now everything about her would be as it was last night, when I was looking at her like a half-starved puppy might look at a juicy, unreachable steak. On purpose I dispensed with the whole circus that I've always put on for similar occasions, since I was telling myself: This won't be one of those. There wasn't supposed to be a hint of routine.

Those select record albums that had never failed before were left right in the cabinet. We just listened to whatever was on the radio. As soon as we stepped into my room, I switched on the ceiling light, not even glancing at the floor lamp with the blue shade, which a few weeks ago would have struck me as sheer stupidity. We sat politely at the table, she in the armchair, I on the sofa, and we talked for a while about the lousy play we'd just seen. Her views were very intelligent, but of course I was already aware of that, she was a bright young woman. After an hour or so I discovered in the cupboard half a bottle of wine, left over from my last birthday. We finished it, but I can swear there was no ulterior motive. The longer I looked at her, the better I liked her. I would've bet my life it was going to be that way forever.

It did occur to me how crude and blunt I'd always been whenever someone else was sitting at the table. But those were such different situations. From the start everything was somehow transparent, the other girl always knew why she'd come along, and I knew that she knew. It was a game played with all our cards on the table. Yet in the theater last night I didn't even dare to hold her hand.

An uncle on my mother's side had told me once that true love makes you shy, and applied to both of us that seemed to be positive proof I was nearing the end of the line in a hurry. I was so inhibited I was getting afraid of standing there like some idiot in her eyes. I didn't want to do anything wrong, for God's sake. I kept on thinking that I didn't want to do anything wrong. It went so far that finally I didn't know what was happening. I couldn't even come up with the next word or gesture, the right ones. Then suddenly I felt certain it'd probably be better if it didn't happen right then. Why, I don't know even, but now I tell myself that I considered it utterly impossible that it could happen today. And so in these straits I just took as undeniable wisdom the saying, something to the effect that all good things take a long, long time.

She asked if anything was bothering me, and if so, I really ought to tell her. I seemed so preoccupied, so entirely different than usual, she said. Obviously I couldn't tell her what was going on inside my poor head, but I couldn't just sit silently forever, so I told her I liked her very much. She was glad about that. Now, she didn't say, "Oh, I'm so glad," or anything of the kind, and her whole face didn't brighten up. She just looked at me with those eyes, one of which is just a little lighter than the other, until I knew she was glad. At that point most of the others would have said, "Oh, you're just saying that." Or they would have asked, "Is that really true?" She said nothing at all; actually she's a very quiet girl.

As soon as we had sipped the last of our wine, she got up from her chair, went over to the floor lamp with the blue shade, switched it on, turned off the ceiling light, and sat down on the sofa next to me. My heart nearly stopped. At that instant I realized that all of my deliberations about putting things off until later, just now, about good things taking a lot of time—I knew right then all of that was screwed-up nonsense. Here she was, acting much like Esmeralda had acted from time immemorial in my dreams, like that other girl whom I've known for an eternity, but who had just acquired through her a real name and a face. It is simply incredible what a difference it makes whether you switch on the blue lamp yourself, or someone else does.

When I put my hand on her shoulder, it trembled. My hand, I mean. Someone was reading the evening news on the radio. I've never heard anything that could have left me more indifferent. I even forgot to kiss her, I was so idiotically content. And you can believe it or not, I'd give anything if it were possible to preserve such a moment. Of course, I realize that you can't spend your entire life sitting in blue light on a sofa, gazing at one another, that's quite out of the question. But I don't mean that either. I mean, if somehow you could save this feeling, this indefinable peace of mind.

When I awoke next to her this morning, it took me a while to get my bearings. Her head was resting on my arm, and my arm had gone to sleep, that's probably what woke me. I pulled my arm carefully away, without waking her, and got up to get a drink of water, my tongue always feels like leather in the morning. It was still very early, and I lay down again and tried to go back to sleep. But it was no use. The floor lamp was still on, as I discovered quite by accident, for the room was as bright as day. In our excitement last night we had forgotten to lower the venetian blind.

I've had plenty of time to look at her closely. Her mouth was slightly open, even though she was breathing through her nose. Now, don't think that I would have suddenly started finding some fault with her, there wasn't any bump on her nose that I might have overlooked earlier. No rash or pimples on her skin, it was as smooth and clear as milk or new snow. If anything, she was almost more beautiful than yesterday. One of her hands was resting on top of the covers, palm up, fingers slightly curled. It looked like a hand that was about to catch some small object. She was sleeping so soundly and peacefully that anyone could be envious. I thought of how beautiful it was with her yesterday, in the blue light, and for a few seconds I thought I would have to wake her. I even had my hand on her arm, but I drew it back and fell asleep again.

Translated by Brian L. Harris

Hans Bender

The Wolves Are Coming Back

The town had been called Krasno Sheri since the Revolution. It lay twenty kilometers from the nearest city in a great forest that was intersected from east to west by a highway.

The starost of Krasno Sheri had gone to get seven prisoners from the camp in the city. He rode in his two-wheeled cart, a sweat-stained horse on the shaft. Between his knees he had a rifle with a long barrel and a rusty sight. In a box behind the seat lay the prisoners' supply sack full of bread, salt, corn meal, onions, and dried fish.

The prisoners walked to the right and the left on the strip between the wheels and the edge of the fields. When the road ended at the first woods, the starost got down. He fastened the reins to the back of the seat and walked along behind the prisoners.

They kept moving at the horse's gait. All prisoners move slowly. They lowered their heads; only one of them held his head up, turning it here and there, curious, suspicious.

"I have a rifle," the starost thought. "They have no rifle. My rifle, of course, is not—"

The prisoner stopped. He let the three walking behind him pass by until the starost was abreast of him.

"Good day," said the prisoner.

Since the First War the starost had not seen any Germans. These Germans were different from the Germans then. He saw that the prisoner was young. He had eyes the color of bright blue water.

"Are there wolves in the woods?" the prisoner asked.

"Wolves?" The starost thought the question over. "Yes, there were wolves. Now there are no wolves here anymore. You drove them away with your war. The wolves ran off to Siberia. At one time the woods were alive with wolves, and no one would have dared to go along this path alone in winter. I saw the last wolves in the first winter of the war when the guns of Vishni Volotshok thundered overhead."

"The war has been over for five months," said the prisoner. "The wolves could have come back long ago."

"Let them stay where they are," said the starost. "In Siberia. Siberia, that's where they belong."

The prisoners and the starost walked through the woods until evening. Often there was a break in the woods, a meadow lay in between, a strip of uncultivated land with dry underbrush, then the woods began again, a tangled, disorderly woods with low deformed trees and prolific brushwood.

In Krasno Sheri the people came out of their houses and stood dark before their doors. The starost distributed the prisoners. To each house he gave one, and the young one who had asked about the wolves and could speak Russian he took to his own house.

An oil lamp stood on the table. In its light a boy and a girl were sitting, looking with round eyes at the door where the prisoner waited on the threshold.

A woman came through the door to the next room.

"His name is Maxim," said the starost as he took off his fur coat. The prisoner went over to the children at the table. Books lay open before them with handwritten letters and photographs.

"And what are your names?" the prisoner asked.

The boy got up quickly and shoved his book across the table so that it fell to the floor. He went to the corner of the room and turned his back to the prisoner. The girl looked up and smiled.

"What is your name?"

"Julia," said the girl.

"Julia, a pretty name," said the prisoner.

"His name is Nikolai," said the girl.

The woman put bread on the table and placed two bowls of soup next to it. The starost sat down, the prisoner sat down. They blew on their spoons and ate. The woman remained standing by the stove and now and then said something about work, food, the neighbors, the weather.

The boy picked up his book, sat down at the corner of the table, and began to read to himself in an undertone: "Hail to the father of all the children, Vladimir Ilyich Lenin!—Hail to the father of Little Pioneers, Josef Vissarionovich Stalin!"

Above the boy's head the gold paper that framed the angels of the Trinity glittered.

In the morning the prisoners, the collective farmers, and the girls went into the fields. The starost broke up the glass-hard clods with horse and plow. The water in the crevices was frozen. The film of ice cracked. The potatoes were cold. The girls and the prisoners beat their hands against their armpits, and their breath frosted before their mouths.

The sun rose high over the woods, slid into the blue-green pure silk sky that stretched far over the horizon. Crows scrawled on it with their tattered Cyrillic script.

The village lay in the middle of open fields, encompassed all around by woods. The road to the east was a slim trail passing through them. Children were walking along the road, small and distant, but their voices resounded close by like cups being placed upon a tray.

"They are going to school," a woman said to the young prisoner. "On the other side of the woods is Rossonov. Rossonov is bigger than Krasno Sheri."

"Are Julie and Nikolai with them?" asked the prisoner.

"Yes, they are with them," the woman said.

The prisoner waved. The children waved. They swung their bundles of books. The children wore fur hats and quilted jackets. There was no way to distinguish among them which was Julia and which was Nikolai. They all waved.

When the children came back along the road from over there, the sun was descending into the woods in the west. A big field had been harvested. The sacks and baskets had been carted away, and all those who had worked were returning, weary, with aching backs and cold faces, in anticipation of a room, a fire, and hot soup.

The children again were sitting at the table behind their open books.

Julia said: "Maxim, we saw a wolf track!"

"What did you see?" the starost asked.

"We saw a wolf track," Julia said.

"Who saw it?"

"First Spiridion saw it, then Katarina, then I saw it, then Nikolai."

"I saw it before you did," said Nikolai.

"A rabbit track is what you saw," said the starost.

"No, it was bigger," said Julia. "Real deep holes, big as apples, and in front claws had pressed into the earth."

"What were the tracks like, Nikolai?"

"Like Julia said. Like apples. And claws, too."

"Nonsense," said the starost. "The wolves are in Siberia.—Now, let us eat."

Before the last field was harvested, snow fell. The plow was stuck fast in the frozen earth, and the prisoners sat with the people where they were staying, lost in gloomy thought. The children were at school. The starost and his wife were sitting at the table. The prisoner was standing at the window, looking at the field.

The starost said, "If it stays this cold, tomorrow we will make ssamogonka. What do you think of that, Maxim?"

"Why not?"

"Good, we'll make ssamogonka tomorrow," said the starost.

"I don't want any," said his wife.

"You don't need to drink any," said the starost. "Maxim and I will enjoy it that much more."

Suddenly, across from the window on a hill an animal was standing, a thin, long-legged animal with a large head and slanting eyes, resembling a dog, but not a dog.

"There!"

In the exclamation of the prisoner there was so much fear and dread that the starost and his wife came quickly to the window and barely caught a glimpse of the animal as it turned and disappeared in the whirling snow.

"Yes, it is a wolf. That's the way they look. The children were right," said the starost.

"And the children are on the way!" the woman cried out.

"The wolf is here, and the children are there," said the starost. But it was unconvincing.

"You have a rifle! Why don't we go out?" said the prisoner.

"My rifle—"

"It's not loaded," said the woman.

The starost uttered a vulgar curse.

"I have no ammunition, Maxim," said the starost. "They didn't give me any in the city. Not at the depot and not at the camp. I didn't want you prisoners to know it."

"Then we'll take an ax, a hatchet, a scythe, or sticks."

"You don't know the wolves, Maxim. But if you want to come along—"

They walked on the road to the east, and when they came to the summit, they noticed that they had not put on their coats.

The starost breathed heavily. The flakes of snow hung on his eyebrows, his beard. An old man.

"The children should have been here long ago," he said.

They went on. It was quiet, with only the crunch of the snow. From the distance they heard the voices of the children.

The starost called: "Julia!—Nikolai!"

The prisoner called: "Julia!—Nikolai!"

Then the children called, too.

The starost and the prisoner walked faster, the children walked faster. Like chickens when the dog is barking among them, they fluttered between the men, Julia, Nikolai, Katarina, Ludmilla, Sina, Stepan, Alexander, Ivan, Nikita, and Spiridion, ten children in fur hats and quilted jackets, bundles of books in their stiff fingers.

They all talked at once about wolves in the woods, about snapping sticks, howling, and a network of tracks in the freshly fallen snow.

While they were standing on the road talking, the wolves arrived. They saw their eyes first, dangerous, cheerless lights in the curtain of snow. Their heads were drawn forward, their ears stiff, a wreath of bristling hair around their necks, shaggy cement-gray bodies with bushy tails. Like a wedge they burst from the underbrush over the fields north of the road.

The children swallowed their last words and clung together behind the men. The starost held the ax high, the prisoner held the scythe high. Their scalps tightened and their thoughts blurred.

The wolves ran past along the road, a mute, surging pack. Row upon row, back next to back, silently, on their long legs. Surely beyond this pack there were other packs lost to view in the whirl of snow. Many animals went past so closely that their ribs were visible, bones, muscles, sinews under their mangy coats, and their tongues that hung long out of their mouths. Hunger drove them, hunger blinded them to the prey next to their trail.

The darkness grew, and still there was no end to the army of wolves. How long did they pass by? How many were there? For hours. All the wolves of Siberia.

The night enclosed the starost, the prisoner, and the children. For a long time they did not dare to relax, to move, to speak.

The starost was the first to speak. He said: "The wolves are coming back. They've caught the scent of peace."

Translated by Jeanne R. Willson

Peter Bichsel

There Is No Such Place as America

I have the story of a man who tells stories. I have told him repeatedly that I don't believe his stories.

"You're lying," I said, "you're fibbing, you're making things up,
you're pulling my leg."

That didn't impress him. He continued unperturbed, and when
I called out: "You liar, you fibber, you yarnspinner, you legpuller!"
he gazed at me for a long time, shook his head, smiled sadly, and
then said so softly that I almost felt ashamed of myself: "There is
no such place as America."

Just to comfort him, I promised to write down his story.

It begins five centuries ago at the court of a king, the King of Spain.
A palace, silk and velvet, gold, silver, beads, coronets, candles,
manservants, and maidservants; couriers who at dawn run one
another's bellies through with swords, who the night before have
chucked the challenging glove at one another's feet. On the turret
watchmen who blow fanfares. And messengers who leap from their
horses, and messengers who throw themselves onto the saddle,
friends of the king and false friends, beautiful and dangerous
women, and wine, and all around the place people who couldn't
think of anything better than to pay for all that.

But the king too couldn't think of anything better than to live
like that, and however one lives, whether in great style or in pov-
erty, whether in Madrid, Barcelona, or anywhere, in the end it's
the same daily routine, and one gets bored with it. People who live

anywhere, for example, imagine that Barcelona is a fine place, and the people of Barcelona want to travel to Anywhere.

The poor imagine that it would be fine to live like a king, and they suffer because the king thinks that being poor is the right thing for the poor.

In the morning the king gets up, at night the king goes to bed, and all day long he is bored with his cares, with his servants, his gold, silver, velvet, his silk, and he's bored with his candles. His bed is a splendid one, but there isn't much you can do in it except sleep.

The servants bow low to him in the morning, as low one morning as the next, the king is used to it and doesn't even notice. Someone gives him the fork, someone shoves his chair in, and people who speak to him call him Your Majesty, with a lot of other fine phrases added, and that's all.

Never does anyone say to him: "You idiot, you nitwit," and everything they tell him today they've already told him yesterday.

That's how it is. And that's why kings keep court fools.

They're allowed to do what they like, and say what they like, to make the king laugh, and when he can't laugh at them anymore he has them executed or something like that.

Thus he once had a fool who jumbled up words. The king found that funny. The fool said "Stajesmy" instead of "Majesty," he said "laplace" instead of "palace" and "mood gorning" instead of "good morning."

I think that's silly, but the king thought it funny. For a whole half year he thought it funny, till July seventh, and on the eighth, when he got up and the fool said "Mood gorning, Your Stajesmy," the king said: "Rid me of the fool!"

Another fool, a short, fat one called Pepe, pleased the king for only four days. He made the king laugh by smearing the chairs of the ladies, gentlemen, princes, dukes, barons, and knights with honey. On the fourth day he smeared honey onto the king's chair, and this didn't make the king laugh anymore, and Pepe was no longer a fool.

Now the king bought himself the most horrible fool in the world. Ugly he was, skinny and fat at the same time, lanky and dumpy at the same time, and his left leg was bandy. No one knew whether he could speak and kept silent on purpose or whether he was mute. His eyes had a malicious expression, his face looked bad-tempered;

the only pleasant thing about him was his name: he was called Johnny.

But the most horrible thing was his way of laughing.

It began quite small and glassy deep down in his belly, blubbered up, gradually changed to a burp, made Johnny's head flush, almost stifled him till he burst, exploded, quaked, yelled; then he stamped his feet as well and danced and laughed; and the king was amused, the others turned pale, began to tremble and were afraid. And when the people all around the palace heard this laughter they closed their doors and windows, fastened the shutters, put their children to bed, and stopped up their ears with wax.

Johnny's way of laughing was the most horrible thing in the world.

No matter what the king said Johnny laughed.

The king said things that could make nobody laugh, but Johnny laughed. And one day the king said: "Johnny, I'm going to hang you."

And Johnny laughed, roared away, laughed as never before.

Then the king decided that Johnny was to be hanged tomorrow. He had a gallows put up, and he was serious about his decision; he wanted to hear Johnny laugh in front of the gallows. Then he ordered all the people to watch the nasty spectacle. But the people went into hiding, bolting their doors, and in the morning the king was alone with the hangman, with his servants, and with laughing Johnny.

And he shouted at the servants: "Bring the people here!" The servants searched the whole town and found no one, and the king was angry, and Johnny laughed.

Then at last the servants found a boy, whom they dragged in front of the king. The boy was small, pale, and shy, and the king pointed at the gallows, commanding the boy to watch.

The boy looked up at the gallows, smiled, clapped his hands, was amazed, and said: "You must be a good king to have built a little seat for the pigeons; look, two have already perched on it."

"You're an idiot," said the king.

"I'm an idiot, Mr. King, and my name is Colombo, my mother calls me Columbine."

"You idiot," said the king, "someone is being hanged here."

"Well, what's his name then?" asked Columbine, and when he heard the name, he said: "A lovely name, so his name is Johnny. How could anyone hang a man with such a lovely name?"

"That's because he laughs so hideously," said the king, and he ordered Johnny to laugh, and Johnny laughed twice as hideously as the day before.

Columbine was amazed, then he said: "Mr. King, do you find that hideous?" The king was surprised and couldn't think of an answer, and Columbine went on: "I don't particularly like his way of laughing, but the pigeons are still sitting on the gallows; it didn't startle them; they don't find his laughter hideous. Pigeons have sensitive hearing. You'll have to let Johnny go."

The king thought this over and said: "Johnny, take off."

And Johnny, for the very first time, spoke one word. "Thanks," he said to Columbine, smiling a good human smile, and went away.

The king no longer had a fool.

"Come with me," he said to Columbine.

The king's manservants and maidservants, the counts and all the rest, though, thought that Columbine was the new court fool.

But Columbine wasn't merry at all. He stood there and was amazed, seldom said a word, and did not laugh, he only smiled and made nobody laugh.

"He isn't a fool, he's an idiot," people said, and Columbine said: "I'm not a fool, I'm an idiot."

And people laughed at him.

If the king had known about that he would have been angry, but Columbine never mentioned it, for he didn't mind being laughed at.

At court there were strong people and clever people, the king was a king, the women were beautiful and the men brave, the chaplain was devout, and the kitchen maid industrious—only Columbine, Columbine was nothing.

When somebody said: "Come along, Columbine, have a fight with me," Columbine answered: "I'm weaker than you."

When somebody said: "What's seven times seven?" Columbine answered: "I'm more stupid than you."

When somebody said: "Are you plucky enough to jump that brook?" Columbine answered: "No, I'm not plucky enough."

And when the king asked: "Columbine, what do you want to be?" Columbine answered: "I don't want to be anything, I'm something already, I'm Columbine."

The king said: "But you have to be something," and Columbine asked: "What are the things one can be?"

Then the king said: "That man with the beard, with that brown leathery face, he's a navigator. A navigator is what he wanted to be and that's what he's become, he sails across the oceans and discovers countries for his king."

"If you want me to, my King," said Columbine, "I shall be a navigator."

That made the whole court laugh.

And Columbine ran away, out of the throne room, and cried: "I shall discover a country, I shall discover a country!"

People looked at each other and shook their heads, and Columbine ran out of the palace, through the city and over the field, and to the peasants who stood in the fields and watched him run, he called out: "I shall discover a country, I shall discover a country!"

And he came to the forest and hid for weeks in the undergrowth, and for weeks no one had any news of Columbine, and the king was sad and reproached himself, and the courtiers were ashamed of themselves for having laughed at Columbine.

And they were glad when many weeks later the watchman on the tower blew a fanfare and Columbine came over the fields, through the city, in by the gate, went up to the king, and said: "My King, Columbine has discovered a country!" And because the courtiers didn't want to laugh at Columbine anymore, they put on serious faces and asked: "Well, what is it called, and where is it?"

"It isn't called yet, because I've only just discovered it, and it's far out in the ocean," said Columbine.

Then the bearded navigator got up and said: "All right, Columbine, I, Amerigo Vespucci, will go to look for the country. Tell me how to get there."

"You sail out to sea and then keep straight on all the time, and you must sail on till you get to that country, and you mustn't give up," said Columbine, and he was very frightened, because he was a liar and knew that there is no such place as that country, and he could no longer sleep at night.

But Amerigo Vespucci set out on his search.

No one knows where he sailed.

Maybe he also hid in the forest.

Then the fanfares sounded, and Amerigo returned.

Columbine blushed and didn't dare look at the great navigator. Vespucci stood in front of the king, winked at Columbine, took a deep breath, winked again at Columbine, and said very loudly and clearly, so that everyone could hear: "My King," that's what he said, "my King, there is such a country."

Columbine was so pleased that Vespucci had not given him away that he ran up to him, embraced him, and exclaimed: "Amerigo, my dear Amerigo!"

And the people thought that this was the name of the country, and they called the country that doesn't exist "America."

"You're a man now," said the king to Columbine, "from now on you'll be called Columbus."

And Columbus became famous, and everyone gaped at him and whispered to others: "That's the one who discovered America."

And everyone believed that there is such a place as America, only Columbus wasn't sure but doubted it all his life, and he never dared ask the navigator to tell him the truth.

But soon other people sailed to America and soon after very many; and those who came back claimed: "There is such a place as America!"

"As for me," said the man who told me the story, "I've never been to America. I don't know whether there is such a place as America. Perhaps people only pretend there is, so as not to disappoint Columbine. And when two tell each other about America they still wink at each other, and they hardly ever say America, but usually say something vague about the 'States' or 'over there' or something of the sort.

"Perhaps people who want to go to America are told the story of Columbine, on the plane or on the boat, and then they go and hide somewhere and come back later and spin yarns about cowboys and skyscrapers, about Niagara Falls and the Mississippi, about New York and San Francisco.

"In any case they all tell the same story, and tell of things which they knew about before the journey, and that's very suspicious, you'll admit.

"But people are still debating who Columbus really was.

"I know who he was."

Translated by Michael Hamburger

Wolfgang Borchert

On That Tuesday

The week has one Tuesday.
 The year has half a hundred.
 The war has many Tuesdays.

On that Tuesday
 in the school they were practicing the capital letters. The school-
mistress had glasses with thick lenses. They had no rims. They
were so thick that her eyes looked quite gentle.

Forty-two girls sat in front of the blackboard and wrote in capital letters:

> FREDERICK THE GREAT HAD A DRINKING MUG
> OF TIN. BIG BERTHA SHOT AS FAR AS PARIS.
> IN WARTIME ALL FATHERS ARE SOLDIERS:

Ulla touched her nose with the tip of her tongue. Then the mistress nudged her. You've spelled "soldier" with a J, Ulla "Soldier"
is spelled with D. D as in "ditch." How many times have I told
you. The mistress picked up a book and put a cross by Ulla's name.
You will write out the sentence ten times before tomorrow, nice
and neat, do you understand? Yes, said Ulla and thought: Her and
her glasses.

In the playground hooded crows were eating the thrown-away
food.

On that Tuesday

Second Lieutenant Ehlers was summoned to the battalion commander.

You must take off the red scarf, Herr Ehlers.

Sir?

Yes, Ehlers. That sort of thing doesn't go down with the Second.

I'm going to Second Company?

Yes, and they don't like that sort of thing. You won't get away with it there. Second Company is a stickler for dress. With that red scarf the company'll just cut you dead. Captain Hesse never wore such a thing.

Is Hesse wounded?

No, he's reported sick. Didn't feel well, he said. Since he's been a captain, he's become a bit slack, Hesse has. I don't understand it. Always used to be so smart. Well, Ehlers, let's see what you can do with the company. Hesse trained the men well. And you'll take off that scarf, is that clear?

'Course, sir.

And see that the men are careful with their cigarettes. Any decent sniper must have an itch in his trigger-finger when he sees those little fireflies flitting about. Last week we had five shot in the head. So just watch out a bit, eh?

Very good, sir.

On the way to Second Company Lieutenant Ehlers took off the red scarf. He lit a cigarette. Company Commander Ehlers, he said aloud.

There was a shot.

On that Tuesday

Herr Hansen said to Fräulein Severin:

We must send Hesse something again, too, Severin, my pet. Something to smoke, something to chew on. A little literature. A pair of gloves or something. The boys have a damn bad winter out there. I know what it's like. Not for me.

Hölderlin perhaps, Herr Hansen?

Nonsense, little Severin, nonsense. No, much sooner something a bit more cheerful. Wilhelm Busch or something. Hesse was always more for the light stuff. Likes laughing, you know that. My God, little Severin, how Hesse can laugh!

Yes, he certainly can, said Fräulein Severin.

On that Tuesday

they carried Captain Hesse into the delousing station on a stretcher. On the door was a sign:

WHETHER GENERAL OR GRENADIER
YOUR HAIR STAYS HERE

They shaved him. The orderly had long thin fingers. Like spider's legs. They were rather red at the knuckles. They rubbed him down with something smelling of drugstores. Then the spider's legs felt for his pulse and wrote in a fat book: Temperature 106.9. Pulse 116. Unconscious. Typhus suspect. The orderly shut the fat book. Smolensk Isolation Hospital was written on it. And underneath: Fourteen hundred beds.

The bearers picked up the stretcher. On the stairs his head dangled out of the covers and swung to and fro with every stairstep. Shaven and shorn. And he it was who had always laughed at the Russians. One bearer had a cold.

On that Tuesday

Frau Hesse rang her neighbor's bell. When the door opened, she waved a letter. He's been made captain, Captain and Company Commander, he writes. And they've forty below. The letter took nine days. "To Frau Hauptmann Hesse" he's written on it.

She held up the letter. But her neighbor didn't look at it.

Forty below, she said, the poor boys. Forty below.

On that Tuesday

the chief medical officer asked the superintendent of the Smolensk Isolation Hospital: How many are there a day?

Half a dozen.

Dreadful, said the chief medical officer.

Yes, dreadful, said the superintendent.

They didn't look at one another as they spoke.

On that Tuesday

they were doing *The Magic Flute*. Frau Hesse had painted her lips red.

On that Tuesday
Sister Elizabeth wrote to her parents: Without God one could never endure it. But as the assistant superintendent approached, she stood up. His walk was bowed, as though he were carrying all Russia through the room.

Shall I give him a little more, asked the Sister.

No, said the assistant superintendent. He said it so softly, as though he were ashamed.

Then they carried Captain Hesse out. There was a tumbling noise outside. They always bump like that. Why can't they lay the dead down gently. Every time they let them bump like that on the ground. One said that. And his neighbor sang softly:

> Zicket-zacket upidee
> Snappy is the Infantree.

The assistant superintendent went from bed to bed. Every day. Day and night. All day long. Throughout the night. Bowed, he walked. He carried all Russia through the room. Outside two bearers stumbled away with an empty stretcher. Number 4, said one. He had a cold.

On that Tuesday
in the evening Ulla sat and wrote in her exercise book in capital letters:

IN WARTIME ALL FATHERS ARE SOLDIERS.
IN WARTIME ALL FATHERS ARE SOLDIERS.

Ten times she wrote it. In capital letters. "Soldiers" with a D. Like ditch.

Translated by David Porter

Rats Do Sleep at Night

The empty window in the lonely wall yawned blue-red, full of early evening sun. Dust clouds shimmered between the steep-stretched remains of chimneys. The wilderness of ruins was dozing.

His eyes were shut. Suddenly it grew still darker. He knew that someone had come and was now standing in front of him, darkly, quietly. Now they've got me! he thought. But when he blinked a little, he saw only two somewhat poorly clad legs. They were standing in front of him, rather bandy, so that he could see through between them. He risked a little blink up the trouser legs and saw an elderly man. He had a knife and a basket in his hand. And a little soil on his finger tips.

This is where you sleep, eh? asked the man and looked down at the tumble of hair.

Jürgen blinked at the sun between the man's legs and said: No, I don't sleep. I have to keep guard here.

The man nodded: I see, that's why you've got the big stick there, I suppose?

Yes, replied Jürgen bravely and held fast to the stick.

What are you guarding, then?

I can't tell you that. He held his hands tight around the stick.

Money, I'll bet, eh? The man set the basket down and wiped the knife to and fro on the seat of his trousers.

No, not money at all, said Jürgen contemptuously. Something quite different.

Well, what then?

I can't tell you. Just something different.

Well, don't then. And of course I won't tell you what I have here in the basket. The man kicked the basket with his foot and clicked the knife shut.

Pah, I can imagine what's in the basket, observed Jürgen disdainfully, rabbit food.

By jiminy, you're right! said the man amazed, you're a smart lad. How old are you, then?

Nine.

Aha, think of that, so you're nine. Then you certainly know what three times nine are, eh?

Sure, said Jürgen, and to gain time he added: That's real easy. And he looked through the man's legs. Three times nine, huh? he asked again, twenty-seven. I knew that right away.

Correct, said the man, and that's exactly the number of rabbits I've got.

Jürgen gasped: Twenty-seven?

You can see them. Lots of them are still quite young. Would you like to?

But I can't. I have to keep guard, said Jürgen uncertainly.

All the time? asked the man, at night, too?

At night too. All the time. Always. Jürgen looked up the bandy legs. I've been here since Saturday, he whispered.

But don't you ever go home at all? You have to eat, don't you?

Jürgen lifted up a stone. There was half a loaf lying there. And a tin box.

You smoke? asked the man, do you have a pipe?

Jürgen firmly clutched his stick and said timidly: I roll cigarettes. Don't like a pipe.

Pity. The man stooped towards his basket. You'd have been welcome to look at the rabbits. Specially the young ones. Perhaps you'd have chosen one for yourself. But you can't get away from here.

No, said Jürgen sadly, no, no.

The man picked up his basket and straightened up. Well, if you must stay here—pity. And he turned around. Then Jürgen said quickly: If you won't give me away, it's because of the rats.

The bandy legs came back a pace: Because of the rats?

Yes, they eat dead bodies, you know. Of people. That's how they live.

Who says so?

Our teacher.

And now you're guarding the rats? asked the man.

No, not them! And then he said quite softly: My brother, he's lying under there. There. Jürgen pointed with his stick at the fallen-in walls. Our house got a bomb. All at once the light in the cellar was gone. And he was, too. We shouted and shouted. He was much smaller than me. Only four. He must be here still. He's so much smaller than me.

The man looked down on the tumble of hair. And then he said suddenly: Yes, but didn't your teacher tell you that rats sleep at night?

No, whispered Jürgen and all at once looked quite tired, he didn't say that.

Well, said the man, he's a fine teacher, if he doesn't even know that. Rats do sleep at night. You can safely go home at night. They always sleep nights. As soon as it gets dark.

With his stick Jürgen made little holes in the rubble.

Lots of little beds those are, he thought, all little beds. Then the man said (and his bandy legs moved restlessly): Do you know what? I'll just go and feed my rabbits now, and as soon as it's dark, I'll come and get you. Perhaps I can bring one with me. A little one, or what do you think?

Jürgen made little holes in the rubble. Lots of little rabbits. White, gray, gray-white. I don't know, he said softly, and looked up the bandy legs, if they really sleep at night.

The man climbed over the remains of the wall out onto the street. Of course they do, he said from there, your teacher ought to pack it in, if he doesn't even know that.

Then Jürgen stood up and asked: Can I really have one? A white one maybe?

I'll see what I can do, shouted the man, already walking away, but you'll have to wait for me here. Then I'll come home with you, see? I'll have to tell your father how to build a rabbit hutch. For you'd have to know how.

Yes, shouted Jürgen, I'll wait. I'll have to keep guard anyway, till it gets dark. I'll wait for sure. And he shouted: We've still got some boards at home. Box boards, he shouted.

But the man was already out of earshot. With his bandy legs he was running towards the sun. It was already red with evening and Jürgen could see how it shone through his legs, they were so bandy. And the basket swung excitedly to and fro. There was rabbit food in it. Green rabbit food, a little gray from the rubble.

Translated by David Porter

The Bread

Suddenly she woke up. It was half-past two. She considered why she had woken up. Oh yes! In the kitchen someone had knocked against a chair. She listened to the kitchen. It was quiet. It was too quiet, and as she moved her hand across the bed beside her, she found it empty. That was what had made it so particularly quiet: she missed his breathing. She got up and groped her way through the dark flat to the kitchen. In the kitchen they met. The time was half-past two. She saw something white standing on the kitchen cupboard. She put the light on. They stood facing one another in their nightshirts. At night. At half-past two. In the kitchen.

On the kitchen table lay the bread plate. She saw that he had cut himself some bread. The knife was still lying beside the plate. And on the cloth there were bread crumbs. When they went to bed at night, she always wiped the tablecloth clean. Every night. But now there were crumbs on the cloth. And the knife was lying there. She felt how the cold of the tiles crept slowly up her. And she looked away from the plate.

"I thought there was something here," he said and looked around the kitchen.

"I heard something, too," she answered and thought that at night, in his nightshirt, he really looked quite old. As old as he was. Sixty-three. During the day he sometimes looked younger. She looks quite old, he thought, in her nightdress she really looks pretty old. But perhaps it's because of her hair. With women at night it's always because of their hair. All at once it makes them so old.

"You should have put on your shoes. Barefoot like that on the cold tiles! You'll catch cold."

She didn't look at him, because she couldn't bear him to lie. To lie when they had been married thirty-nine years.

"I thought there was something here," he said once more and again looked so senselessly from one corner to the other, "I heard something in here. So I thought there'd be something here."

"I heard something, too. But it must have been nothing." She took the plate off the table and flicked the crumbs from the tablecloth.

"No, it must have been nothing," he echoed uncertainly.

She came to his help: "Come on. It must have been outside. Come to bed. You'll catch cold. On the cold tiles."

He looked at the window. "Yes, it'll have been outside. I thought it was in here."

She raised her hand to the light switch. I must now turn the light off, or I shall have to look at the plate, she thought. I dare not look at the plate. "Come on," she said and turned off the light, "it must have been outside. The gutter always bangs against the wall when there's a wind. I'm sure it was the gutter. It always rattles when there's a wind."

They both groped their way along the dark corridor to the bedroom. Their naked feet slapped on the floor.

"It is windy," he said, "it's been windy all night."

As they lay in bed, she said: "Yes, it really is pretty cold."

Then it was quiet. Many minutes later she heard him softly and cautiously chewing. Intentionally she breathed deeply and evenly so that he would not notice that she was still awake. But his chewing was so regular that it slowly sent her to sleep.

When he came home the next evening, she put four slices of bread in front of him. At other times he had only been able to eat three.

"It's all right to eat four," she said and moved away from the lamp. "I can't digest this bread properly. Just you eat another one. I don't digest it very well."

She saw how he bent deep over the plate. He didn't look up. At that moment she was sorry for him.

"You can't eat only two slices," he said to his plate.

"Yes, I can. I don't digest this bread properly in the evening. Just eat. Eat it."

Only a while later did she sit down at the table under the lamp.

Translated by David Porter

Thomas Brasch

Flies on Your Face

The shift is over about five. At a quarter after I'll be at the gate. Will you pick me up?

What else? he said, I'll be at the gate at five.

He stroked her cheek, bent down and kissed her on the neck. Then he turned around and left.

I should have told her. Tomorrow she'll come from her shift, and I won't be there. She'll think I forgot. She'll wait until five thirty and then she'll cry. She'll think I was with someone else. When I was traveling with Harry, she called him three times. I should have told her. Or some story—that I'm going on a trip, then she wouldn't have to wait tomorrow. She'll find out anyway eventually one way or another. Either I'll write her from over there or I'll be dead. Maybe I'll be dead by five tomorrow. How that sounds! Maybe I'll be dead tomorrow. Today I say that tomorrow I'll be at the gate at five and tomorrow at five I'll be lying in the morgue. Or sitting in front of a policeman. One from here or one from over there? I should have told her. Tell your fairy tales to someone else. You certainly don't think that I believe you. What do you want over there? she would have said, looked at me, and turned away. Then I would have gone to the place anyway and would have tried it. But it would have been different from now.

I'll ride somewhere or other. It's over six hours still. Somewhere I'll get off and sit down on a bench. Maybe I'll have another drink and then go to the place. I've got to think about something else. I'll go to school over there and sometime or other I'll get her, and we'll live together. When it's safe, she'll come. I'll get everything ready. Or I'll be dead.

Excuse me, Hiddensee Straße, can you tell me where I have to get off? I'm a stranger here.

The small man smiled at Robert.

I don't know—Hiddensee. I don't know. I'm a stranger here, too. Maybe you can ask the driver.

Thanks a lot, the small man said and smiled again.

The man began to press forward to the driver, and Robert got off.

She'll wait tomorrow, and day after tomorrow she'll make a long-distance call. My mother will be fearful. The first thing she'll think of is the fuss she'll get at work. Or she'll think of father: If he were still alive, this would not have happened. And maybe I'll be dead. But if I make it, then everything'll be different. I'll call. That's it. Mother, I'll say. No, first I'll call at work. Hello, I'll say. Yes, Robert, where are you? Why weren't you at the gate? You just can't ... And then I'll interrupt her and say, very calmly, as though nothing had happened: I'm in the West. And nothing more. I'll wait for her to say something. Just simply wait.

Hey there, you, hey! Just stop for a minute! Yes, I mean you!

It's over. They've been watching me the whole time. They know about everything from the beginning.

Robert felt the sweat spurting in his armpits. He turned around. A man was looking out the window of the new apartment block and stretching his arm downward.

My pillow's lying down there. It fell out. The elevator's broken. I'm not good on my legs anymore. Can you bring it up to me? Fifth floor on the right: Werner. The door is ajar.

All right, said Robert, picked up the pillow and went toward the building. Two boys were standing in front of the elevator and Robert followed them in. They poked one another. Werner, said one of them, and both laughed. Robert got out on the fifth floor and went down the corridor, opened the door at the end of the hall and walked into the apartment. The smell of old cooking fat came to him.

Leave the door open, he heard.

Robert walked past the cooking alcove into the room. On the rumpled bed the old man was sitting dressed only in pajama pants and an undershirt.

Did you fly? Five floors in half a minute. Not bad.

The elevator's working, said Robert and laid the pillow on the easy chair.

I should have known that, but they don't inform you when the thing's working again.

The old man shoved his legs over the edge of the bed and look'ed at Robert.

Do you want some tea? You can get a glass. I'll put some water on.

No thanks. I have to get going. Don't go to any bother.

Bother!

The old man laughed. Nothing bothers me anymore.

I have something to take care of, said Robert.

I understand. You're thinking: This guy's not in his right mind. First he has me bring up the pillow, and now I'm even supposed to take a seat in his dirty apartment.

Between every word he took a deep breath, and to Robert it seemed as if he heard a whistle in the man's voice.

You can't be in such a hurry that you can't keep an old man company for ten minutes.

Robert took a seat in the easy chair and looked around. The old man was looking for his shoes, found one, and finally went barefoot into the kitchen alcove.

He knew that the elevator was working. What am I supposed to say to him? It doesn't matter. Six hours. Better to sit here than get the jitters on the street in front of every policeman.

The old man began to cough. He was standing at the sink, letting the water run into a kettle. The coughing grew in intensity and suddenly the old man dropped the kettle and vomited into the sink.

And now he's throwing up.

Robert went into the kitchen alcove.

It'll be all right in a minute, the old man whispered, and his body trembled.

Then he vomited again, and Robert saw the red clumps in the sink. The old man leaned his head against the wall. Tears ran down his face. His pants slipped down. He grabbed for them, but he couldn't get hold of them. Robert bent down and pulled them up again. The old man's trembling increased.

Now he's falling over.

Robert grabbed him by the shoulders and his bent knees and picked him up and carried him to the bed. The old man had closed his eyes.

How light he is.

Robert shoved the pillow under his head and covered him up. Then he went to the door.

I can't help him, either. Why should I stay here? That damned elevator has to be somewhere.

Are you looking for someone? Robert heard a voice behind him.

The gray-haired woman was standing in an apartment door drying her hands on a dish towel.

I was headed to Herr Werner's.

You're just coming from there, aren't you?

Maybe I missed the nameplate. Maybe I read the name wrong.

The woman shoved the dish towel under her apron.

What do you want with Herr Werner?

I'm supposed to bring him something, from his sister.

She took a step toward him.

What? He has a sister? That can't be true. That's the limit! She ought to come herself instead of sending someone. Her brother won't last much longer, you can tell her that. He isn't exactly in good shape. In his mind, I mean. All day long he marches around his room in a goose-step. Or he gets strangers in his room. Now he's even started singing at night. Singing—what am I saying! He crows. And suddenly it turns out that he has a sister. You just tell her, she . . .

Robert turned around and went back.

You tell her! Her brother's conking out here and she sends some people or other. She ought to be ashamed of herself.

The old man was asleep. Robert covered him up and looked at him. His face was wrinkled, covered with beard stubble; a deep scar ran from his ear to his chin. His fingernails were long and dirty. Now he moved and groaned. He pushed his cover back and Robert saw his narrow, hairy chest that rose and fell at irregular intervals. His athletic shirt was spotted and ripped at one place. Robert shoved the old man's blanket up under his chin and sat down in the easy chair again. He pulled a cigarette out of his pocket and lighted it.

And what if he dies? A doctor? The police: What are you doing in this neighborhood? Where do you know this man from? You won't believe a word I tell you. A pillow. Haha. You're not serious. Where are you headed? Where do you work? I don't at the moment. That's interesting. Follow us. Clear up this matter.

Robert threw his cigarette into an empty vase, stood up, went to the bookcase next to the door, took out a book, and read:

Far from Moscow.

He opened the book up in the middle:

You will take it there yourself, Comrade Sjatkow, together with comrades Umara and Batmatev, will hand this valuable gift to Comrade Stalin personally, answered Pissarev. Again applause threatened him such as the Adun and the ancient Taiga had never heard.

Robert closed the book and put it back.

Now that, too. What a man! The classic pair: young citizen in flight meets a veteran of the workers' movement.

Robert took the picture frame from the shelf. Out of a newspaper photograph men in leather jackets looked at him with shouldered rifles and stars on their caps.

Red Front, said Robert.

I was there, too, Robert heard and turned around.

The old man had pushed his back against the head of the bed and was looking at him.

I was there thirty-eight years ago. In Spain. Give it to me.

Robert went to the bed and handed him the picture.

I cut it out of the *Berlin News*.

The old man lay down on his back and held the photograph before his eyes with both hands.

Thirty-eight years ago, he whispered, and I was there.

Fine. Shall I make you tea?

You probably don't believe it. But it's so. I was there, and whenever I see the picture, I feel like I did then. It was a great time. Others accomplished nothing more in their life but two children and three days' leave. It's different with me.

I'll make tea. Robert went into the cooking alcove.

Did I sleep long? asked the old man.

Not long, said Robert, and let the water run into the kettle. Just a couple of minutes.

He looked for matches.

I'm sorry about before.

Robert set the kettle on the flame.

Where's the tea?

The old man had turned to the wall and was still looking at the picture.

Below in the cabinet.

Robert poured tea in the pot. Then he sat down on a stool in the cooking alcove and waited.

Whenever I see the picture, I think about it. I see the stars on the caps and right away I also hear the shots and see the flies on the dead faces.

Yes, yes, said Robert.

He watched the old man speaking, but he no longer listened to him. After a few minutes he got up and poured boiling water into the pot. He took two glasses from the shelf, went into the room, and sat down again in the easy chair.

You can't forget a thing like that, the old man said and turned to Robert.

Stop it! I know that refrain. I had it played to me in kindergarten already.

The old man looked directly at him.

What's the matter with you?

Nothing. Nothing's the matter with me. I just know what's coming next and don't want to hear it for the thousandth time.

Oh, I see, you don't want to hear it, said the old man. But you do want to hear your babbling music, your electric dah-bee-doo-bee-di.

Never mind. I know that refrain by heart. The next thing, you'll say that we're know-it-alls. That we get it stuffed from behind and just open up our mouths.

That's the way it is, said the old man.

Nobody asked you. That's the answer you want to hear, isn't it?

Go the window! Go on!

What now?

You'll see.

Robert went to the window.

What do you see? Just tell me what you see. Thirty years ago you'd have seen nothing but rubble and trash. And what do you see now?

Boxes, said Robert. A giant prison with lawns.

Oh you do, the old man yelled, I suppose ruins are more beautiful, freezing is probably better.

Stop it! All right! I told you that I know that game. I'm leaving, yell at your beautiful new walls.

Robert walked to the door.

Wait! called out the old man. It's my fault. I wanted to tell you something else. I was in Spain. We fought and we know what for. I saw flies on the faces of the dead. I was a young man. But they got the better of us. When it made no more sense, we headed across the border. It wasn't easy, but when it couldn't go on, we had to go across the border.

Good, said Robert and sat down in the easy chair again, let's play this game to the end. So you had to go across the border, and you did go. What border can I cross, when it makes no more sense?

What do you mean by that?

Don't pretend to be dumber than you are, said Robert and looked straight at the old man. That's part of this parlor game. You had your part, now I have mine, and it goes: I can't do what you could. Finally you all build a wall around the beautiful houses.

If we hadn't built it, you'd all be over there now, where it glistens and sparkles. The old man leaned back.

Or maybe not, said Robert.

What do you want over there? What to you want from them?

Nothing at all. I don't want anything at all from them. But better there than here far away from Moscow. So, and now you can go to the phone booth. Police is 110.

The old man stared at him.

What's the matter with you? Who did anything to you? What do you want, anyway?

Robert got up and stood in the middle of the room. It seemed to him as though he had said those things a hundred times already and listened to his own voice at the same time.

What do I want? he yelled—to cut this umbilical cord! It's strangling me! Do everything differently. Without factories, without automobiles, without censors, without time clocks. Without fear. Without the police.

He hit the bookcase with his fist, but the weariness remained in his voice.

To start all over again in an open countryside.

Just sit down, said the old man.

I know, Robert continued yelling, all of that was already there, that all sounds sentimental, none of that's new. If I knew something better, I wouldn't be standing here now.

He let his arms fall. The old man got up, took the record player out of the bookshelf, and set it on the table in front of the bed, went to the cabinet, and took a record from the drawer.

Sit down, he said, you're trembling.

Robert let himself fall into the chair.

In Spain our cause was going bad. Falling back was all we did, a hard metallic voice was singing. And the fascists then were roaring: Fallen is the city of Madrid.

Madrid, Robert heard the old man singing along.

Those were the days of the Eleventh Brigade and its flag of freedom . . .

Robert saw the old man close his eyes.

Five more hours. I'll go to the border. They will shoot. I'll lie there with flies on my face.

It was quiet again in the room.

The old man opened his eyes.

Sometimes you think that it doesn't matter to you, he said softly. There's nothing more that makes you glad. Your friends are dead or don't know you anymore. It could be all the same to you, but suddenly you're afraid. Sometimes I think it would have been better had I fallen in battle in Spain. But I'll die here, in bed next to the record player.

Robert got up and put the tone arm on the record again.

In Spain our cause was going bad, the voice sang again.

We have nothing in common, said the old man.

Robert turned the loudspeaker knob as far as it would go, and the music drowned out the old man's voice.

But we do, said Robert, we're both afraid of flies on our faces.

Nonsense! yelled the old man, bent over frontwards and suddenly looked at the door.

Robert turned around. Next to the wardrobe stood the gray-haired woman from the hall. She walked through the room, went up to the table, and raised the tone arm from the record.

Have you finally lost your mind? the woman yelled at the old man. Do you have to listen to the stuff at full blast? There are people who want to have their quiet when they come home from their shift. I'm going to speak to your sister!

The woman turned around.

Have you fallen for his big stories? she said. He probably also told you that he was a freedom fighter. In Russia or Spain or with the Indians. A glorious past. Citations and medals. Don't make me laugh!

The old man jumped up. His hands were trembling.

In his whole life he never got farther than Oranienburg, and now he drags young people up here every day, pretends to be a great man, and stuffs those garbage disposals with his newspapers.

Robert saw the old man take a step toward the woman.

See that you get out of here, you fascist, you Nazi crow. Women like you put Hitler in power, plunged this land into misfortune, and now they devour butter-cream cakes all day long.

Both of them looked at one another with hate-filled faces. Robert reared against the cushion and looked at the clock.

Translated by A. Leslie Willson

Hans Christoph Buch

Fritzleben, for Example

1

My name is Fritzleben because my first name is Fritz and I am still living. My real name is different, but names are just noise and smoke. An American would say, "Just call me Fritz," dear Reader, for I am the living example of the successful unification—or should I say reunification?—of my fatherland, which was divorced by the higher power of the Allies. It was a genuine miracle, not some commonplace economic miracle that catapulted me from the Geological Institute in Potsdam to Antarctica, or more precisely to the Weddell Sea, where I have been stuck for several days at 76° south latitude and 23° west longitude in pack ice that closes its ring of siege tighter and tighter around the ship, just as it was in old travel accounts.

The ship is called the *Almirante Irizar*. It is named after a courageous navy officer who, in 1903, rescued the expedition of Dr. Nordenskjöld, a Swede, which was frozen solid in the ice. The ice breaker, which sails under the Argentine flag, was built in 1978 in the Wärsilä Shipyard in Helsinki. It is 119.5 meters long, 25 meters broad, and 225 meters high. Its draft is 9.5 meters, its maximum speed 8.8 m/sec (16.5 knots), and its cruising radius is 36,000 nautical miles at water temperatures from −2.9° C to 29° C, and air temperatures from −30° C to 30° C, in case you wanted to know its exact specifications. The ship weighs 4900 metric tons. Aside from its load of 2,500 metric tons, which consists mainly of drinking water, frozen beef, potatoes, and kerosene, it has 225 sailors and officers and 36 Polar researchers on board, one of whom is my humble self. "Researcher" is actually a bit of an exaggeration, because the women and men—yes, you heard it right; we have women on board, too—are really only technicians, or to be more exact, measuring technicians, who enter data into computers that they have previously gotten from other computers or the opposite, data such as water and air temperature, prevailing wind direction, ocean currents, and ice drift, not to forget the ominous ozone layer, which is becoming more and more porous. Any decent weather satellite measures all that today. The computers have long since been able to manage without their users, exchanging their data from monitor to monitor via modem or fax. Of all the measuring technicians, who tinkle around on their laptops day and night like piano virtuosos, there is only one who may justifiably call himself a Polar researcher, aside from the algae freak who stores the macro algae fished out of the ocean by his pretty assistant in his cabin's minibar and constantly annoys us with the question, "How big is your minibar?" Did you know, dear Reader, that ocean water freezes at −3° C and that the gelatin used in Jell-O molds today is made from algae? But I digress. The only true scientist abroad this ship is me, the seagull expert, Dr. F., ornithologist from Jena and Potsdam, which was previously the GDR, who had the fortune of discovering a tagged skua in the chalk cliffs of Rügen. Such a discovery is made only once every hundred years, and with that catch, which met with great approval in the scientific press, nothing more could stand in the way of my career. The GDR wanted international recognition, and my request to move to Antarctica, which had been denied for many years, was generously granted. Don't forget that the South Pole, as seen from Potsdam, was in the West, and that the trip there went through Cape Town or the Canary Islands, where ideologically insecure citizens could be tempted to go over to the capitalist enemy. In addition, there were one or two black marks on my record, and so another year passed before the Secret Police gave the green light for me to be put on the ice breaker *Akademik Fedorov* from Leningrad to Bellingshausen in March, where I spent my first Antarctic summer under the wings of our Soviet friends.

I remember, as if it were yesterday, the feelings I experienced as I went ashore at Gomera, where Columbus set sail to the New World, and took in the aroma of Spanish oranges. But that was nothing in comparison to the heavenly, no earthly, perfume that greeted my nose on the beach of Bellingshausen as I waded through a colony of donkey penguins, ankle deep in their droppings—or were they Adelia penguins?—and was attacked by a skua for the first time, which dive bombed me like a Stuka or MIG-17, to drive me from its hunting ground. Skua are intelligent creatures, just like the penguins whose eggs they pilfer and whose intestines they tear out of living bodies when a young bird wanders into the wrong colony. Penguins and skuas live together in symbiosis, like seals and icebergs. The skuas defend the penguin colonies against intruders and demand their tribute in return, like wolves from sheep herds. It resembles a sort of health police—but I have strayed much too far from the starting point of my story. In any case, I already knew when I first went ashore in Bellingshausen, quietly creeping over the stony beach so as not to wake the sleeping seals, that I had finally reached the place I belonged. Neither Germany, East or West, nor the country where the lemons bloom is the Blochian homeland for me, the place where no one has ever been. My Arcadia is the inland ice of Antarctica, which is not eternal, only a few million years old, geologically speaking still young. More precisely, my Arcadia is in the Schirmach Oasis, which is totally unrelated to the critic of the same time, at the foot of the Wohlthat Mountains, which are named after the Reichspost Minister who founded the Schwabenland Expedition in a dry valley mapped in 1938, whose existence was dismissed for a long time as a Nazi phantom until our Soviet friends set up their bases, first Lazarevskaya and the Novolazarevskaya, after the first one disappeared in the ice, the base I could see when I raised the East German flag with the hammer-and-sickle emblem over the Georg Forster Station. That sentence was way too long! Before I get more deeply lost in the underbrush of my story—underbrush is actually overstated, because nothing grows here except for mosses and lichens—I prefer to tell my story from the end. In retrospect, every detail reveals its hidden meaning. I spent the ninth of November in the radio room of the Georg Forster Station, seated in front of the short-wave radio the British used to convey to us the latest news from Berlin from their base at Halley Bay, a thousand kilometers away. We celebrated the opening of the border with Rotkäppchen Sekt that we had saved for special occasions, and our Soviet friends contributed Moskowskaya or Stolichnaya. At that time they were still drinking real vodka on their station, not the homemade stuff. The next morning—in retrospect, the events, which in reality lasted weeks and months, shrink to a few days—the next morning we were awaked by the noise of an Alouette helicopter that landed unannounced on the helipad. I had not yet slept off my intoxication, and then a man wearing sunglasses and coveralls come up to my bed, held a calling card from the Bremerhaven Institute for Polar Research (AWI, for short) under my nose and wanted to know where the boss was. I have forgotten the man's name. I know only that he wore an anorak made of super lightweight fleece, in German *Faserpelz,* while we were still dragging around in down at the time. I offered him coffee and Armenian cognac that we had used to celebrate the fall of the Wall, and after a short tour of the station, he informed me that our prefabricated barracks imported from the GDR did not comply with the safety standards set down in the West German building code because they were made of wood and therefore flammable. The Georg Forster Station, he said, along with its entire inventory, which he ordered me to list carefully, would pass into the possession of the West German government, which as of that moment would be responsible for the safety of the GDR researchers but would be unable to guarantee their continued employment, because no money was available in Bonn's research budget. From the mouth of that man, whose name, thank God, escapes me, I heard the word "liquidation" for the first time, a word that constantly sounds in my ears. I found out what was behind the word only years later, after the mummy had been unwrapped from its wrappings and bandages.

2

Re: "Fritzleben"
Decision of the German Literary Foundation on the request for financial support of Project "Fritzleben."
Result: The request is rejected because the project named above does not appear to members of the Committee to be worthy of support.

Reason:

(1) The Author: An author by the name of Hans Christoph Buch is not known to the German Literary Foundation of Darmstadt.

The name appears neither in the *Critical Lexicon of Contemporary German Literature* edited by Heinz Ludwig Arnold, nor in the author index of PEN, nor in the membership lists of the media union (IG "Printing and Paper"). It is apparently a pseudonym the author or authors of the submitted prose fragment are using in an attempt to attach themselves to the success of Lutz Tilger, who was born in 1963 and whose novel Fritzleben was recently praised by Marcel Reich-Ranicki's "Literary Quartet," although Lutz Tilger received only a consolation prize in the Ingeborg Bachmann Competition. Whoever is hiding behind the pseudonym H. C. Buch, and it is unimportant whether there are one or several authors, the author or authors of the submitted manuscript have done themselves a disservice, since their request for support from the German Literary Foundation in the form of a yearly stipend with twelve monthly installments of 2,000 DM is obviously unjustified. (2) The Work: The submitted prose piece, apparently intended to be the beginning of a novel, did not convince the members of the Committee, since the text in and of itself has an indecisive, redundant, and heterogeneous effect. The author or authors could not decide whether they wanted to write a book about Germany or about the Antarctica. The demand for unity of time and place, which has been valid from Aristotle to Reich-Ranicki and was recently confirmed by the "Literary Quartet," is not fulfilled, for a novel about the reunification cannot take place simultaneously at the South Pole: either Germany or Antarctica. Both together do not work. Apparently the author or authors of the text submitted for examination wanted to leave all options open, for the attached index of characters (see enclosure) is so extensive that no inferences about the course of the action or the protagonists of the novel can be made. In addition, none of the characters presented in the index appear in the text. There is not a single attempt made by the author or authors to comply with the demand to create characters typical of the time period under historically accurate circumstances, which is raised correctly time and time again by Marcel Reich-Ranicki. The text sways indecisively between West German arrogance and East German sentimentality, and no clear politico-ideological direction can be recognized. Moreover, it is teaming with linguistic and factual absurdities. The Committee took the trouble to consult an Atlas and a biology book, and it came to alarming conclusions. (1) Skuas—they are aggressive seagulls—live in the North and South

Polar regions as well as on the islands extending from the Polar sea: Greenland, the Aleutians, Kerguelen, etc., but they have never been spotted, much less caught. (2) The ships of the Soviet Antarctic fleet were strictly forbidden to dock at Cape Town and other ports of the Republic of South Africa up until recently. Instead, they had to refuel in Maputo. (3) The previously Soviet, now Russian, station of Bellingshausen is in the western part of the Antarctic Peninsula, whereas the Schirmach Oasis is located on the northeast coast of Antarctica. Not to mention stylistic blunders: What business do Anglicisms such as "algae freak" and "Just call me Fritz" have in the stream of consciousness of a GDR citizen, who, the authors would like to have us believe, slept in pack ice through the fall of the Wall and the reunification, and what, for heaven's sake, does "How big is your Minibar?" mean—perhaps an allusion to Botho Strauss' *Big and Small!*? In addition, the references to the polar researchers' excessive consumption of alcohol appear unbelievable, when one considers that vodka freezes at −40° C and salt water at −3° C, not to mention the health risks of methyl alcohol. One begins to suspect that the author or authors themselves had too much to drink when they committed their ill-conceived text to paper. Asking the members of the Committee to read the text was, to put it mildly, asking far too much. In conclusion, it is not the task of the German Literary Foundation to promote the abuse of spirits common among writers by granting them generous stipends instead of effectively combating alcoholic consumption in the old and new lands at the federal level.

Signed

(illegible)

Translated by Thomas Lawshae

Hans J. Fröhlich

An Angel of Death

Lili, no doubt about it, it was her.

A week ago he had met her again at the opera. She had been living in Rome for two years. She had ostensibly come to Berlin because of the matter of some inheritance. He had often thought about her in recent months. For a short time she had been his patient, or at least had consulted him without ever having been treated by him. A letter from her had led to a vehement argument with his wife and was finally perhaps even responsible for her death, insofar as any responsibility at all can be considered in such an unfortunate chain of coincidences and mistaken ideas. Even Lili's first visit had thrown him off balance. Unannounced, in a white, bare-shouldered float, she had appeared in his consultation room with a Siamese cat under her arm, had dropped into the armchair in front of his desk as if exhausted from a long walk, and, stroking the cat, without looking up, asked for a glass of water.

The sudden presence and appearance of this bizarre but enchantingly beautiful and girlishly delicate person had torn him for the moment out of all connection with professional reality. Such an angelic, supernatural creature comes only once into any life. It was not virtuousness but anxiety over endangering his marriage to an abnormally jealous woman five years his senior, who was inclined to depression, that kept him from falling in love with the girl on the spot. Besides, he would never have allowed himself to get involved with a patient. He was in his mid-forties and had so far always conducted himself as a doctor in a correct and irreproachable manner. As with other women who came to him, he wanted to see in this one, too, only a patient, and in order not to let his confusion show, he had asked her the reason for her visit and inquired about previous illnesses. She could not remember being seriously sick, she had been anemic as a child, ate very little and, because of the danger of anorexia, had twice been sent to a sanatorium on the advice of a physician. But now she had come because she had recently been suffering from terribly troubled sleep, both in falling asleep and while she was sleeping. At night she would lie awake in bed for hours, turning and tossing from one side to the other, unable to quiet her thoughts, constantly making the effort by counting off numbers or by arbitrarily evoking beautiful scenery in her head to force sleep to come. But when she finally succeeded in falling asleep, she was immediately afflicted by frightful dreams of persecution from which she would start up, tormented by fear of suffocation, and spend the rest of the night awake in bed with all the lights on and the windows open, supported by pillows and bolsters or else, with knees trembling from fatigue, wander around the house until dawn. But the worst was that now from pure fright she did not even dare go to bed anymore, often stayed up until far past midnight, sitting in a chair and reading or trying to read, often the same page three or four times because turning the pages was intolerable, and naturally then on the following day she couldn't even see for weariness, though not sleep either. On the one hand complete exhaustion, on the other inner agitation, so that she expected a total collapse of her nervous system. Earlier, when she was between ten and twelve years old, loss of appetite, aversion to any kind of sustenance, now incessant insomnia. Whether there was not a connection there, she asked herself now and then, whether insomnia was not another form of appetite loss.

He listened to it all, occasionally making a note, and then said what she had described was not at all unfamiliar to him, since he at times also suffered from sleep problems, especially when there was a full moon. This was, however, only a reassurance with which he aimed to exhibit his understanding. Actually, it was difficult for him to believe her, although, on the other hand, it had not occurred to him to consider her a liar; and as if an evil spirit had prompted him, after a well-timed pause he had said that she had really detailed her nocturnal distress very impressively, but that the sleep difficulties were certainly not the only reason for her visit. He had naturally not expected to elicit a more substantial affliction with this remark but had also not expected that she would jump up indignantly and leave without a word.

Nevertheless, he was relieved by her departure, since the short visit had already plunged him into considerable confusion. But scarcely a week had passed when she came again, this time without the cat, and in a black leather suit, and startled him with the declaration that she had actually made incomplete statements the week before, because she had not mentioned that her father had recently died in an airplane crash. She should have begun with that, since her difficulty in sleeping probably originated with his death. She had seen her father the last time ten years ago, since he had lived in America after his divorce. In the beginning she had suffered a great deal because of the divorce and had never forgiven her mother for marrying again—a paper manufacturer. She had kept up a correspondence with her own father until the end, actually, but inwardly become more and more alienated from him without ever admitting it to him. Meanwhile, she regretted her insincerity, particularly because she suspected that her dissimulation had not at all escaped him, even if—perhaps because he felt guilty about her— he had never allowed how much this estrangement oppressed him to show. He had constantly represented himself as being a caring and solicitous father, and in the end left her his entire, not inconsiderable, estate. However, she could perceive in this arrangement of her inheritance only an unbridled sentimental perversion in any case, as if he had wanted to assure himself of her lifelong attachment in this way, to purchase her love at last. In a fit of rage and in order not to increase the inheritance still more by the profit from interest, she had closed all his accounts and taken the money home and hidden it in her apartment. Madness to keep such sums in a private home, to make the apartment into a hiding place, and consequently to live in a hiding place literally. Madness.

She had repeated the word madness a few more times, then became silent and had sat there before him, looking totally drained.

He asked her why she didn't go on talking. He was suddenly extremely uneasy because he was afraid the confidences could perhaps be his undoing.

She had said all that was necessary, was her reply, and now he would certainly accept the fact that she suffered from insomnia and had come to him for that reason alone.

She had given him possible reasons for her insomnia, she continued, possible reasons for her fear of suffocation, too. A psychologist would certainly be very pleased, but he was a general practitioner, he could take her blood pressure, do an EKG, have her lungs x-rayed. . . . What did she expect from him? He was, as she could tell, convinced that nothing was the matter with her, that she was organically sound, and she would certainly not assume, after all, that her problems could be disposed of with some sort of pill.

Heaven knows she hadn't come to him to have pills prescribed for her. She could get those, if she needed them, without a prescription. She had turned to him with confidence in her desperate situation, but if he refused even to examine her—there were other doctors.

This time her visit left a sting behind.

It was clear to him: He had failed and not just as a doctor. And what distressed him the most: He couldn't talk to anyone about it. Least of all his wife, because of whom he had conducted himself so impossibly toward this young woman.

One day almost three months later he had gotten a letter from her. Since she had still not received a bill from him, she was taking the liberty to send him a check for three hundred marks. And in a postscript: She had gone through a rather turbulent time. A month ago her mother had died. She really needed to recuperate and had the intention of staying for a while with a friend in Palermo. But she needed very much to talk to him first. Then printed: When and where can we meet? Call me!

In spite of some hesitation he did so and made an appointment with her for the late afternoon of the next day in a café. She had arrived punctually, in jeans and with a triumphant smile around her mouth. How nice that he had come. But she had counted on it completely. He could not imagine what she had been through, what had been expected of her.

She had never had a good relationship with her mother, who had been pampered throughout her life, a person who was already spoiled by her parents, who had never grown up and always wanted to remain the admired child she had once been when between the ages of eleven and sixteen she had delighted the concert-going public of Lodz and Warsaw with her piano playing. She herself, however, had known her mother only as a woman of infinite indolence, extremely unfit for life, who lay in bed until noon and spent the rest of the day on a sofa in a silk dressing gown without ever touching a piano key. The extent of this pathological indolence that approached the brink of physical degeneration was indescribable, and she (Lili) could not blame her own father for not wanting to live for long with such a woman, who had become increasingly shapeless. In the end the paper manufacturer, too, had also divorced her mother; beforehand, however, trying in every way possible to seduce her (Lili), which he had certainly not succeeded in doing. She didn't want to say this man was responsible for her insomnia now either, in spite of the fact that there was a lot of tension there, but after the death of her mother she felt better, freer, more liberated for the first time, and wanted to tell him that was why she had written him and asked for a meeting, and that he had come she could certainly take as evidence that he forgave her certain caprices.

There was nothing to forgive, he told her, and besides he had come only to give her back her check. He had no claim on her for any fee.

On no account would she take the check back. She had taken up his time and did not expect any favors.

Still he could not be persuaded to keep the check, and he had torn it up before her eyes, but in doing so seemed to have done what she secretly wished. How she interpreted his gesture, which was meant to be generous or perhaps only correct, could have become clear to him when she addressed him, apparently inadvertently, in informal terms and, when they said goodbye in front of the café, had suddenly embraced him like an acquaintance of long standing. He became aware of what had transpired within himself only at that moment weeks later on the day his wife had found Lili's letter in his jacket pocket and he, suffering pangs of conscience, had been honorable enough not to deny the meeting with his patient outside of office hours.

It had been a mistake to deviate from his rules of conduct and meet Lili; it had been foolish to have stuck her letter in the side pocket of his jacket instead of destroying it at once. On the other hand, after his wife had found the letter, he saw no reasons why he should conceal the harmless meeting with Lili in an unobjectionable café. He had a clear conscience, had done nothing reprehensible, and if he had failed to mention this meeting before, it was only so as not to give her the wrong idea. But since the letter had fallen into her hands (accidentally, as she maintained), he considered it fitting to abandon his consideration and to tell her about the afternoon meeting of more than three weeks before. He had hoped in this way to prevent any further and far-reaching speculation. But to his wife this unexpected candor was nothing other than the cynical admission of infidelity already consummated.

He was familiar with her intense, uncontrolled outbreaks of jealousy, and he attributed them to her severely depressive inclination. Usually, however, he had succeeded in quickly calming her again with soothing talk. But this time he had made a mistake in justifying himself only halfheartedly, for he was not able to traduce Lili only for the purpose of refuting the massive imputations.

He had never deliberately lied to his wife, and he had not managed this time either to lie and deny feelings that he had had for Lili since her first visit, although he had not wanted to admit it until this moment. And he could acknowledge these feelings to himself much more easily, since he knew this enigmatic and somewhat eccentric creature was long since far away and that he would, if possible, never see her again.

It was his frankness that had brought his wife's jealousy to the boiling point, his frankness and that he had wanted to spare the other woman.

She had often left the house late in the evening after such arguments but had always returned after two or three hours. But this time he had waited the whole night for her return; and when she had not come back by the next morning or the whole next day, he had called her mother in the firm belief that she was staying there. But she was not at her mother's, she was also not at her sister's, and she was also not at her best friend's. In spite of a certain uneasiness when she had not even returned in three days, he had still not been afraid for a moment that anything serious could have happened to her and had even more completely excluded the thought that in her desperation she could have done any harm to herself.

Actually, it had been an accident after all, an accident with fatal results, and a week ago, after a surprising encounter at the opera, after which they had gone to get something to eat, he had explained that to Lili, to his relief and hers. An accident in an Austrian health resort and already a year and a half in the past. Lili, nevertheless, seemed not to understand what her letter had to do with the death of his wife, whose existence she had only now learned of, and as if she were obliged to console him, she had grasped his hand and said how strange it was that all of a sudden two bereaved persons were sitting across from each other and, almost amused, added: two widowed persons. And then she was suddenly as if transformed and told him that her trip to Italy had completely changed her life. In Palermo her friend's friend had fallen in love with her— a young Roman attorney with whom she had shortly thereafter moved to Rome. She had told him clearly from the beginning that their relationship was only temporary and that she had no intention in any event of marrying him. He (Fulvio) had accepted that to begin with, too, but after a few weeks had not wanted to hold to the arrangement any longer and had importuned her more and more passionately, at times accompanied by huge threats, to agree to marriage. She had been close to leaving him, even though she really was very fond of him. But then suddenly he had had to have colon surgery, and after his release from the hospital it had been clear to her that from then on she was just going to be playing the part of a nurse. He himself, however, at least in the beginning, had firmly believed that he had gotten through the worst with the operation and that he would soon be completely restored to health. But actually he got worse from day to day, and finally he could no longer leave his bed. In this situation there was, naturally, nothing else for her to do but to stay with him till the end, convinced, certainly, that it would be over for him quickly. But there she had underestimated his will to live. Not only did he inconsiderately continue to expect and demand that she sleep with him, but even more stubbornly than before insisted that she marry him.

Finally, completely exhausted, and lacking any will of her own, she had given up opposing him and agreed to marry him on his sickbed in a civil ceremony. *Madness!* On the other hand, why shouldn't she have fulfilled this last wish for him? And in fact his condition became rapidly worse from day to day. But in spite of what was no doubt unbearable pain, he could not be prevailed upon to enter the hospital again. Three or four times a day, since he did nothing for himself anymore, she had to change the bedclothes, and that went on for more than three months. Compared to that, her mother's death had actually been child's play. Really, only out of pure human kindness, in order to spare him an even longer and more degrading illness, she had finally laid a rather large number of sleeping tablets on his nighttable in the hope that, if the pain were no longer bearable, he might take them in his extreme distress. But he had apparently not believed he was dying until the end. Madness, all madness! And now, without ever believing herself really to be married, she was a Roman widow and lived in the apartment Fulvio owned in the diplomatic district. Her first friend, from whom she had gotten the Siamese cat, had died of blood poisoning, her beloved cousin of pneumonia, and now Fulvio: of cancer of the colon. Obviously she had bad luck always to get involved only with doomed men.

It was not this last sentence that had shocked him; it was also not the story about Fulvio: It was the tone in which Lili had told it, a mixture of indifference and pretended solicitude. And all of a sudden this woman he had thought of with longing so often in recent months had become sinister to him in an alarming way. A half an hour previously he had still intended to invite her to his apartment after they had eaten. Now he was happy he had not yet expressed his intention and was totally relieved when he heard that she had to fly back to Rome already on the next day. Still, he had accompanied her back to her hotel, wished her a pleasant flight and all good things for the future, and had then gone home, convinced he had acted correctly, since a relationship with this woman could only have ended disastrously for him, too.

Two weeks later he witnessed an event that was incredible to him: A torrential downpour had begun when he was on his way to his office, and he had gone into a store to buy an umbrella. As he was paying at the main register, he heard that the police had just caught a young woman who had repeatedly been spotted stealing small items by the house detective, but today she had tried to hide a dozen men's watches in her handbag. Suddenly someone called out: "There she is!"

He looked around and couldn't believe his eyes: The one who had been arrested was Lili. No doubt about it—it was her. In spite of her dark glasses, he had immediately recognized her. How come she was still in Berlin? And his next thought was: I must help her! And he was about to say to the officer: "I know this woman. She is a patient of mine. Let her go!" But then he stood there indecisively and was at last convinced that this time, too, he could not help her.

Translated by Jeanne R. Willson

Martin Grzimek

The Liar

Dunraven, versado en obras policiales,
pensó que la solución del misterio
siempre es inferior al misterio.
El misterio participa de lo sobrenatural y aun de
lo divino; la solución, de juego de manos.

—Jorge Luis Borges, "Abenjacán
el Bojarí, muerto en su laberinto."

Not too long ago something so strange happened to me that I feel
compelled to recount it. The story involved a former fellow student
of mine I'll call Langenthal. In spite of the fact that I can recall
every detail of our last encounter quite clearly, I have to admit that
what I know both of Langenthal and his life is based mostly on
second-hand information. I had exchanged no more than a dozen
words with him in earlier days, and he was not even a close acquaintance, let alone a friend. But he was a striking figure, both in
appearance and in behavior, so that I, and others, tended to pay
more attention to him than he probably deserved. In order to pro-
vide at least a brief background to my story, then, I want to begin
with Langenthal's student days, and I hope I will be forgiven if my
description tends to be a bit vague and subjective. On the other
hand I'm prepared to swear in any court that the following account
of our recent meeting, which occurred quite by chance, is both
accurate and true.

When I first met Langenthal, around twelve years ago, he was a student of philosophy like me, except that he was just beginning his course work, while I was in the process of gradually bringing my own studies to an end. I was taking advanced seminars, racking my brains over Hegelian logic, Marxist theory of value, Kirkegaard's concept of despair, and Schelling's philosophy of art. I listened to university lecturers explain the immemoriality of being, entangled myself in proofs of God's existence, pondered various theories of transcendence, and struggled with the doctrine of the incommunicability of identity and non-identity. On more than one occasion it seemed to me that I was being introduced to the analysis of eternal cosmic turbulences rather than attempts to bring a little order and sense into the confusing complexity of real worlds.

But of course there were moments, and sometimes even hours or days, when, after lengthy study and meditation, I was intoxicated by the feeling that I had grasped the most profound implications of some difficult text. If I ventured to express to friends my exultation at this knowledge and was asked to explain the matter to them, I quickly realized how slender was the tightrope of insights upon which I was about to perform my high wire act. I had placed more trust in the balance of dark words than in the skill and dexterity of my own language, and so I was always happy if no one asked me to explain myself, but instead accepted in impressed silence the *Eureka!* I had let slip so lightly.

Of course I seldom dared to take part in discussions at seminars or lectures, since the others who did so seemed to prove by their intellectual prowess just how little I had understood, in the final analysis, of the matter at hand. Today, from the distance lent by years and experience, I would maintain, even at the risk of being accused of arrogance, that most of those who elucidated major theories and reduced both their fellow students and even the professor to a state of respectful silence didn't understand much more about them than I did. Lacking all sense of shame that might have led them to confess how often human thought is at a loss, they were like jugglers in a circus of the mind, drawing applause with the simple whirl of their words. Like many others, I allowed myself to be impressed by them, forgetting my own abilities in my admiration for these conceptual artistes, and at the same time asking myself why I couldn't do the same: Why couldn't I raise my hand

and, with utter conviction, explain that the appearance of existence contains a negation of the negation of the negation ...

Perhaps this summary may serve in retrospect to explain why Langenthal made such an impression upon me, and not just on me alone. For, in the first of his long years of study, he managed not only to participate in such disputes at an apparently high level, but also to speak out boldly and articulately. Even more astonishing was the fact that, without having fulfilled the prerequisites by sitting through several semesters, he suddenly appeared in upper-level seminars to which even advanced students were often admitted only after special interviews with the professor in charge, and with documentary proof that they were adequately prepared. Doors that remained closed to more than one doctoral candidate opened before Langenthal as self-evidently as if he had been born with the right to stride straight through the holy portals of philosophy. And there he sat: young, with curly blond hair, broad shoulders, and a deep tan, leaning back nonchalantly. For the first few sessions of the seminar he would sit quietly, take notes, leaf through the book, study certain passages in the text, apparently lost in thought, or nod in agreement with the words of the professor. Then he would suddenly raise his hand and ask a question that would put the seminar leader on the spot, forcing him into extended explanations which demonstrated that Langenthal's intellectual level required a response beyond the ordinary.

Anyone who has ever dealt with professors who have made a name for themselves outside the narrow confines of the university knows that their lectures and class subjects become, by reason of a certain conceited arrogance, a type of private lake in which they alone may swim, and their reaction is quite predictable when someone else, particularly an unknown newcomer, steps into the same water. They don't drive him out, but fix their attention instead upon the alien swimmer, pointing him toward the farthest shores, and, when they see that the intruder is becoming accustomed to the water and has gained a measure of self-confidence, they lead him to a dangerous, cold area and watch, from a proper distance and with no little pleasure, as the competitor swims along, thinking himself safe, toward the falls ahead ...

But back to Langenthal. He was not yet twenty back then, and the perfect picture of nonchalance. While others were still stubbornly chewing over the same text after years of study, he sprang across the glacial crevasses of philosophy so adroitly, with a mixture of pugnacity, cleverness, knowledge, and arrogance, that he was soon surrounded by a crowd consisting in equal parts of those who admired and those who envied him.

It should not be forgotten that during the period of which I am speaking, this field of study was taken very seriously and not regarded simply as a matter of fashion or as a hobby. To choose to study philosophy was to make an existential decision to place the spiritual values of life above the profane values of the quotidian, and to join ranks in the spirit of "struggle." In this sense one was undertaking an intuitively political and quasi-revolutionary course of study. At stake was the unmasking of lies, the demystification of the world of appearances, the representation of relationships in terms of material conditions, and special interests in terms of the concurrencies of power. We were to learn to see beneath the surface, to meditate rather than regurgitate, to prefer the serious over the merely amusing, and to prefer life itself over "the art of life," and having learned all this, to use that knowledge to alter the present and reinterpret history.

As a result the practice of philosophy had, in its outer form as well, something monastic and spartan about it. Those who had chosen this field of study, denying themselves the certainty of a steady income in the future, were unlikely to be wealthy, and had they been they would never have admitted it. The naked, abstract truths of ancient or modern treatises were engraved as visible furrows upon the thoughtful brow, and the first gray hairs were there to demonstrate that in spite of all temptations of the flesh, the head should always be held erect above the body below. The doctoral candidate who could not come to terms with the problem of the Ego in Fichte, and therefore placed his father's hunting rifle in his mouth and pulled the trigger, was no more uncommon than the student who wore the same shirt day in and day out for the simple reason that, involved as he was with more essential matters, namely Kant's *Critique of Pure Reason*, he simply forgot to change it.

Langenthal contradicted this stereotype in a startling way. Although he, too, sat for hours studying in the library, brooding over a single sentence and oblivious to his surroundings, he took the liberty of entering the classroom in the latest bright-colored fashions, and as if they weren't enough, with a thoroughly attractive young woman in a low-cut dress on his arm. The effect was that of two bright, joyful parrots perched among the old gray owls of wisdom. Or he would travel, uninvited of course, to philosophical congresses at which experts were gathered from all over the world, would speak up from one of the back rows of the auditorium, breaking into the official discussion at the podium, then stride up to the microphone to the general astonishment of those present, state his objections in a clear yet novel manner, and earn the applause of the professional world and its elderly, white-haired representatives with their high foreheads and their serious mien—only to be seen that very same evening by his fellow students, pulling up in front of the concealed door of a fashionable discotheque in his open sports car and entering as easily into the mindless underground world as he did into congress halls strictly reserved for the academic elite.

A specific intellectual depth and a certain type of decadence existed side by side in Langenthal, or rather were united in him, and, it seemed, successfully so. For just as I was finally ready to prepare for my exams, the word was spreading through the Institute that Langenthal had already started his dissertation and was assured of a position as assistant professor upon its completion, thus entering upon a career of which others whose backs were long since permanently bowed from sitting hunched over their books could only dream. And while I was satisfied simply to have passed my exams with some degree of success and without any real problems, reports were piling up that Langenthal was being invited to the private homes of various professors who wanted to converse with him among a small circle of friends over a good meal and a glass of burgundy. A kingdom was thus opened to him that was known to most students only by hearsay, a kingdom whose anteroom I was now about to leave by completing my own studies. The old saying I had grown up with, that knowledge is power, a concept I had attempted to undermine during the course of my studies, seemed to be confirmed in the most astonishing manner by Langenthal's steady and irresistible rise.

I left the university and began to earn my living beyond its walls, gradually forgetting all about Langenthal. Now and then I would see him walking jauntily down the street in his gym shoes, proud and resolute. As I saw less and less of him, however, my interest in him faded.

I became involved in other things and finally settled into a minor position at a lexicographical institute that promised some security and decent colleagues. A few of them had been fellow students, and since in addition to their jobs they still attended evening lectures arranged by the philosophical faculty, or in some cases were still working on their dissertations, I was brought into contact once more with the past. It was through them that I heard Langenthal's name again, for the first time in almost two years. I was surprised to hear of him in connection with the Institute or the city, since I had long imagined him teaching in one of our great universities.

The details I began to pick up were disturbing, although I must admit that they also aroused a certain satisfaction in me, for they seemed to confirm and justify a mistrust I had harbored from the outset. Word had it that Langenthal had run aground. His rapid rise had been followed by an equally spectacular collapse that had turned him into a depressing example of what happens when one is unable to face the competitive pressure of our career- and success-oriented world. It seems he had now been tossed aside, a worthless object on the fringes of society.

Now that Langenthal had been brought to my attention, I started noticing him occasionally, when I was in the old part of town. His youthful freshness was gone. He still had long, curly hair, but his face seemed shapeless and bloated, his eyes clouded and dull, his body slack and sluggish. It was said that he drank heavily, and no one knew where his money was coming from, since his parents refused to support him any longer. I was advised not to have anything to do with him. On the one hand he was unpredictable, and on the other he was obstinate, and kept getting all mixed up because he had apparently lost the ability to concentrate. Only when he drank enough did his old strength and superiority seem to return. Nevertheless, whether he was seen walking through the park or sitting with a bottle of beer at the window of a pub, he always had a book of philosophy with him, as if he could retain some part of his old identity in this way. At times months would pass without his being seen in the city, then he would reappear in his old, worn-out clothes, drinking, talking, or simply sitting around looking lonely.

That was his situation when I ran into him a few days ago, when some friends and I entered a pub at the edge of town around ten o'clock in the evening. Since I had never before been in that particular pub due to its location, you can imagine how surprised I was to find Langenthal there of all places. Nevertheless I acted as if I didn't recognize him, while at the same time involuntarily seeking out a place from which I could observe him. He had a book in front of him on the table, with a glass of beer beside it. He sat with his back to us, his legs stretched out at a slight angle, and gave the impression that he was resting, meditating, or simply day-dreaming. The only time he changed his posture was when he looked over his shoulder to order another beer.

The presence of my former fellow student in the pub put me in a strange mood. I listened to the conversation at our table with only half an ear, since I kept thinking about Langenthal. What could have brought him here, I thought. Did he live in this neighborhood? Is that why he seemed so at home sitting there? Why wasn't he looking around, why wasn't he leafing through his book? Had he even noticed me? And, if so, had he recognized me?—The longer I observed Langenthal, the lonelier he seemed. His immobility was oppressive and seemed to reinforce the grim simplicity of the room, with its beer-hall furniture, bare walls, and cheap vases with artificial flowers.

Around eleven o'clock I had to pass by Langenthal on my way to the men's room. On my way back I stopped at his table and spoke to him. I still can't figure out what made me do it. But I do know that the first thing I asked him was whether he still remembered me.

"Of course," he said. "You took your exams with. . . ."

That was a long time ago, I replied, astonished by his easy manner. I asked him what brought him to this particular pub.

"It's quiet here."

Yes, and the wine was said to be good.

"I don't drink wine, but the beer isn't bad either."

I asked him how things were going.

"Not bad. I can't complain. As long as I've got a good book to read, things are fine."

And what was he reading now?

"Husserl."

Having said the name, he lifted the book with his left hand, revealing a signet ring and chewed fingernails, and turned it for a moment so that its spine was visible. Then he returned it to its former position. I had just enough time to read the word *phenome-*

nology. Then he lifted his glass with the same hand and finished his beer.

"Would you like to join us at our table for a bit?"—I had been staring at Langenthal's hand, not even looking him in the eye, and yet I asked this question. It was out, I couldn't take it back, and I hoped immediately that Langenthal would simply decline.

"Why not?" was all he said.

I looked at him in shock.

Langenthal stood up. He was shorter than me, and I noted that his waist was hidden beneath a roll of bloated flesh. His neck was fleshy, too, almost fat, as was his face, and I was struck for the first time by his unhealthy, spotted skin.

I led the way, pulled a chair up next to mine, announced to my friends that a former fellow student of mine was joining us, and introduced him. "This is Langenthal," I said, as if he were a famous person, but in truth I couldn't remember his first name.

"You've forgotten your book," I said, as Langenthal was about to sit down.

"Oh yes, Husserl," he replied, "he'll be all right on his own for awhile."

From that moment on I simply didn't know what to do. I was annoyed with myself. I had obviously been bothered seeing Langenthal sitting by himself. But now I realized how shallow my sympathy had been, a conventional response, and my invitation nothing more than a polite charade. Because I was having a good time with friends, it seemed I felt compelled to rescue a lonely figure from his relative isolation. On the other hand it may have been curiosity that motivated my supposed kindness, or even a hidden desire to see a fallen angel close up, and perhaps learn from him firsthand the reason for his fate.

But the more I realized how egocentric my good-naturedness had been, the less I was able to get Langenthal involved in the conversation, or even to address myself directly to him. Instead I behaved exactly as he did. I sat in silence beside him and sipped from my glass while he quietly drank his beer. We both listened to the discussion, which was becoming more animated under the influence of the wine. For the most part it moved from one topic to another by chance or random association, ending in mutual teasing or degenerating into long, drawn-out descriptions.

As is always the case with such evenings, when everyone is in a good mood over nothing, the back and forth of ideas and the raised and lowered voices mingle together freely until the fragmentary conversations, interrupted by laughter and loud toasts, finally reach a point at which the exuberance of the group experiences a sudden reversal, and everyone falls silent in exhausted satisfaction, as if there is really nothing more to talk about, as if they need to catch their breath before starting up again. In short, silence descended upon the table. But whenever silence spreads over such a talkative group, the new situation seems so uncomfortable that someone just can't stand it, and suddenly comes out with a question or remark that has no other purpose than to get the conversation going again.

In our case the wife of one of my friends couldn't take the pressure of the silence that had settled over us and—what could have been more natural?—turned to Langenthal, who was sitting to her right, and asked him what he was doing. I was the one who winced at this question. Langenthal himself sat quietly with his legs stretched out before him, looked at the woman calmly, albeit with a somewhat glassy stare, and said, "I'm just listening."

The woman became embarrassed. That wasn't what she meant, she said, she'd only wanted to know what he did for a living, or whether he was still a student.

"Yes, I'm still a student . . ."

"And what are you studying?"

"At the moment I'm studying Husserl's theory of retention."

"Retention?" The woman laughed. "Retention? Never heard of it. What is it?"

Now everyone at the table was staring at Langenthal, and I was racking my brain to figure out how I could keep him from launching into an exegesis of Husserlian theory, as I feared he might. But Langenthal didn't answer the question, at least not in the manner one might have expected. He drew his glass of beer toward him with his left hand and began to revolve it in his fingers. At the same time he stared down in front of him as if he were thinking it over. Even as he finally began to speak, he kept turning the glass.

"You know," he said, without looking at the woman, "the only reason I'm sitting here at the table is because you're here. I can't forget your face. Actually I always see it before me. Yet you're not at all the person I'm speaking about. You just happen by chance to resemble another woman who doesn't live here, but up north, or perhaps somewhere else completely now, for all I know."

Langenthal drank and fell silent, as if he didn't care to say more.

"What about this woman?" his neighbor asked.

Langenthal continued speaking, as if the question had been unnecessary: "Everything here reminds me of the evening I saw her for the first and only time. It was in a small town in the Harz Mountains. A group of people suddenly came in the door of the pub and sat down at my table, since there were no other chairs free. They immediately began talking, and I sat there and listened to them. The woman was part of the group, and at some point she began telling about what had happened to a friend of hers. This friend had gone to a movie one evening, had a drink afterwards, and then got into her car to drive home. She lived in a village about ten kilometers away, and a long stretch of the road passed through the forest.

"As she's driving along, she suddenly sees something lying in the middle of the road. At first, of course, she thinks it's a dead animal or something, but as she comes closer she sees it's a man, lying on his back as if dead. She's not stupid, however, and so she doesn't stop. Instead she drives slowly around the man, thinking it might be a trap. Even so, about ten meters farther on she stops, asking herself if the man might really be in need of help. So she shifts into reverse and sees by her back-up lights that the man is still lying in the road and hasn't moved. Then she takes a flashlight from the glove compartment, shifts back into neutral, steps out, and shines the light on the man, on his head, which is turned toward her on its side. She thinks it might be best to wait until another car comes along, but she steps closer to the man, who still doesn't move. His mouth is open, but his eyes are closed. She thinks he might really be dead, or at least that he's been hit by a car, because of the way his limbs are twisted. Since the man is absolutely motionless, she bends over him, and suddenly he jumps up!"

At this point Langenthal paused and emptied two-thirds of his glass. He still had a bit of foam on his upper lip when he continued:

"Naturally, the woman was scared to death. The man had already grabbed her by the jacket, but she was able to tear loose and run to her car screaming, with the man after her. She jerked open the door, jumped behind the steering wheel, slammed the door shut, shifted into gear, and gave it the gas. The woman who was telling the story said her friend didn't really know what she was doing, she just acted by instinct and fled in a panic, without ever looking in the rearview mirror, just staring straight ahead, frightened out of her wits. When she finally arrived home, she collapsed over the steering wheel and could do nothing but cry. She was completely devastated. After she's finally calmed down a bit, she starts to get out, opens the door, and notices something fall to the ground. Thinking it may have been something that was in the car, she bends over and picks it up. She holds what she has up to the light and sees that it's two fingers, not whole fingers, just the upper joints, still soft and warm, scarcely bleeding. She screams and throws the fingers down. She calls the police, who then find all four fingers of the man's right hand. The woman severed them when she slammed the door as he tried to stop the car. It was a long time before the woman could be calmed down, and even then she was overcome by nausea when she saw the severed fingers lying in a plastic bag on her living room table. At any rate, that's what the woman told her friend about what happened that night, and that's what the friend told, just as I've tried to tell it."

Langenthal fell silent. Those of us at the table stared at him for a long time, until the woman next to him asked, "And the man?"

"I've no idea," said Langenthal with a shrug. He straightened up in his chair, lifted his glass of beer to his mouth, and spoke the following sentence directly into it: "That's all the woman said. The man still hadn't been found. He probably just disappeared into the woods."

Only then did he place the glass to his lips and finish it off with one swallow.

What happened next took place very quickly. But, after the lengthy description, and before I finally come to the end of my last encounter with Langenthal, I mustn't omit mentioning that he sat beside me and told his tale quite calmly, almost indifferently, in a much more relaxed and careless tone than I've been able to represent here. Much of what he said I've only paraphrased, for, to be honest, only the last sentence sticks in my memory with any real accuracy. That may be because it seemed that Langenthal meant the last sentence, "He probably just disappeared into the woods," to describe himself as well, since it appeared he was going to get up and leave both us and the pub.

It was one of my friends, however, who not only kept things from breaking up so rapidly but also dissipated the tension that at least I, and I believe others as well, felt upon hearing Langenthal's tale, and in the most strikingly banal manner. Langenthal had barely emptied his glass when my friend said that story had been around a long time. He'd seen it himself in some supermarket magazine or read it in a book, or maybe he had heard someone else tell it, he wasn't exactly sure anymore: In any case, there was no point in Langenthal trying to fool us into thinking he'd heard it from a friend of the person it happened to. "Why lie about it?" my friend concluded, and looked away from Langenthal, as if by doing so he could demonstrate how little he thought of him.

I think my friend's remarks disillusioned us all a bit, and Langenthal's credibility was suddenly destroyed, particularly since he went back to his table without replying, picked up his book, and seemed completely defeated. But instead of heading for the door, he turned back toward us, shoved the chair he had been sitting on aside with his foot, and began searching for something in the right-hand pocket of his jacket. He paid no attention to us, and his face betrayed no emotion. Finally, he lifted his right arm and the first thing I saw was a bank note, and then, as he dropped it on the table and asked us in a flat voice to pay his bill for him, I saw his right hand, with the ends of all four fingers missing. We all saw it. We all saw the bank note slip from between his thumb and the stumps of his four fingers and fall to the table top, we all saw his mutilated hand long after he had left the pub.

The sight of that hand paralyzed me even more than the others. No one would have considered trying to follow Langenthal. But I had to face a host of questions that evening, since I was the one who had brought him over to our table and apparently knew him. My stumbling and fragmentary replies must have seemed enigmatic to my friends, and I myself was at a loss to establish a connection between what had just occurred and my scanty knowledge of Langenthal's rise and fall as a student of philosophy. For days my colleagues in the lexicographical institute wouldn't believe my story of the encounter with Langenthal, for none of them who knew him had ever noticed that four fingers were cut off of his right hand. No one could prove the contrary, of course, since no one had seen Langenthal since then. I agree it's unsatisfactory— but that's the way this story actually ends.

As for me, all I can say is that it left me in a state of some confusion. All this had one good effect, however: I've started reading philosophy books again. And, of course, at the moment the book lying in front of me on the table is the one Langenthal had with him, by Husserl. I'm having a difficult time working my way into the theories of time and the limits of recollection that form the central core of the text. Starting over again is always difficult and perhaps as impossible as preventing a musical tone we once have heard from fading gradually from our memory until at last it completely disappears. And yet we continue to believe we can recall it. By the way, Husserl calls this phenomenon *retention*. And for the sake of completeness we should add, in closing, that lawyers render the concept literally as *restraint,* while psychologists understand it simply as *attachment deficiency,* or the inability to form stable relationships.

Translated by Breon Mitchell

Hannah Johansen

Virginia

"I can't stand it anymore," Virginia said. Her name wasn't Virginia, we just called her that. And every time Virginia said: "I can't stand it anymore," one of us was in the vicinity who said: "You can stand anything." Then we all laughed. I don't know what she did, when she was alone. Perhaps then the thought never occurred to her to say that she couldn't stand it. Or she was able to give herself the necessary answer. It was possible that she didn't need us at all. It was possible that she just wanted to do us a favor and, so to speak, keep us in a good humor in that she offered us the opportunity to shake our heads over her and say to her: "You can stand anything." It was possible. It was not a certainty.

Virginia was terribly slim as the vogue demanded. That didn't look bad on her, but we would have liked her even if she had been fat.

I believe we called her Virginia from the beginning because she smoked. She smoked the strongest stuff she could find. She smoked so continuously that not one of us will admit to ever having seen her without a cigarette, while we gradually gave up smoking because we could no longer endure the thick smoke. She did not stop. Nothing could be done about it.

Once, when we shared an office with one another, I asked her what her name really was.

"Regina," she said. "Or Verena. I've forgotten."

"How can you forget that?"

Virginia slammed a dusty file shut and laughed.

"What must be, must be," she said, and the cloud of dust from the documents mixed with the smoke of her cigarette.

At that time we were put by twos in small offices. Only a few men worked on our floor. We were lucky, for we could open the windows and didn't have to wait, like the others in the new building, until the air conditioner blew out on us some sort of air-mix concocted in the pipes. With us the windows stood more or less constantly open, at least at the times Virginia shared the office with us. At first I was happy having her in the vicinity. We laughed a lot, and we worked a lot. After a while I wished, just as the others before me had wished, that Virginia would pack up her belongings and move to another office. "I can't stand it," she said. I could also scarcely stand letting her go, but the amount of smoke was making me sick. It was the same with the others, and consequently Virginia moved rather often. In this way a certain amount of discontent developed in our department, but since we always settled things among ourselves, scarcely anything about this discontent penetrated into the upper floors. It was better that way, for discontent is not looked upon with pleasure. Not even then. Today it would be an impossibility. But today everything is different anyway; we stay where we are and do what we can.

Today only about half of us are still there; the others have fallen by the wayside because of a series of restructurings, so that half of the corridor is now occupied by another department made up of nothing but male area-experts.

In that year, when scarcely an eye could penetrate her cigarette smoke and we were again planning a move, things were better for us. Virginia said, "I can't stand it." We said, "You can stand anything," and that was it. We liked her, and that was enough for us.

We didn't know much about her otherwise. She was not married, and she had never said anything about a boy friend. I didn't even know how old she was. One day when we had just closed the office door behind us, I asked her.

"Twelve," Virginia said.

I laughed although I had not understood the joke.

One day when Sybil complained that she could no longer endure the tar-laden air, Virginia said she didn't want to move anymore.

What to do?

The situation was not at all as difficult as it looked. We said to ourselves, why should it always be Virginia who moved. That's why we all began to roam around and Virginia stayed where she was. I have to add that these office changes had nothing unfriendly about them. For when the smoke became too much for one person, then another one looked forward to Virginia. She had something about her that we enjoyed. And each time, when someone moved, we had a party.

"When I was twelve," she told me one evening, "I forced my parents to move to the country."

"How is that possible?"

"First they didn't want to," said Virginia. "They objected with all their might."

"And then?"

"And then it worked out after all. A lot of things work out when you use force."

She looked at the floor, hopped from one foot to the other, and we laughed so that it resounded through the deserted halls.

"It's unbelievably quiet in the country," she said when we had calmed down again. I was not so sure about that, but Virginia continued: "No shared walls to the rear, no music outside the windows, if you know what I mean. No drunks."

I nodded.

"No broken glass. No rattling of garbage cans. No cemented-over places."

I nodded.

"No bushes growing out of the cracks either. In the stone. Understand?"

"Why did you absolutely want to move to the country, Virginia?"

"Just for that reason."

"And now?"

She laughed again. "Long ways away," she said and looked at her shoes.

At this moment I had the suspicion that, except for work, the subway, and home, she never went anywhere.

"One ought to be able to fly," I said.

Virginia nodded. "What would you do if you could fly?"

"Fly away," I said, "far away." We had gotten to the stairway and looked over the landing down the shaft. Virginia nodded again.

She dropped her cigarette down and lit a new one. She looked like eighteen.

She must certainly be in her mid-twenties, I thought, as she stood next to me like that and stared off.

"Thirty," she said as if she could read my mind. "Next week."

Actually she could read minds as little as I could. The next thing she said, but not to me and very slowly: "She was not even a virgin."

Who?

I had no idea of, course, what that meant. How could I, after all?

"Come on," I said because I had no idea what she was talking about.

Something was the matter with her. She was incredibly pale. For a while she had complained when our male colleagues stood in the hall in front of the cafeteria with their beer bottles. Now she began to cry out. "There're four," she screamed. The men stared at her full of disgust. When it was two or three, we could calm her down. But if it was four, then we had to actually take her by the arms and carry her off by force.

"Come with us," we said. "Don't yell."

"I can't stand it," she screamed.

"You can stand anything," we said to get her to laugh. But she didn't laugh. We held her tight. She was thin and had unbelievable strength in her with which she fought against us.

"Come on," we said. "Be quiet."

Virginia bit her lips until they were bloody. She kicked. In the halls, in our arms, she didn't calm down for a long time.

On the days that followed she didn't laugh at all anymore. She only worked. Once she threw up her whole lunch. Once she lost consciousness. Once she stuck a knife and fork in her purse and went after the men. We had to keep an eye on her all the time. Then it stopped, and she was astonishingly quiet.

On the day she turned thirty, she threw herself down the stairwell. Why? What could we say? We maintained we didn't know. Three days later the funeral took place with strange conversations.

Her silence was not refilled.

Translated by Jeanne R. Willson

Marie Luise Kaschnitz

Long Shadows

Boring, everything boring, the hotel lobby, the dining room, the beach, where her parents lie in the sun, falling asleep, letting their mouths hang open, waking up, yawning, getting into the water for a quarter of an hour in the morning, for a quarter of an hour in the afternoon, always together. You see them from behind, Father's legs are too thin, Mother's are too fat, with varicose veins, they come to life in the water and splash around like children. Rosie never goes swimming when her parents do, while they swim she has to look after her sisters, who are still little but not sweet anymore, just silly geese, who fill your book up with sand or lay a jellyfish on your bare back. It's dreadful to have a family, other people suffer because of their families, too, Rosie sees that quite plainly, for example the brown man with the little gold chain, the one she calls the Shah. Instead of remaining under an umbrella with his family, he hunches over the bar or steers a motorboat, wild passes at breakneck speed, and always alone. A family is a nuisance, why can't you come into the world already grown up and immediately go your own way. I am going to go my own way, says Rosie one day after lunch, and discreetly proposes buying postcards in town, picture postcards, which she is supposed to write to her schoolmates, as if she would think of sending cards to those stupid brats in her class, Greetings from the blue Mediterranean, how are you, I am fine. We want to come too, scream her little sisters, but thank God no, they're not allowed to, they have to take their afternoon nap. Well, just up the road to the market-place and right back again, and don't speak to anyone, says her father, and walks off after her mother and little sisters, with his poor, crooked clerk's back, he went out on the water in a boat today, but he'll never be a sailor. Just up the road, you'll see the town situated up above, with its walls and towers stuck onto the mountain, but her parents have never been up there, it was too far away for them, too hot, which it most certainly is, no shade near or far. Rosie doesn't need any shade, what for anyway, anywhere is fine with her, fine with her skin, gleaming with suntan oil, provided that no one tries to tell her what to do and no one asks her anything. When you are alone, everything becomes grand and curious and begins to belong to you alone, my road, my mangy black cat, my dead bird, disgusting, eaten up by ants, but it absolutely has to be picked up, mine. My long legs in faded linen pants, my white sandals, one foot in front of the other, no one is on the road, the sun is blazing. Up there, where the road begins to climb the hill, it begins to form a snaky line, blue snake in golden vine leaves, and the crickets are chirping like crazy in the fields. Rosie takes the shortcut through the garden plots, an old woman walks toward her, a mummy, oh my God, the things that are still running around loose here that should have been in a grave long ago. A young man overtakes Rosie and stops, and Rosie puts on a stern face. The young men here are importunate loafers, you don't need any parents to know that, what do you need any parents for anyway, the devil they paint on the wall took on a totally different face long ago. No, thank you, Rosie says politely, I don't need any company, and walks on past the young man, as she has watched the young women do here, stiff back, vertebra on top of vertebra, chin pulled in, eyes cast down darkly, and he only mumbles something fawning, which sounds infinitely absurd to Rosie's ears. Vineyards, cascades of pink geranium blossoms, nut trees, acacias, beds of vegetables, white houses, pink houses, sweat in the palm of her hands, sweat on her face. Finally, she reaches the top of the hill, the town as well, the good ship Rosie catches the wind in her sails and glides through streets of shadow, past fruit stands and flat, tin tubs full of colorful, glittering, round-eyed fishes. My market, my town, my shop with herds of toy animals and a firmament of straw hats, with racks full of postcards, too, from among which, for the sake of form, Rosie selects three glaring-blue seascapes. Farther through the marketplace, no oohing-and-aahing thoughts at the sight of the citadel and the church façades, but interested glances at the modest shop displays, also into the ground-level bedrooms, where mawkish pictures of the Madonna hang above heavily orna-mented, cast-iron, double bedsteads. Almost no one else is on the street at this early afternoon hour, a small, shaggy dog of indeter-minate breed is yelping up at a window where a boy is standing, making faces at him. In her pants pocket Rosie finds half a roll left over from her second breakfast. Catch, Good-for-nothing, she says and holds it out to the dog, and the dog dances around comically like a trained monkey. Rosie tosses the bread to him and then immediately chases him away from it, the ugly creature hopping around on two legs makes her laugh. At last she squats down in the gutter and scratches his dirty, white stomach for him. Hey, the boy yells down from the window, and Rosie yells Hey back, their voices echo, for a moment it is as if the two were the only ones awake in the hot, drowsy town. It pleases the girl that the dog follows her when she walks on, not to be questioned but to have some company, to be able to talk, come along doggy, we're going to go through the gate now. The town gate is different from the one Rosie used to enter the town, and the road certainly doesn't lead down to the beach, but uphill instead, straight through the oak forest, then runs along the scary slope high up above, with a full view of the sea. Her parents were planning a family walk up there and then on to the lighthouse; it is comforting to know that, behind the face of the mountain, they are lying on their beds in their darkened room just now. Rosie is in another world, my olive grove, my orange tree, my sea, my little dog, fetch the stone. The dog performs and barks on the melting, dark-blue asphalt ribbon, then he runs a short way back toward the town, someone is coming around the bend of the cliff, a boy, the boy who was standing in the window making faces, a stumpy, suntanned child. Your dog? Rosie asks, and the boy nods, comes closer and begins to tell her about the area. Rosie, who understands a little Italian from her holiday in the Tessin, is pleased at first, then disappointed, since she could have determined for herself that the sea is the sea, the mountain the mountain, and the islands the islands. She walks faster, but the stocky boy tags along at her heels and keeps on talking to her, everything that he points out with his short, brown fingers loses its magic, all that remains is a picture postcard, like the ones Rosie had purchased, electric blue and toxic green. He should go back home, she thinks, and take his dog along with him, suddenly she does not find any pleasure in him anymore either. When she sees a path branch off to the left of the wood and lead steeply uphill between the cliff and the brush, she stops, pulls from her pocket the few coins remaining from her purchases, says thanks, and sends the boy away, immediately forgetting all about him to enjoy her adventure, the mountain path, which soon loses itself in a thicket. Rosie has finally really forgotten her parents and sisters, and also herself as a person, with a name and an age, Rosie Walter, student, tenth grade could do something more; but no more of that, a roving soul, defiantly in love with the sun, the salt air, with being able to do things and with allowing things to be done, a grown-up person like the Shah, who unfortunately never goes out for a walk, otherwise she could meet him up here, and without a lot of stupid chatter, keep watch with him for steamers passing by in the distance. The path turns into steps, which wind on around the cliff, Rosie sits down on a step, touches the fissured stone with all ten fingers, breathes in the mint, which she crushes between the palms of her hands. The sun glows, the sea sparkles and flashes. Pan is sitting on the furze hill, but Rosie's schooling is deficient, she doesn't know anything about him. Pan creeps behind the nymph, but Rosie merely sees the boy, the twelve-year-old, my God, there he is again, she is very annoyed. He comes leaping soundlessly down the steps of the cliff on dust-gray feet, this time without his dog.

What do you want, says Rosie, go home, and she starts to continue on her way, which is just about to lead along the cliff wall for some distance without any railing, below lies the abyss and the sea. The boy doesn't start up again with his Ecco il mare, ecco l'isola, but he will not go home again either, he follows her and then emits a strange, almost supplicating sound, which has something so inhuman about it that it startles Rosie. What's the matter with him, what does he want, she thinks, she wasn't born yesterday, but that just can't be it, he is twelve years old at the most, a child. It may well be that the boy has heard too much from his older friends, his big brothers; there is that talk in town, a constant, half-whispered conversation about the foreign girls who are so amorous and complaisant and who roam the vineyards and olive groves all alone, no husband, no brother to pull a gun, and the mere mention of the magic word *amore* can coax their tears, their kisses. Such are the conversations of autumn, the conversations of winter, in a cold, sad café or on the wet, gray, thoroughly lonely beach, conversations that rekindle the blaze of summer. Just wait, little one, in two years, in three years, one of them will come for you, too, she'll walk across the marketplace, you'll be standing at the window, and she'll smile up at you. Then simply run after her, little one, don't be bashful, take her, what do you say, she won't want to, but she will really just be playing a game, she will want to.

Not that at the moment the boy, the master of the apish little dog, would have remembered such advice, the winter's grand song about love and summer, and the two or three years are by no means past. He is still Peppino, with the runny nose, the one who still gets a thump on the ear from his mother when he dips his finger in the jelly jar. He can't play the man like the big boys, winking salaciously and yelling ah, bella, now, when he is about to try his luck with a girl, the first who ever smiled at him and coaxed his dog to come to her. His luck, he doesn't even know what that is, the rumor and gossip of the older boys, or does he know all of a sudden, when Rosie draws back from him and slaps his hand away, and with her face quite pale, presses herself against the wall of the cliff. He does know, and because he can't demand, he begins to plead and to beg, in the language which foreigners understand, which consists entirely of infinitives. Come to me please, embrace me please, kiss please, love please, blurted out all at once with a trembling voice, by lips that have saliva dripping from them. When at last Rosie laughs, though she is still frightened, and *says*, Nonsense, what are you thinking about, just how old are you anyway, he retreats, then, before her very eyes as they say, sheds his child's skin, develops angry wrinkles in his forehead, and takes on a wild, greedy look. He mustn't touch me, he mustn't do anything to me, thinks Rosie and looks around in vain for help, the road lies far above, behind the cliff, not a soul is to be seen walking along the zigzag path at her feet, and any cry down below by the sea would be drowned out by the noise of the breakers. Down below by the sea her parents are taking their second swim now, where can Rosie be, she only wanted to buy picture postcards for her schoolmates. Oh, the classroom, so dark and cozy in November, you painted that very prettily, Rosie, those bluejay's wings, that should go up on the bulletin board, we'll pin it up. Rosie Walter, and on the back a cross, your dear fellow student, killed at the blue Mediterranean, how is better left unsaid. Nonsense, thinks Rosie, and tries again in her maladroit words to speak to the boy, but at this moment even adroit words would not have succeeded any better. The small Pan, pleading, stammering, blazing, wants to have his nymph, he rips his shirt off, his pants as well, suddenly he stands naked in the hotly glaring hollow of stone in front of the yellow bush, shocked into silence, then all at once it is very still, and from below you can hear the garrulous, indifferent sea.

As Rosie stares at the naked boy, she forgets her fear, he suddenly appears so lovely with his brown limbs, his bathing-suit belt of white skin, the corolla around his black hair, wet with sweat. Except that now he is stepping out of his holy, golden halo and coming toward her, his long, white teeth flashing, now he is the wolf from the fairy tale, a wild animal. You can protect yourself against animals, Rosie's own narrow-chested father did that once, but Rosie was still little then, she had forgotten it, but now she remembers it again. No, child, no stones, you only have to look at dogs right straight in the eye, like this, let him come closer, right straight in the eye, you see, he's trembling, he cringes down to the ground, he's running away. The boy is a stray dog, he stinks, he has been eating carrion, maybe he has rabies, very still now, Father I can do it, too. Rosie, who has been cowering against the wall of the cliff, slumped down like a little pile of bad luck, straightens up, grows, grows out of her child's frame and looks at the boy angrily, straight in the eye, for many long seconds, without blinking a single time and without stirring a limb. It is still, terribly still, and suddenly there is a stupefying scent of millions of unpretentious, honey-sweet, herb-bitter furze bushes, and amid the stillness and the fragrance the boy finally collapses, like a doll with the sawdust running out of it. It cannot be comprehended, you can only assume that Rosie's terrible gaze must have had some sort of primordial power in it, the primitive instinct of self-preservation, while the primitive instinct of lust lay behind the last, wild gesticulations of the boy. Everything new, everything freshly awakened on this hot, sunshiny afternoon, sheer new experiences, the passion for life, desire and shame, these children, awakened by the spring, yet not to love, but to longing and fear instead. Ashamed, the boy retreats before Rosie's basilisk gaze, step by step, whimpering like a sickly infant, and Rosie, too, feels ashamed, likewise from the effect of that gaze, which she would perhaps never find the courage to repeat later in front of a mirror. The boy, who had swiftly turned around and, with his clothes in his hand, run soundlessly back up the steps of the cliff, sits down at last, and suddenly his little dog is there again, with his carefree, cheeky bark, the boy sits on a low wall, buttons up his shirt and mumbles to himself, angry and blinded by tears. Rosie runs down the zigzag path thinking she should feel relieved to have gotten out of that this time, no, these fathers, you can really learn a lot from fathers, but she basically only feels sad, stumbling along among the spurge bushes and the white thorn bushes, blinded by tears. Your fellow student Rosie, I hear, has just returned from Italy, yes, thank you, it was very nice. It was nice and dreadful, and having reached the shore, Rosie rinses her face and neck in the sea water, thinking I will not say a word about it in any case, and then saunters off along the margin of the waves toward her parents, while up above on the road, the boy slowly trots home. And during all of this so much time has passed that the sun already hangs low over the mountain, so that both Rosie and the boy cast long shadows, long ones, widely separated from each other, across the tops of the young pines in the abyss, across the already paling sea.

Translated by Suzanne and Carl Clifton Toliver

Barbara König

Waiting for Wisdom

Dining car on the way to Mainz. I have traveled this stretch so often in past years that I know it by heart. I know the breakfast, too, the coffee, the soft-boiled egg, and the other plastic-wrapped delicacies, but it's different this time. This time I see myself from outside. Why did I never do that before? Why wasn't it important enough to me? And I do know so many people. Men as well as women who constantly see themselves from outside and obviously are quite happy doing that?—so see myself with the eyes of the other: a slightly older woman, not pretty, not ugly, but none of that plays a role any more, just because she's a slightly older woman.

The waiter comes by and I order a schnapps, although I don't like schnapps. That shows me that I'm in a state of shock. Incredible, when I think of the reason: the short minute in the train station this morning. Sitting at the ticket window was a curly blond young man whom I had never seen before; he looked like he was seventeen, but that might be because of my advanced optics—I believe now, while outside the Ulm cathedral rises from the roofs and the unaccustomed schnapps burns its path into my stomach— so the youth asked very politely what my wishes were and added, a further act of consideration: "Senior pass?"—There it was, no more than that, but for me it was a blow of the fist in the pit of my stomach that knocked the air out of me. I could have given all kinds of answers, for example: Oh no, I just turned fifty-nine! or: listen, my dear, you'd better leave that to me! or quite simply: No!—instead of which I managed nothing but a mild shake of my head and as though benumbed afterward the way to the platform and to the train and in the train the way to the dining car. There I sit now, flabbergasted and dismayed: the episode was so terribly banal, outright childish. Actually it shouldn't have bothered me at all. And now that's the second shock on this morning: that I'm shocked.

Still in the dining car. I have eaten breakfast and look at the Swabian Jura mountains, how they split up the swaths of fog and surprisingly let it converge again. I don't think, don't feel, and yet know all of a sudden: That's not the way it was. What happened there was neither childish nor banal, it was death itself, who spoke to me there, curly headed and blond and politely through the window: "Do you finally understand, ma'am—the matter is closed!" It was the clutch from the grave, horror itself.

Eleven o'clock at night in my lonely hotel room. That's an hour I ordinarily enjoy a lot—a cigarette, a small glass of tonic water, perhaps a couple of notes—but not tonight. Tonight I want simply to sleep. And the session ran pleasantly, and the dinner, too. I was cheerfully disposed to divert myself—and very probably the others, also—from my sudden blemish of age, and was successful, too. But now it's night, and I would love to have had something alive with me, human being, cat, or dog, main thing being that it was warm and breathing, whether in the bed or under it, and no matter how many legs it had.

At home again. Looked in my old diaries for some solace; spread out three or four square yards of paper over the floor, before I even found a place with that theme. Not a word of solace: "Woke up and was seized by terror: the person I have been seems to disappear before my eyes into a bottomless shaft from which, if at all, it will emerge again as an antipode, covered with spider webs in a world overgrown with gray mold, where even the erstwhile sun is nothing more than a running Camembert, every blossom fallen from a decaying bouquet, every animal either an owl or a howling jackal, no people in sight, and if there are, then as slithering ghosts; I myself mirrored in a glazed glass: I'm approaching forty."

That was twenty years ago. The nightmare couldn't have lasted long, for already after a few months later I began to look forward to my first baby, and the joy stayed and stayed. Number of years had nothing to do with growing old, only with growing—I was simply happy.

Then another passage: "Berlin, Erdener Street, my forty-fifth birthday. I danced with Milo Dor, and he said: 'My dear lady, I'd give three fifteen-year-olds for you!' Funny thought." Why do I find it only half as funny today? Because in the meantime it would be four fifteen-year-olds, or even three twenty-year-olds, or, God forbid, even two thirty-year-olds? Or just because I'm afraid that offers of that kind are gone forever anyway?—Pause. I have washed two hair brushes and a comb and polished my nails. Now I have my reply, too: by right I should be completely indifferent as to who would like to trade how many young creatures for me or not—and I am, too.

Midnight. Actually, I should go to bed, instead of which I am driven between the bookcases, looking for a contemporary who could say to me: This is the meaning of growing older, and that's it. What I find are the familiar friends who all together resist growing old: Max Frisch, Canetti, Italo Svevo. And even the really clever women: Grete Weil, over seventy and still skiing, and the man at the lift says with admiration: "My esteem, ma'am!"—and she writes "He hasn't the slightest idea how deeply that hurts." Or Simone de Beauvoir, who observes the strange face in the mirror with repugnance, the wrinkled skin, bags under the eyes, and yells: "How did I get this way? That's not me!"

Ask me now how they might have felt after they put their lamentation and their fury down on paper: better at any rate, and maybe they had arrived at a new insight that could help many. But the reader will never find that out, for authors (especially the good ones) are egotists; they write only what they want to rid themselves of, and then they enjoy the fruits alone.

Woke up exasperated. It was still dark; downstairs shivering, made tea. After a look at the leaden lake between meadows, sitting on the bar stool in the kitchen ate toast and marmalade and found out the reason for my exasperation: me myself. How can I let myself be depressed so protractedly by a simple number that fixes age?! Even if I know how tremendously relative those numbers are!

After all, I have experienced it: At eighteen I loved a grizzled old man of thirty-six, and at fifty-nine I danced with a kid of thirty-five. At eighty I could theoretically flirt with a contemporary of seventy. Bewildering.—Adele Sandrock comes to mind, who celebrated her seventy-fifth with a gloomy countenance. One of her admirers trilled: "But sweetie! Seventy-five, that's not old!" And Sandrock, in her deepest bass: "Not for a cathedral!"

I laugh; the spell is already broken. Besides it has gotten lighter; the lake has changed from lead to silver, and I've breakfasted, too.

Shrove Tuesday at the Gossers. Many lovely women with smooth faces. From the distance they looked like mid-twenties, near up like mid-forties, in reality they are old. That puzzles me at first: How can Frau Karg, whom I haven't seen for a long time, now look ten years younger than she did five years ago? Then I'm glad: Wonderful, such a victory over decline, and at the same time hope for us all. In the end, disquiet remains: Something's not right. I listen to Frau Karg talk brightly about her trips—she did that five years ago, too, except that then it wasn't Kashmir but the Caribbean—and suddenly I know what bothers me: She's wearing her new face like you wear a new dress when you know it doesn't flatter you: self-conscious, cheerful. Except that, like a dress, it has become an object, pretty but exchangeable.

Again a voice on the radio that speaks about the dignity of growing old. It seems to me as though I had heard that a thousand times since my childhood, and since my childhood I haven't known what to do with it. What is dignity? Hard to say. The man on the radio doesn't know either.

Probably it was Proust who wrote: "Time is a process of counting that corresponds to nothing in reality."

Back from Cologne and still partly depressed, partly disgusted by the experience in the hotel. And actually it was nothing more than an everyday incident that earlier wouldn't have occupied me for a minute. But since I know that I'm getting old everything is different.

Such an ordinary little scene: during the morning after breakfast I'm packing my suitcase. I open my jewelry case, in which the pin with the two sapphires lies, but the pin isn't there. So I begin to look for it. Meanwhile I feel distrust shooting out of me in all directions, ready to tear the mask off the face from any person happening to be in my vicinity. Exhausted I collapse into an easy chair, overpowered by the power of evil that suddenly surrounds me—then I think of checking in the closet and, of course, the pin is stuck there on the dress I had worn during the evening. My suspicion deflates; I'm ashamed of myself. And still, as I finish packing, in control and totally myself again, in my opinion, there I notice it: a trace of mistrust remains. Now I sit there and wonder whether I will continue to look at each and all with suspicion that will thicken with years ever more into certainty. Horrible thought.

Next day. My friend Kaminchen has calmed me down. What do you want, she said, I'm at least as mistrustful as you are, and I have my reasons. Believe me, people have stolen from me so often that I can't manage being trustful of humanity. As emphasis she tells me the story about her cousin in Berlin who went to the bathroom in the department store, set her purse down on the floor in front of her and had to watch as a hand reached in and pulled it out from under the door. It was one of those doors that ends a foot above the floor. Her cousin took only a minute to leave the toilet, but that minute was enough for the thief to disappear with her purse in the milling crowd of store customers. She asks a lady in the wash basin area whether she had seen a woman with a dark-brown leather purse, but she knew only about an improbable housewife with a rather large shopping bag. Hopeless case. Her cousin reports the theft in the store office, borrows two marks for the subway just to get home, there rings the building superintendent's door so that he can let her in her apartment, arrives finally exhausted and first pours herself a schnapps. Then the telephone rings: Here the So-and-so Department Store, leather ware department: Your purse has been turned in to us. You can pick it up. No, I don't know what's missing; I just was told to call you. Her cousin grabs the extra key and another purse with money and takes a taxi to the department store. The blond girl in the leather department doesn't know anything about her purse, nor does her colleague who is called over. Finally in the store manager's office she is told clearly: The call cannot possibly have come from us, for if it had we would have notified you—Again a taxi, and home again Even while entering her apartment she knows: She has been taken. The wardrobe stands open, her new winter coat is missing, and inside in the living room even more is missing, and particularly in the bedroom: the money from the chest and her jewelry from its case. "Believe you me," Kaminchen says, "if I tell my cousin about your misgivings, she'll have a laughing fit."

Actually I ought to be reassured: Everything seems to be just fine with me, just not with humanity.—I sit there now and wonder what the reason is that I'm not at all reassured.

Once in my young years I was sitting with a friend in a boat on the Rhine, and my friend asked: "Have you ever thought about how you would most like to die?" "I just know how I wouldn't like to die," I said, "and that's in a casket in which I've been buried alive.—And you?" "I'd like to be shot to death at the age of ninety by a jealous husband," he said.

Guests in the evening, the married couple G in a good mood: in two months they both stop working. "What will you do then?" I ask, and they reply as though with one mouth: "Travel!"—They want to see all the places they ever dreamed of and for which at first they lacked the money and later the time. "Preferably the whole world," says Frau G. I say that I envy them, and they ask how come, for I could do it too, wouldn't have to . . . "Sure," I said, "but I don't envy your trips, rather your relish for it—I once had it too, but now it's getting less and less."

Ambivalencies. More and more often it happens that I wake mornings between four and five and can't go to sleep again because I am tormented by anxieties and pursued by furies; then after tossing and turning I get up and sneak downstairs—the nasty condition that is called "pre-senile flight from bed." Whereupon I run out of the house and into the garden, barefoot over the grass, and stop at the roses, the lavenders, the yellow poppy, the marigolds, smell the phlox and understand what I have missed during my whole life, what everybody misses who sleeps away these early hours.

Bad Wörishofen. I could imagine that: a life in the hotel. Preferably like here, in one of the big old edifices that exist everywhere in the world and have preserved the flair of yesterday, besides attract a certain kind of guests, those who, like me, have the flair of yesterday.

This is what Frau Goethe wrote to her son in November, 1793: "above all things, in accordance with my rank and prominence I must have a lodging—so that in the last years of my life I am not belittled. For in the fifth act there should be applause and not whistles of derision."—Rank and prominence could be ignored, but the last sentence is good.

So, assuming I were very old and alone, then a hotel like this one would surely be too expensive for me in the long run—in case one could still speak of the long run—but perhaps I could find an old edifice that is cheap, without carpets in the hall, without central heat, possibly without a private bath. That I can live like that I have proved, of course, and more than once. Except that back then it was an adventure, temporally limited as are all adventures, and with the prospects of improvement. That prospect will no longer exist. To be really old, perhaps slow moving, perhaps too blind to read, perhaps also not completely right in my head—and then poor, too? No. That's too unreasonable, not only for me, that just can't be. Dignity, I think, the word that I never could do much with—here it fits.

Later. This was a hard afternoon. Rode my bicycle for a whole two hours through this peaceful landscape, and while doing so rid myself of one of my favorite ideas about myself: grand independence. No, I'm not that anymore and perhaps I never was really. That hurts. Such a galling, galling disappointment.

When Mama turned fifty, in the last year of the war, radiant and happy, in spite of the bad times, she quoted one of her favorite sayings: "If you don't want to get old, hang yourself while you're young!" And one of her birthday guests, Monsieur Schmitt, who had been dragged along, bent over the carrot cake and added in his half-whispering way: "—or become a soldier."

Sat on the floor the whole afternoon in my large closet between mounds of pullovers and the sort, for that's my new sport: tossing ballast overboard. Astonishing the lightness it give me, the joy! At least as much as going shopping did before.

Found a quotation: "The delightful feeling of being the right age: when I look at the junk all around me and can say to myself: You don't need that anymore!"—No, that wasn't a wise man of our new affluent society, that was Wilhelm Raabe, about 1900 or so.

Met a woman in the supermarket. She too, as the saying goes, will never see sixty again. Nevertheless she's still a very pretty woman, it's just that earlier she was a beauty. And we're already on the subject. "Time was," she said, "nine out of ten men turned around and looked at me on the street, and now it's just one." I laugh. That was a mistake: "Anyone who hasn't herself experienced that can hardly imagine such a thing," she says. Serves me right. We go our own ways amicably. I look after her, carrying her sack to the parking lot, with her head sunk, as though she had to hide a disgrace. I'd like to be of help to her, just don't know how.—Beautiful women age badly.

Looking for a lost letter found the photograph of Manés Sperber as an old man and thought suddenly with delight about what I described in one of my early diaries as "horrible suspicion": that old age is the real condition of mankind and that everything else before that is just a cover up by certain vital substances, muscles, hormones and so forth, all for the preservation of the species. When all that falls away, then what remains is what it is.—Handsome Manés Sperber.

Afternoon in the rest home, with Dr. R., Renata's last uncle. I met him in the large hall. "You won't mind if I remain seated," he said, "the small conventions have no value for me—old age, you understand." "No problem," I said and sat down. "Not for you," he said, and then, with open malice in his voice: "Not yet." I handed him the book I had brought for him. He turned it in his hand. "Beckett," he said, "of course, I read him a long time ago." I reached out my hand, but he said: "Why shouldn't I read it again?" and laid the book next to him on the cushion. "You look like him," I said. He seemed to know that already, for he simply nodded.—"I'm supposed to bring you greetings from Renate," I said after a while. "Pointless," he said, "she would never have sent you to me without sending me greetings. Did she have anything else to say?" "Just that she's doing fine, and that she will visit you in the summer." "So nothing," he said. "What do you expect?" I asked. "Well, that communications contain something worth communicating," he said. Now I noticed that I began to find him despicable. Incredible that the man was once a doctor! "Obviously," I said, "Renate found it worth communicating to notify you of her visit for the summer." "She would have been quite right," he said, "if she hadn't made that communication to me already in her Christmas letter." I couldn't think of anything to retort, and he used the opportunity for an impertinent question: "How old are you? Sixty?" That was too much. I was about to get up and leave, but I didn't. I remained seated and said, very cautiously so as not to show any emotion: "No, not yet. But soon. And you?" "Old enough to be your father," he said. "No thanks," I said.

All of a sudden he laughed, loudly and uncontrollably, everything about him laughed, his scrawny figure, his wrinkles, above his eyes. I realized how he might have been thirty, forty, fifty years before. Meanwhile other visitors streamed into the hall, each of them with flowers or a present in the hand. "All heirs," said the doctor, "and all are waiting for someone to die. If you have money, then they're waiting for the money; if you have none, then they're waiting to be rid of you. The best thing is that you have a large income that dies with you: then they wish you a long life because they can then pocket some for a long time." "Maybe," I said, "there's another possibility you've forgotten, namely, rich or poor—to be loved!" That brought me nothing but contempt. "That miserable desire to be loved! From the cradle to the bier, always just that! And no one wants to be loved, although that would settle everything else." "Do you want to be?" I asked. But his outbreak seemed to have used up his energies; he started to get up. "Of course not," he said with clenched teeth, so it seemed to me, "but I don't expect anything from others either."

Next day. Woke up with the desire to become a wicked old woman. That contradicts all my goals up to now, admittedly, but I can suddenly imagine that it would be a pleasure. I'm just afraid it must be right for you, you must practice it inside all your life so that in your old age you can do it.

September. I'm practicing. In the shoe store I try on the garish sandals. "Aren't they somewhat too youthful?" I ask, "after all,

I'm sixty!"—wait for the incredible astonishment of the salesgirl the contradiction. But the salesgirl shrugs her shoulders and says: "That doesn't matter, you can wear these sandals at any age."

The first letter from friends: What do you plan for your round-numbered birthday? Will you be at home or on a trip? Probably they want to send flowers. And it's always the "round" one, although I can't imagine anything more pointed, more prickly.—So eight more days and I'll have become not a year but ten years older. Afterward I'll resign myself, get used to my new age, until the new horror appears, the next zero! And that, starting with thirty, decade for decade the movable terror.

10 October. So. Yesterday I turned sixty. And now? Nothing. It was simply a birthday, with an extraordinary number of letters, flowers, and presents, that's true, but otherwise—nothing spectacular, neither inside nor outside. And that very thing's the miracle: I DON'T SEE THE PROBLEM ANYMORE!

Was there ever a problem? What was I afraid of for a whole year? I read my diaries and don't want to believe myself—such insanity! Now I'm free and easy as never before, that's the reward for anxiety. Then, sitting among flowers, letters, cooking dishes, the thought strikes me: probably it will be exactly the same way with death—years on end the fear of it, and finally the time has come, I die, die, have died. Look around and ask: Why that big, lifelong fear? I don't see the problem anymore.

December. Shock, relapse, catastrophe: The teeth are gone. Just when I had finally come to terms with being old, so relaxed and solemn. Gone. Two molars must go, the third still has a chance. "Well, all right," I say, "then we'll do a bridge." "Not necessarily," says the dentist, "we've got to see if the fourth will stay." "And if it won't?" I ask with mouth already dry. "Then you'll get a partial prosthesis," says the doctor. A horrible word. I stare at him. Irretrievable. Disgusting. Never more uninhibited while eating, talking, laughing. "Piece by piece I'm mislaying myself": Montaigne. Catastrophe.—But with all of that, there's a part of me that's amused. Hardly believable, but that's the way it is. A part that sees the decline and laughs! "I won't be able to give any more readings," I say. Now the dentist laughs, too: "If everyone who has false teeth could appear on stage no more," he says, "then they'd have to close the theater." I manage a tortured smile. "Oh, well," I say while I twist myself out of the chair, "maybe the fourth one will stay."

Later. Terrible mood, miserable day. Now ice-cold rain instead of snow. Gray and chilly, that fits. And: what happened of any note? Two or three teeth will be leaving me, that's all. There are still enough left, aren't there? Anyway, this may just be the beginning, of the end, of course. A nightmare has begun.—Teeth falling out in a dream: bereavement, it said in the dream books of my childhood. So again fear of dying seems to lurk behind everything. "Weariness of material things," I tell my brother with a shrug, who has a soft disk and is a physicist besides.

Next day. Fine, now it's starting to amuse me. Growing old and everything—almost everything—that's connected to it amuses me! Such an amazing discovery. I told the dentist about it, but he warned me: "I wouldn't tell that to anyone. There are too many people who are pained by it. They wouldn't understand." "But maybe it would be just the thing to show them that possibility?"— "They wouldn't consider it a possibility," he said.

Waiting for wisdom: gradually it had to show itself.

Translated by A. Leslie Willson

Gerhard Köpf

The Bottles of Venice

You can visit Venice only in the wintertime, best of all at New Year's. Then the narrow streets are still more or less passable and you don't keep stumbling into a Japanese. I stopped off at the Gritti Palace Hotel and on the first evening pored over the guest list, which lay in a prospectus in my room. The Agah Khan, Churchill, de Gaulle, Giorgio Armani, Truman Capote, Graham Greene, Rubinstein, Toscanini, Bogart, Chaplin, all the beautiful people had signed the *Libro d'oro*. Suddenly I also came across the name Jean Seberg. At once I saw her before me again. As a newspaper vendor in *Breathless* she was wearing a short-sleeved T-shirt on which, front and back, the *New York Herald Tribune* stood. She looked absolutely enchanting.

As a young man who was undyingly in love with the pharmacist's daughter from Marshalltown, Iowa, that struck me to my heart so deeply that I went to the nicely outfitted bar to have a drink. My heart pounded for a long time, as though it were about to burst forth from my chest. I wasn't exactly dressed properly for the Gritti Bar, for I was wearing cowboy boots, jeans, my fisherman's vest with the thousand pockets, and a red-checked woodcutter's shirt. It wasn't difficult for me to choose the seat with the best view of the bar. To my right were sitting a spectacled black man with a Van Dyck beard and a spectacled blonde. Very much in love. I missed a bar pianist as an imaginary conversation partner.

I was solo.

I spent half the night drinking, until a man came up to me and introduced himself as Hermann Schiefer. I liked him very much at first sight. We left the counter and sat down by the blaze in the open fireplace. I told him about my grandmother, who had nomad fever, and about my stay in Venice. Schiefer, who had for a time taught at the University of the Holy Heart of Jesus in Milan and there, faced by ignorant students, had discovered his passion for the subjunctive, but now was working on a wine lexicon, a comprehensive, encyclopedic work, ordered a Barbecarlo for us, one of the oldest and most distinctive wines of Oltrepò Pavese in the south of Lombardy, vintner Lino Maga. We toasted one another, and Schiefer said: "That's a new experience for you, isn't it?" And I praised the wine.

I was playing with a half-empty whiskey bottle, and I stuck my finger in the neck of the bottle.

To my question about how he had gotten the curious idea of putting together a wine lexicon, since such things already existed in abundance, he replied with a story:

"This story took place years ago, and I tell it only because you got so excited about the bottle we have. So imagine a man—let's call him Ganzenmüller for the sake of simplicity—on his way from Potenza to Matera. If he can, he wants to reach Tarent, but probably that detour would take too much time. A really significant detour: He had not imagined it like that. San Gelsomino is the name of the village where Piatgorsky lies buried. Actually he doesn't know the people very well, but he once promised to take a photograph of the grave, their son's grave, which they never saw: It's hard to refuse something like that. San Gelsomino is not on the map. It must lie somewhere between Poggio and Cazzano, somewhere in that desolate region. He looked for the name for quite a while on the road signs, but there's not much to them there. Apparently the natives know their way well enough, and there are hardly any tourists to get lost here. He hopes his car will get through. For some time it has been having a problem, hesitates, doesn't drive too well. Maybe it's the carburetor. A breakdown in this locale—that would be the end, no garage far and wide, maybe not even a telephone.

"Piatgorsky, fallen in war. What nonsense to wage war here, in this land, where, by God, there was nothing to gain!"

Schiefer interrupted his story and ordered an extremely attractive Frescobaldi. Silently we drank, silently we gave homage to the wine with nodding heads and rolling eyes.

Again I stuck my finger in the neck of the whiskey bottle. This time I couldn't get it out. Jack Daniels wouldn't turn loose of me. But that didn't bother me at the moment. Maybe I was already too drunk. I listened attentively to the person opposite me:

"Obviously Ganzenmüller had taken a wrong turn. Here in this nameless locale on the hill, the road stops. You couldn't tell that from the bottom. It leads only to a few houses and no farther. Maybe he'll do better by asking. Good thing that he knows Italian, at least.

"It is midday—dazzling, dusty brightness. Aridity and heat. A time in which time stands still. The houses look run-down, even poorer than anywhere else. Apparently they haven't been painted for centuries. All the window shutters are closed. You might be led to believe the place was abandoned, were it not for a dirty white chicken taking a bath in the dust. Ganzenmüller knocks on a door. Nothing stirs. He tries it again, louder: in vain. The door is locked. He looks around. Shall he try somewhere else? He calls out, 'Hello!' into the hot stillness. 'Hello! Is anyone there?'"

I could not get my damned finger out of the neck of the bottle and turned the bottle back and forth, but nothing helped. Continuing to drink didn't get me loose. Before my eyes flickered the image of Hemingway and the face of Jean Seberg. They were acting so familiar with one another that I became very jealous. Again and again I tried to pull my finger out of the bottle, but couldn't manage it. My conversation partner seemed not to notice it at all and kept on with his story:

"For a long time nothing stirs, but then a door does open, farther along, on the oppose side of the lane, and a black-clad old woman comes into view. She steps out for a moment, looks at him, and disappears again. No matter, he crosses over, knocks, enters. The room is almost dark. For a moment he sees nothing. 'Take a seat,' comes from a corner. He feels his way, makes out a table and chair, and sits down.

"'I've gotten lost,' he says. 'I'm looking for a small place. It's called San Gelsomino. It must be here in this area. Do you know where?'

"'You're German,' says the woman."

Again Schiefer interrupted his story and ordered, this time, to my surprise, a horrible Amselfelder, which I would preferably have spat right out again. It was a terrible brew, served preferably by unspeakable wives of dyspeptic professors, that made me belch sourly. My finger being in the neck of the bottle made me more and more nervous. I drank with one hand and tried in a ridiculous way to grip the bottle between my legs and free my finger. I pleaded with Jean Seberg for help, but she didn't hear me. I felt thoroughly wretched. What could I do to get my finger out of the bottle? Helplessly I look across at my conversation partner, but he seems to take no notice of my predicament. As I glance at him pleadingly he continued his story:

"Ganzenmüller can see her now; his eyes are getting used to the gloom. She is wearing a headscarf, black as the rest of her garment, like all old women in this land.

"'Yes, German. Did you recognize my license plate?'

"She is silent.

"'San Gelsomino,' says Ganzenmüller. 'How do I get there?'

"She gets up and disappears into a nearby room. He hears her puttering about. She comes back with a bottle and a glass, sets both down before him, and pours.

"'Have a drink. You must be thirsty. A wine from this region. You speak Italian well for a German.'

"'I need to. I'm traveling on business. Do you know where San Gelsomino is located?'

"'Yes.'

"'Oh, good!' He takes a drink. 'Where?'

"'What do you want in San Gelsomino?'

"'Photograph a grave. Acquaintances have asked me to. Their son died in the war and lies buried there. A German officer.'

"'His name is Piatgorsky,' she says.

"'Yes,' he replies stunned. 'Did you know him?'

"The woman doesn't answer. For a while it is quiet in the room. A fly is buzzing.

"'You are in Gelsomino, signore.'"

Schiefer orders again. This time he gets a Südtiroler Bauernfeind for a short intermission. My friend warded off my objections to such gall and said with a wily smile that life was full of variety.

That bothered me little at the moment. I couldn't get my finger out of the damned bottle. I was already imagining having to live out my days with my finger stuck in the bottle. All the shaking and turning and sweating and squeezing was of no use, none, none. Gradually my rage turned into miserable desperation. I stuck the bottle under the nose of my companion, but Hermann Schiefer only smiled and presumably took it for the wearied prank of a drunk. It made no impression upon him. Instead, he continued narrating:

"The hot quiet dribbles through the closed shutters. Ganzenmüller has the feeling of hearing a clock ticking, but there is no clock here. He empties his glass: he slurps, in order to hear something. Actually, I shouldn't be drinking any alcohol, he says to himself, in this heat. It's no help against thirst, and I have to drive.

"'So this is it,' he says aloud, just to say something. 'Then I have to search no further.' Maybe, he thinks, I'll still get to Tarent.

"'No,' the woman replies. 'You've arrived.'

"It would be impolite to leave right away. Also, he must still ask her the way to the cemetery. Outside, murderous heat broods. It feels good to sit in the coolness awhile.

"'Tell me about it,' says the woman.

"'Tell you? About what?'

"'Surely you were also in the war.'

"'Yes.'

"'In Italy?'

"'Yes, also in Italy.'

"'And killed people?'

"'I had to. To survive. Me or the others. You had no choice.'

"She nods: 'I know. It's always the same. They all have to, nobody knows why, and God lets it happen.'

"'This Piatgorsky,' says Ganzenmüller. 'Did you know him while he was alive? Such a coincidence,' he says. 'It's a small world.'

"'Coincidence? Now that you're here?'

"'Me? How so? That's just a coincidence, too. On vacation you meet people, complete strangers. You mention that you have business in southern Italy, and then you're asked about a fallen soldier.'

"'That's no coincidence, signore. I've been waiting for you.'

"Waiting? What does she want? The wine is going to his head, or is she talking nonsense?

"'What do you mean by that?' he asks.

"He tries to give his voice a casual tone.

"She doesn't answer.

"He tries something else: 'Did you know Piatgorsky?'

"'Know him? Saw him when he was dead. Before that, he shot and killed my husband and my son. He alone had survived, the last one in his patrol. He defended himself to the end and kept shooting as long as he could instead of surrendering.'

"For a while it is again quiet in the room.

"'I didn't know him,' says Ganzenmüller. 'Fellow countrymen, a coincidence. Besides, it was a long time ago.'

"'That doesn't matter.' She says that soothingly, as though she had to comfort him."

She pours for him again, waits until he has drunk, pours again.

"'Did you notice that I'm not drinking with you?'

"'Oh,' he says, 'I thought you didn't want to.'

"'With a guest you drink, though.'

"'So why not, then?'"

It bothered me that Schiefer interrupted again and ordered from the waiter an Est! Est!! Est!!! di Montefiascone that was as suitable as a fist in the eye. Even the wine's name made me ill.

"Are you trying to kill me?" I protested. "That's murder!"

Schiefer replied: "Just drink. It belongs with this story."

But I resisted.

Schiefer tried to change my mind.

I didn't want to.

At that moment I would have drunk anything, just not that poison.

At Schiefer's last words my finger was still stuck in the half-empty whiskey bottle that was hanging heavier on me than a millstone. I was near tears: from sentimentality, from drunkenness, from desperation. Helplessly I looked at Schiefer and began to pray: Dear God, let me think of something to get my finger out of this bottle. Do something to get me loose from it.

"What's wrong with this damned bottle," I yelled.

"It goes against my grain to explain to a fallen man the depth of his plunge. If necessary, I would try soap on it," said Hermann Schiefer. His voice sounded odiously soft and unmoved, and he said that, according to tradition, a German bishop, in other reports a Dutch cardinal, as others say, a Bavarian baron, who liked to drink wine, had sent his chamberlain ahead on a trip to Rome and had ordered him to try the wine in the inns and taverns along the way and to write the word Est on the wall of the building involved, and in Montefiascone the servant is said to have written the word three times, he liked the wine so much, whereby the bishop or cardinal or baron had been just as enthusiastic and supposedly drank himself to death, which lets us surmise that the wine of the time must have been of a different quality from that of today.

But I wasn't interested in such sufficiently familiar historical digressions, rather solely in my finger in the whiskey bottle, perhaps also in the end of Schiefer's story, which he finally could no longer keep from me:

"'There are two bottles,' she says. 'So that God's will may be done. If it's not His will, then you will go on living. If it were up to me, you wouldn't. Two for two, that's fair. I always knew that you would come one day. You, or somebody else. And now you have come. But I've let too much time go by. My hate has lessened. At first there was only one bottle prepared, the one with the poison. Poison in the empty bottle. Pour in wine, when the day arrives. But then I had doubts. It is written: Vengeance is mine, sayeth the Lord. I put a second bottle beside it, without poison, and confused the two so often in the dark until I could no longer tell them apart: When I saw you driving into the village before, I filled the bottles with wine.'

"She takes the emptied bottle in her hand, turns it, and says with a voice as though she were speaking of the possibility of a change in the weather: 'Now it depends.'

"'Does the poison work quickly?'

"'No, slowly. It would be futile, if you tried to do something now. It goes right into your blood. They would come too late. I even knew the name, but these Latin words, you forget them.'

"'Does it taste bitter? Or how does it taste?'

"'I don't know. I never tried it, after all. I believe they told me it was completely without taste.'

"'If I die, what will happen to you then? We're no longer at war. Did you give that a thought? They will condemn you.'

"'No. It will never get out. They don't know people here. A foreigner, who's driving around in the land and dies: heat stroke. It won't be investigated. But even if it is—I'm old. I don't care about anything. Not much.'

"'I'm innocent,' he says. 'I never saw Piatgorsky.'

"'That doesn't matter,' she says softly. 'My son was also innocent. He just ran past. He was only thirteen. He would be taking care of me now.'

"'What am I going to do?' He's surprised that he asks her that, her, a woman who wants him dead.

"'You did want to photograph the grave? Come, I'll show you the way. The cemetery is outside the village. You have to go there on foot.'

"When they walk out into the bright day, it seems to him that what he experienced in the dark couldn't be true in the light. A bad film, and now it's over. But the usher is still there.

"'When will it have its effect?'

"'I don't know exactly. Maybe in half an hour.'

"'Do you notice anything ahead of time?'

"'I don't think so. But I don't know.'

"'What will you do, if I get away? Wait for the next German?'

"'Of course not.' She stops, looks at him, and says: 'I'll drink the other bottle then myself.'

"'Why?'

"'As penance for my hate. Because God was against me.'

"Sweat appears on Ganzenmüller's brow. Can't he even hope without penalty that he got the wrong bottle?

"'Don't do it,' he says. 'That would be silly.'

"'Oh,' she replies with a deprecatory gesture, 'what do you know about it?'

"She accompanies him to the village exit and shows him the path to the graves. 'Up there, straight ahead. You can't miss it.'

"Then she goes back. He looks after her, as, black between the white walls, she becomes smaller and doesn't turn around toward him a single time."

Today I no longer know how I finally got rid of the bottle.

Translated by A. Leslie Willson

Günter Kunert

Fabulous Monologue

I'm not denying anything. Anyway, it's all superannuated. I admit that I've eaten several foresters since 1730. Their horrible taste, mostly tobacco, staghorn, and unwashed loden, can be counted punishment enough for my appetite. Yet I haven't touched a forester for a hundred years. It makes me sick now to think of those bearded green creatures, mad about trees, ears brimming with curly hairs and delightedly pricked up to listen to the nerve-shattering racket of the birds. I'm too delicately strung to endure this perpetual screeching cuckooing trilling fluting piping chirping. But the foresters, ever since they've existed, or rather, ever since I've known them, stand spellbound as if they were listening to the subtlest music Liszt Toselli, while the mists of daybreak swirl around them, a first sunbeam falls through rotten boughs, and from the pond, in whose middle I dwell, my hand quietly reaches out and grabs them by their green collars, to put an end to that romantic misery. I'm not denying it. But it's superannuated. And there were never any witnesses. Likely clues, such as remnants of clothing shoulder blades shoes of indigestible leather, dissolved into the boggy ground long ago. And there's no mesh fine enough to catch some infusorian whose reaction to the twittering might disclose in what earlier metamorphosis of matter it originated.

Foresters are bores. Crack their skulls and you'll find nothing inside but huntsman's twaddle. Hardly a scrap of news about the big wide world out there on dry ground. For ages I haven't spoken to anyone.

Not many days ago, something was swimming around down here, an odd creature, the like of which I'd never seen before. It steered with fins instead of feet, two round growths protruded from its back, its face was almost a single large flat eye, and from its mouth hung two curved tubes, from which beads of air kept bubbling. I thought it was a sort of udderless seacow gone astray, until I spoke to it and it stopped, in horror, and rushed madly to the surface. Then I realized: it was a human being. My gigantic iron hand reached out after him, came up against a rapid whirling from the stern of a boat, and, if I hadn't been made of iron, my fingers would have been taken off. As it was, it only scratched away a few layers of the rust with which I was caked. In the past, I used to clean the rust off by myself, and I took pleasure in having a smooth iron rump, but soon I rid myself of this juvenility. The rust came back before long, in any case; so I let it grow, until it formed a thick rough bark all over me, the color of a fire going out. I still remember what that is: a fire. The first time I saw one, which was also the last time, was just after I was born. My birth was quite normal. My pedigree isn't in the least mysterious.

My mother was a simple miller's daughter, but my father came from the very highest society. He wanted to keep his incognito, and really I should keep it too, if my reverence for science and my sympathy for Dr. Mullberger did not compel me to divulge without restraint everything concerning myself.

While the miller's daughter was gathering blueberries in the summer of 1719, merrily filling her basket, who should come riding along the lonely road but a tall gentleman, for whom basket blueberries miller's daughter and dismounting all came to the same thing. Before the heretofore innocent maid, dazed by the sticky heat of the forest, could stand up straight again—it was too late. Without hesitating a moment, the horseman had ravished her from behind. And when she implored the impetuous gentleman to speak his name, so that the child might at least know that much of its father, the right rude words boomed from behind her: "Subordination without ratiocination!"

She knew at once who was the master of her consequent fate: King Frederick William I, who, on this sweatmaking July day in anno domini 1719, was riding from village to village inspecting his subjects—incognito, as he believed. Not long afterward there were signs that his woodland stroll was bearing fruit, and fruit of a puzzling consistency. Such was the weight of the fruit that after only three months the miller's daughter couldn't stand on her own feet. She spent six months in bed, until twins were born: for there were two of us. Me, Johnny Ironsides, and him, Peter Nickelbones. Of him, more in a moment. When the midwife drew me out and held me up, my weight so amazed her that she got frightened and dropped me. He's fallen on my foot, this boy! I heard her scream: ah, she was bleeding, the instep was broken . . . . Miller's daughter, miller's daughter, what have borne? And my little mother replied, in her embarrassment, that the gracious gentleman had looked quite normal, so far as he had been visible at all during the act: a tall stout man in a blue doublet. Clearest of all she had seen his broad shoes with genuine silver buckles. The midwife was groaning: Lord protect us, the children are made of metal! You're a witch, miller's daughter, you've been humped by the devil. . . . And off she rushed to the tax office, to report the matter. Soon there was a trial, which resulted in the death penalty: The miller's daughter, together with her two homunculi engendered with Beelzebub, as she herself confessed on the rack, should be sewn into a stout sack and submerged in the biggest pond far off outside the village. Since she had attempted to ascribe the aforesaid satanic act to the king, she should also be deprived of her civil rights, because of lese-majesty.

So we were submerged: all three of us. Our mother drowned. We metallic sons didn't drown, of course. Breathing with lungs turned out to be superfluous in our case. But we did feel mighty hunger now and then. So we ate fish, and these waters have been lifeless ever since. We grew. With our enormous claws we grabbed the animals that came to the shores for a drink. It was Peter Nickelbones who got the first forester, but we finished him off together. We shared everything. Evenings, as darkness thickened under the water, we would be pensive and speculate about our own materiality, though we could never explain it. Only later was it explained to me by a specialist, after my brother had emigrated to England. Here is how that happened.

All through one roasting summer the level of our pond got lower and lower, it must have been in 1760, and we could hardly stand up without showing ourselves. So mostly we sprawled in the mud, dreaming. A peasant, attacked by the absurd hope of catching a barbel or a stickleback, was seesawing his barge in the rectangular shadow overhead. We hauled him down and learned from the trembling creature that for seven years a war had been going on: the fields were unplanted and people were starving. Questioned more closely, he stammered: It's against Austria! Our generalissimo is King Frederick William the First's son in person!

Our half-brother! We wanted to know if he was made of iron or of copper, or whatever, and the answer was: I don't understand what you gentlemen are talking about, but everything made of metal is being collected nowadays and melted down for cannon and cannonballs.

Wistfully chewing on those skinny peasant bones, we thought how peculiar it was that our half-brother, a certain Fritz, should be made of real flesh and blood. Peter Nickelbones, always a timorous fellow, was afraid of being melted down as soon as the water level dropped a bit farther and exposed us. He was for preventing the violent demise of his personality into a bally militant mass, so he decided to escape that same night down one of the pond's outlets. He seemed to have vanished without a trace, seemed to have sunk out of sight who knows where, until I heard from an Englishman, who was tough outside but nice and tender inside, that my brother was now in Loch Ness. People often saw him, but they didn't try to catch him, because the RSPCA had declared him to be a "Royal Monster" and in need of sanctuary. Our common chemicophysical genesis, a mystery to me because of my defective scientific training, was clarified only in the twentieth century.

My rust bark grew, my iron face was rank with tendrils and algae, from which I freed myself once a year with a scraper; I went through this performance on the surface, among the reeds, protected from view, stooping over the glassy surface of the pond, as I scratched the nasty green mess from my cheeks. Then, one day, hardly had I raised my head, blinking in the bright sunshine, spluttering, and dripping water from jowls and ears, my bones pressing down on the sandy shore, when there was a great shout:

You! You there, you're fouling the lines! You idiot!

I shouted back that the pond was my property, that I was the terrible Johnny Ironsides in person, and that nobody should insult me; but the man in the boat replied: We Germans fear only God in this world! I am Andreas Schulmann, emeritus professor, and I fish wherever the law allows.

I: It's only allowed here because there aren't any fish left. What's the date? I mean: what year is it?

He: It's 1912. You must be a foreigner. Oriental-Baltic, I'd say, with a Mongoloid touch, to judge by the shape of your skull.

I explained that I was born in the region, but he shook his wild white mane: Nonsense. I'm a geneticist. I know you more precisely than you know yourself!

What's a geneticist? I asked him, and he, whizzing his pince-nez around on its black ribbon, explained. He really did seem the only proper person to explain the incomprehensible fact of my birth. Breathlessly he listened to my confession, soon even tears came to his eyes, and he muttered excitedly: A Hohenzollern, a genuine Hohenzollern! This prominent brow, insignia of world-embracing designs, pondering the grandeur of the Reich, that severe nose, the chin—yes, Your Majesty has convinced me! Your Majesty may command of me what he will!

I: How come it's iron I'm made of?

He: A remarkable process, but by no means a mythical one. As far as we latecomers know, His Majesty King Frederick William I had an iron character, which probably functioned as a genetic catalyst. At that time the King was taking a mercury cure for his gout, that is, a quicksilver cure—the kind of thing that underdeveloped medicine might well prescribe. The catalyst of his character must have induced a structural transformation of the quicksilver circulating in his body and in his gonads, changing it into iron, or into nickel. An astonishing and most regal process. The sperm, of the same chemical composition as metal, though alive, could not help but produce metallic beings, a being of iron: Yourself, my Prince!

I was so overcome with amazement that I neglected to consume this important scholar, though that would have been no end of a help for the development of my personality. As it was, I just gaped as he pulled on the oars, called out a respectful farewell, and was swallowed up by the mockingly rustling reeds instead of by me. He was the first person who ever escaped undigested. And this moment of confusion and indecision was the major mistake of my life—as it later turned out.

I bedded myself quietly in the slime again, to contemplate the unveiled enigma of my earthly existence, of which I could only be glad while under water, for on dry land my weight forbids all motion, and then I must have dropped off. For a few years, at the most. I woke up with, and because of, a shock.

Thought I heard distant thunder. Grumpily heaved over onto my other side. Then another wave of pressure finally shook me awake. Inky mud whirled into my eyes, the banging and cracking sounded very clear and close, was under the water, not above it, and brought me to my feet. I surfaced. It was raining out there. On the shore there were some men in black uniforms. One shouted: There he is, captain! And the one so named put a megaphone to his lips and spoke to me:

Now listen here, Comrade Ironsides! I'm Captain Schulmann. My father told me about your grand old German strength. Now that final victory is in sight, we must throw the whole bag of tricks at them. Your metal as well. The nation needs fellows like you. We've got better things than hand grenades for draft dodgers. Depth charges. Blood sweat and tears, get it? We don't let defeatists get away with it, see? Right! Tomorrow morning a truck will come to pick you up. Toothbrush and a change of underwear will do. Sieg heil!

Their dark shapes slid away among the trees. Millions of rain-drops made them invisible. With the forest standing there quietly in the rain before me, a dim three-dimensional curtain, I could hardly believe that anyone had been there. But the element I lived in had been all churned up by the explosions, and was quite opaque. Depth charges, eh? I wondered if perhaps Schulmann Junior were not actually right to ask for my help. Shouldn't I be grateful to the nation for the foresters? After all, it wasn't the nation's fault that they tasted so filthy of cloth and cardboard. Didn't I owe a debt of thanks to my people for those sturdy mushroom-gathering virgins who simply melted in one's mouth? To be German means: to be easily digestible! And: to digest with ease! Despite my iron constitution: depth charges. Hm. Hm? I decided to save that fatherland of mine, though I knew it only in its wetness. Certainly I'd be sent to the coast, to sink enemy ships or whatever. One bang from my fist against its side, and the cruiser would go down to the bottom. I'd certainly get a medal. I saw myself with the Order of the Black Eagle, or the Golden Fleece, firmly soldered to my freshly de-rusted breast, a living victory memorial towering out of the Atlantic swell, billows crashing against me, a Germanic

Poseidon, source and founder of a new myth of the wave-ruling race of Teutons.

Loaded with ambivalent tension, as well electricity, I waited sleeplessly for the next morning. It came. But no Schulmann Junior and no truck. It was my greatest disappointment for decades and reason enough to retire, wounded, into the snug mud and dream there of the world-political role that unexplained circumstances had compelled me not to play. Wouldn't it be better to renounce earthly doings entirely? Never to surface again? Rust mournfully away, to be discovered millennia afterward, an unimposing chunk of scrap iron, from which Prussia's destiny was once suspended? Serves them right: if they didn't want me, they could (not only could, they'd bloody well have to) kiss my ass. Even if it gave them blood poisoning.

For a long time I stuck to my purpose, until something swam down to me, a curious shape, seemed credibly enough to be an udderless seacow gone astray, until I spoke to it and it fled to the surface. Then I noticed: it was a human being. I grabbed at it. Also surfaced. A boat shot away, dragging a train of loud shouting off across the pond: and I felt a shiver of fear. The bigmouths in a speedboat would certainly trumpet abroad their encounter with me. My time of repose was over. Hand grenades, eh? Depth charges? Well, who knows what monstrosities they'd invented.

Down at the deepest level of the pond I waited for what I imagined. I didn't have to wait long: soon the body of a ship passed overhead, big and oval, a rubber ellipse. As I looked upward, a canister came down, hanging by a cord. The lid was open, amber-colored fluid spread from the container in delicate swaths. Then I lost consciousness. Suddenly it was night.

When daylight came again, I was lying on the bottom of a tiled tank, in lukewarm water, the taste of scented soap in my mouth, rid of the algae and limpets that had inhabited my bottom and back, and covered with a net of steel wire. Over the rim of the tank peeped a bald head, bespectacled, bearded, like a seal: it was you, Dr. Mullberger, and you said: Good morning, Johnny Ironsides—How are you feeling? And I replied: Where am I? How did I get here? Then you continued:

You're in a scientific research institute, my good friend. I'd almost given up hope of ever finding you. For twenty years we've had in our strong room an SS captain's report of a meeting with you. The report was never submitted, because that officer was killed. A friend of his, a metallurgist, appropriated the report and, when the war was over, gave it to his firm, which then passed it to us for evaluation. What a time I've had, Johnny Ironside, searching ponds and pools and lakes for you. The captain, you see, had forgotten to give your exact address. Yesterday evening, when I received the news that you had surfaced in Devil's Hollow, there wasn't a moment to lose. At four in the morning we searched the bottom with mine detectors and—bingo! there you were. Down goes the sedative, a hawser around your neck, we drag you to land, hoist you onto the truck, and off we go to the institute. All along the road crowds of nosy people and reporters were rushing the other way: but we had got there first. You can congratulate yourself. No more corrosion for you now!

Every morning Dr. Mullberger appeared at the tank. From varying phials varying liquids dropped into the water. Was it a tincture of hydrochloric acid? An anticorrosive? Whatever it was, I woke up one morning completely smooth and shining, like a stripling. The floor of the tank was covered with a fine, rough coating: my former rust. Proudly I inspected my limbs, from which rays of light were shimmering through the water, so that Dr. Mullberger had to wear dark glasses when he approached me. I asked him every morning why he had taken me away from my home pond, but he always shook his head with a smile and said:

Wait a while, Johnny Ironsides—The future has just begun, Johnny. We need you urgently, my friend. How do you feel this morning?

Thanks, Herr Doktor, I'm feeling fine. I feel so young, just as if I'd been born twenty years ago, not in 1720.

The next morning a girl's face was craning over my bright iron nakedness. As a child of the eighteenth century, I was extremely embarrassed. I cowered; she giggled. She moved a little farther over the rim of the tank, drank some milky nectar from a little tube, and, in doing so, revealed that her shoulders were unclad— and a little bit further. I lowered my eyes, because nothing covered her nice nubilities either. I think that a reddish shimmer passed over my gleaming exterior. The next day I ventured to raise my eyes. And, after a week, I had grown fully accustomed to the sight of her in her utter nakedness. So my astonishment was only slight when she appeared one morning together with a second girl, just as unclad as herself. The first was a blonde, the second a brunette. The third was freckles all over. The fourth was suntanned. By the time the eighth appeared, I wasn't seeing the details anymore, and with twenty of them surrounding my tank I could hardly distinguish between one and the next. I didn't feel hungry for them, not even when the wire net over my head was removed and I could easily have reached out with my gigantic hand and grabbed some breakfast. Absurd: I had lost my wildness. Possibly some appetite killer had been mixed with the water. Or the lukewarm water simply had a lulling effect. I didn't even grab at them while they were splashing impudently about on the surface. Nor when they dived down to me. They came very close, touched me with their small soft paws; and that started something like a steam hammer pounding in my chest. They frolicked around me like mermaids nereids nixies naiads nymphs or whatever names temptation has, until I finally succumbed to their ceaseless onslaught. Nine months later Dr. Mullberger comes up to my tank, nods smiles says: Congratulations, Johnny Ironsides, you've become a father today. Precisely twenty times. Twelve daughters, eight sons.

I: Thanks, Herr Doktor, it's an awkward situation for me.

Nonsense, Johnny. That's what you're here for. Ah, but I'd quite forgotten to tell you why you've been staying at our institute. So: now you know.

I replied that I had confided to him frankly the story of my life, even the thing about the forester, although it was superannuated, whereas he—he had told me nothing about why he had chosen to abuse me. Until now. Until he now gave me the following lecture:

We need people with your constitution. You, Johnny Ironsides, through people like you we can attain the perfection of frictionless historical functions, long sought, and now within our grasp. Homo sapiens, this tearful creature, eternally hungry, eternally unsatisfied, governed by conflicting emotions, will gradually be supplanted by a species born of your seed. Only an iron humanity is destined to rule the cosmos, and I, Dr. Horst Mullberger, shall be its prophet!

He was gesticulating with his right hand, his left was hidden behind his back: a careless move on his part, and I realize that he's concealing a little bottle from me: it contains the amber-colored fluid that I remember only too well. I demand an explanation, he answers curtly:

You've done your duty. You can go back to your pond.

Suddenly yellow fog starts to roll through the water and however far I retreat to the opposite corner of the tank—it still reaches me. As I lose consciousness I see Dr. Mullberger emptying bottle after bottle of the same stuff into the water, and as I pass out I wonder what is the point of this overdose? . . .

Epilogue: Sales advertisement in the *Daily Post:* "About two tons of high quality iron (faulty casting for a statue), price well below cost of scrap: Dr. H. Mullberger, Institute for Macrobiology."

Translated by Christopher Middleton

Siegfried Lenz

Luke, Gentle Servant

To the south the grass burned. It burned fast and almost without smoke, it burned in the direction of the mountains, towards the mountains of Kenya. The fire was abroad in the elephant grass, and it had its own wind, a wind that tasted of smoke and ashes. Once a year they threw fire into the grass, the fire ran along its old routes towards the mountains, towards the mountains of Kenya, and when it reached the mountains it died down, and with it the wind died down, and then the antelopes returned and the jackals, but the grass was gone. Once a year the grass burned, and when it had burned down, the soil was ploughed, dug up and, ploughed, the new ash went to join the old ash, and they threw corn into this soil of ashes and stones, and the corn grew tall and had good cobs.

I turned aside from the fire and drove in a wide curve down toward the river, toward the bamboo forest. I drove slowly between thorn and elephant grass, skirting the fire, and I felt the hot gusty wind on my skin and tasted the smoke. I planned to drive along the river by the bamboo forest, I would overtake the fire, and after overtaking it return to the grassland. It was no great detour, I only had another fifteen miles to go. I would be home before dark, I had to be home before dark.

But then I met them, or they met me. I don't know whether they had been waiting for me. They lay at the edge of the river and at the edge of the bamboo forest, more than twenty men, they streamed out of the bamboo forest, silent, solemn, twenty lean men, and they had small scars on their foreheads and bodies, deadly stigmata of hate, and in their hands they held their Panga knives, short heavy choppers which they use to kill our wives and children, their own people, and their cattle. They surrounded the car, they looked at me and waited. Some stood in the elephant grass, some in front of the thorn bushes, coming no nearer though they saw that I was alone. They held their Panga knives close to their thighs and were silent, twenty lean Kikuyu, and they looked at me gently and quietly with condescending pity. I turned off the engine and remained where I was; my revolver lay in one of the glove compartments. I could see it, but I did not dare take my hands from the steering wheel. They were watching my hands, quietly and apparently without interest they watched my movements, and I let the revolver lie in its shelf and listened to the fire runnning across the elephant grass in the distance. Then one of them raised his knife, lifted it and signed to me quickly, and I got out. I got out slowly and left the revolver where it was, and then I noticed the one who had motioned to me, and it was Luke, my servant. It was Luke, an old lean Kikuyu. He was wearing a pair of old linen trousers of mine, clean but torn by the thorns, Luke, a quiet, gentle man, Luke who had been my servant for fourteen years. I went up to him, I said: "Luke," but he remained silent and looked past me, looked over to the mountains of Kenya, toward the burning grass; he looked across the backs of the fleeing antelope and did not know me. I looked around me, peered into each man's face, probed, tried to remember desperately whether I had not met one of them before who could nod his head and corroborate that it was Luke who stood before me, Luke my gentle servant for fourteen years; but all the faces were unknown to me and repudiated my glance, strange, distant faces, shining in the close heat of the bamboo.

They opened the circle, two men stepped aside, and I went past them, went in among the thorn bushes; the thorns tore my shirt, they tore the creased, yellow skin, they were hard, dry thorns which grabbed at me, hooked themelves into me, and broke. My shirt hung in tatters over my chest. We have a name for the thorns, we call them "wait-a-while." I heard them overturn the car, they left it there and followed me, they did not set fire to it, they left it there and that was enough in this land of deep sleep and of decay, nobody would ever put that car on its wheels again, perhaps someone might push it into the river. I would never use it again.

They all followed me, mre than twenty men walked behind me; we went through the thorn as if we had a common goal, they and I.

Luke walked behind me, I heard his knife fall against the thorn branches, the branches that had been bent forward by my body and that sprang back. Sometimes I stopped so that Luke would catch up with me, I had not yet given up the idea of speaking with him, but he always noticed my intention and slowed his step, and when I looked around he turned to look back or stared over the top of my head. I followed them as far as the river. I was following them, although I walked ahead, and when I came to the river I stopped, stopped before the flat, lazy river that I had already waded twice, twice in mud up to my hips, once in the war and once when the missionary had an accident. It was long ago, but I had not forgotten what it had felt like. I remained standing on the river bank, and they came and stood around me, more than twenty men with heavy Panga knives, strange, rigid faces marked with the small scars of hate. Black river ducks paddled quickly toward the other bank, paddled away and looked back, and I stood in the circle that the river completed, stood in the center of their silent hate. They sat down on the ground, they held their knives on their laps; they were silent, and their silence was as old as the silence of this country. I knew it, I had borne it for forty-six years. When we came from England, this country had received us with silence. It had been silent when we sowed and when we harvested, it had been silent whatever we did. We should have known that one day it would speak.

A snake swam across the river. It came out of the bamboo grove; it held its head rigidly above the water, a small snake with a flat head, vanishing at last into the river bank, and I marked the place where it had disappeared. I turned my head and looked into the men's faces. I wanted to discover whether they too had noticed the snake. I wished to placate them for I was afraid of the moment when they would start to speak. I was used to their silence and therefore afraid of their speech. But they remained silent and stared in front of them; they behaved as if I were their guard, as if they had yielded to me in silence; they were silent as if their lives depended on mine, and they left me standing in the middle until it was dark. I had tried to sit down on the ground, my shirt stuck to my back, my knees trembled, the heat that came across from the bamboo had made me limp, but I had scarcely sat down when Luke made a short, casual movement with his knife. He lifted the tip just a little, and I knew that I would have to stand up. I was certain that they would kill me, and I looked at them one by one, long and thoroughly, even Luke, for fourteen years my gentle servant. I looked at them and tried to find my murderer among them.

When it was dark, some of the men got up and disappeared, but they returned soon after, carrying dry thorn bushes. They threw the bushes in a heap and lit a small fire in the middle of the circle, and one of them sat near the fire and tended it.

I recalled the time I had spent with Luke, he had disappeared only two days before; I thought of his silent pride and of his tendency to complicate life. I looked at the men and thought of their ritual executions, and I remembered that they used to wrap their thieves in dry leaves and set fire to them. In my forty-six years I had heard much of their fantasies, their ceremonies of sacrifice, and their guileless cruelty: one Kikuyu has more imagination than all the whites in Kenya, but his imagination is cruel. We have tried to wean them from their natural cruelty, but we have only impoverished them. We have tried to disparage their secret tribal oaths, their orgies and incantations, and their life has become boring and empty. They want not only to get the land back, they want to get back their magic, their cults, their natural cruelty. I had only to look into their faces to understand this. In their faces lay the thirst for their land and the nostalgia for their old soul, in all those faces touched by the black gleam of the fire. I wondered whether I should flee. I had seen no crocodiles in this part of the river, but perhaps they had only been lying in the reeds on the other side among the bamboo, and perhaps they had slipped into the water in the darkness. I could swim underwater, I was a good swimmer despite my age, and it takes the crocodiles a little while to make up their minds to attack; perhaps I could make it. But the men who had made a circle around me would not simply look on, would not squat silently on the ground and look on as I fled. Alarmed, I probed their faces, I was afraid they might have guessed my thoughts, but their faces were strange and immobile, even Luke's, my gentle servant's. Perhaps they were hoping I would flee, perhaps they were just waiting for me to throw myself into the river—their faces seemed to be waiting for it.

Luke got up and went to the fire. He squatted down, he stared into the glow, his arms rested on his knees, an old, lean Kikuyu sunk in recollection. I could have thrown myself upon him, he was squatting right at my feet, sunk in thought and unconcerned. I would have accomplished nothing, had I thrown myself on him, his knife lay in front of him, its point in the fire, just below his large, lean hands. It looked as if Luke were dreaming. Now two men stepped out of the thorn, two men I had not seen before. They were taken into the circle, two men with bare feet, in cotton shirts, they looked as if they had lived in town, in Nairobi or Nyeri. They squatted on the earth behind Luke, and all eyes were on them; they had brought rolled banana leaves with them, each of them had two large leaves, and they pushed the leaves close to Luke and waited. They were strong, well-nourished men with flesh on their ribs, they did not look like Luke and his companions, who were lean and narrow-chested with thin, dangling arms. Their faces were different too, they did not have that strange, indifferent expression, a look of infinite distances, their faces were goodnatured, their glance quick and probing, revealing that they had lived in a city. I saw this when they stepped into the circle, I also saw how they changed when they saw Luke before the fire: Their faces altered, they seemed to be reminded of distant suffering, and the distance made them strange and abstracted.

Luke took the knife out of the fire. He could not have seen the arrival of the two men, but he must have known that they squatted behind him, he turned towards them on the balls of his feet, I heard the grass creak under his feet as he turned, it was the first sound he had made. Luke nodded to one of the men, and the man to whom he had nodded took off his cotton shirt and threw it behind him, and then he approached closely to Luke and squatted down in front of him, quickly, almost greedily. And Luke lifted the knife and pressed it into his shoulder blade, it hissed when the hot iron touched the flesh, and the man's body reared once, his head flew back, I saw his clenched teeth, his contorted face. His eyes were closed, the lips drawn downward. He did not moan, and Luke, gentle servant for fourteen years, set the knife against another place, seven times he set the knife against the shoulder, the chest, and against the forehead. When he received the second cut, the man trembled, then he had overcome the pain. After the second wound he looked calmly at the approaching knife, offered his shoulder to the knife, stretched his chest toward it, impatient to receive the small cuts, irrevocable signs of conspiracy, stigmata of hate. When he had received the marks, Luke motioned him back, he crawled to his place and squatted down, and Luke laid the knife in the fire and, after a while, nodded to the other man. The second man took his cotton shirt off, the knife plunged into his shoulder, it hissed, there was a smell of burning flesh, and he also became apathetic and quiet after the second time and received seven cuts and crawled back. I heard distant thunder and looked at the horizon, looked up as if there were deliverance for me in the thunder, but it did not thunder again, I saw only the grass fire sweeping toward the mountains. The moon came out, its reflection melted in the lazy waters of the river, the river gurgled against the opposite bank, the sound traveled back to us. The bamboo was silent.

I saw how Luke pulled the banana leaves towards him, he unrolled them carefully, and I noticed a tin can in one of them. He set the can near the fire, it was full, full of some liquid, dark and thick. Luke poured off a little of the liquid and took something out of the other leaf, and I recognized that it was entrails, entrails of an animal, perhaps a sheep, he took them in his hands and divided them and threw some pieces into the can, and then he threw grain and flour into the can and began to sing in a low voice. While Luke sang—I had not heard him sing in fourteen years—he stirred the dough, I observed how he beat the dough and kneaded it, worked it with quiet song, a gritty dough, which Luke finally took into both hands and formed into a large ball. He then pinched a small piece out of the dough ball and began to roll it between the palms of his hands, making it into a small ball. The dough was wet and I heard it squelch between his hands. Luke rolled fourteen small balls, twice seven moist dough balls, and laid them in two rows before him, one next to the other, and when he had finished, Luke nodded to one of the men who squatted before him, and the one he had called came to him, knelt down, closed his eyes, and pushed his head right forward. He opened his mouth and Luke took one of the moist balls of dough and pushed it between his teeth. The fed man's face gleamed, he swallowed, I saw how the ball traveled down his throat, he swallowed several times, his head moved back and forth, back and forth, then he stopped, his lips opened, pressed forwards in mild greed towards the next bit of dough, and Luke pushed another ball into his mouth. Luke, sorcerer and gentle servant, fed him with the dough of hate, fed him seven times and sent him back when he had had his number, and after a while Luke nodded to the second man, and the second man came and opened his mouth and choked down the balls, choked down a vow with the dough, and his face gleamed. He too ate the dough of hate seven times and was sent back. He went back upright, took his shirt, slipped it over his head, and settled into the circle they had made around me. I remembered that seven was their number, the holy number of the Kikuyu, I had often heard of it in forty-six years, now I had seen it. Why had they allowed me to see it, why did they tolerate my presence, my number was a different one, I was the one for whom the wounds were meant, the fresh marks on the men's bodies, I was the object of their hatred, why did they not kill me? Why did they hesitate, why did Luke hesitate to lift the heavy Panga knife against me, why did they not allow me to die the death they had imposed on so many others, had they a special death in store for me? Had Luke, the gentle one, invented a special death for me in the fourteen years he was my servant?

We had spoken little in those fourteen years, Luke had always worked silently and well, I had even invited him to eat with us. Sometimes, when I had watched him from afar at his work, I had gone up to him and invited him, but he had never come, had always found a sinple excuse, he declined my offers with polite sadness. Nobody worked better for me than Luke, my wonderful servant. What kind of death had he thought up for me?

Luke got up and walked past me to the river. Slowly he walked up and down on the river bank, observed, listened, he lay down flat on the ground and looked across the water, he took a stone, threw it into the middle of the sluggish river and observed the point where the stone had fallen, and waited. Then he returned and now came up to me. He stood in front of me but his glance went past me, did not reach me, although it was directed toward me. He stood before me, his knife in his hand, and he began to speak. I recognized his voice immediately, his quiet, mild voice. He invited me to go, he spoke to me as if he were asking a favor. I should go, he begged, the time had come. With his hand he pointed across the river and the bamboo in the direction in which my farm lay; I should go, he begged me, where Fanny lived, who was my wife, and Sheila, my daughter. Luke begged me to go to them, they would need me, he said, tomorrow at sundown they would need me. I should wait no longer. I should prepare Fanny and Sheila, he said, for tomorrow the farm would burn, the great fire would come, and I must not be far away then. He started to turn away, he had said enough, but I would not let him go, I pointed with outstretched hand at the black river, and he read my question from this gesture and gave me to understand that there were no crocodiles nearby, that he had observed the water. I could go, the way was clear.

I looked around the circle of faces, strange, stony faces lit by the weak light of the fire. Luke went back and fitted himself also into the circle, he squatted, and I stood alone in the middle and looked across at the bamboo forest, felt the oppressive heat drifting across, felt decay and secrecy, and I set one foot in the water and went. I went slowly towards the middle of the river, my feet sank into the soft mud, the water rose against my body, against my hips, my chest, black, tepid water, carrying dead bamboo canes and branches, and when a branch touched me I was startled and stood still. I did not look back once. I wondered why they had let me go, there must have been some reason why they had not killed me.

What verdict lay behind their sending me home? I did not know, I could not guess it though I knew many of their tricks, their gentle, cruel cunning—why had they let me go? My foot touched a hard object that lay on the bottom. I jerked back, I would have cried out if they had not been on the bank, I threw myself onto the water and made quicker progress swimming than wading, and I swam into the middle with desperate pulls. It must have been a sunken tree trunk that I had touched, the water remained calm, there was no movement in the river. Slowly I waded on, rowing with both arms—long groping steps through the soft mud: I crossed the river for the third time.

What trick lay behind my acquittal, why had they let me go, why had Luke sent me home? Luke had shown me the shortest way, the way that led through the river and the bamboo forest. I knew that the grasslands began beyond the bamboo, grasslands of toil. I remembered that I would then have to pass the cornfields and go past a farm. I'd make it, I thought, I could walk fifteen miles before the following evening, perhaps McCormick would take me the last stretch in his car, he owned the farm.

The bamboo grew thickly, I was hardly able to make any progress but had to squeeze myself between the canes. It was hopeless. The ground too was dangerous, leaves and branches covered it right up to the stand of bamboo, I could not see where I stepped. Again and again I sank in, sank to my hips and fell forward. It was impossible. I stood still and looked back; the men had gone, the fire was out, I was alone. I was alone in the oppressive heat of the bamboo. I felt my wet clothes against my skin, my knees trembled. I felt that I was watched, I felt eyes on me from all sides, indifferent, waiting, immobile stares. I had no weapons, I must go no farther.

All was silence, only occasionally the stillness was broken, a bird called in the darkness, an animal complained of disturbed sleep; I must go no farther, I knew that at night, without weapons, I would not come out of the bamboo forest alive, the leopard would prevent it, the leopard or something else. I knew I must return to the river and either wait for the morning or move closer to the water. Without weapons and without fire the night was dangerous, I could feel it. The night was a little too silent, a little too gentle, that was not good, and I fought my way through the bamboo stands and creepers back to the river. I wanted to use the night to walk upriver, this would gain me at most two miles, two toiling miles, but I decided to take this way, I wanted to be home before Luke brought the big fire to the farm, I had to warn the girl and Fanny, my wife.

Again I went into the river, the water came up to my calves, then I waded, trying to make no sound, upriver; I made better progress than I had expected. The moon lay on the water, if it had not been for the moon I would not have gone on. The mud became firmer, the farther I went upriver the harder and surer became the bottom. I knocked against small stones in the water, the bushes did not hang so far over the river bank, all seemed to be going well. Sometimes I saw a pair of eyes between the bushes, green and immobile, and I instinctively strained toward the middle of the river. I was afraid, but I had to stifle my fear if I wanted to reach the farm in time. Sometimes the eyes on the river bank followed me along, cold and quiet, they accompanied me upriver. I could recognize no head, no body, the eyes seemed to float above the bamboo, they floated through the bamboo and the creepers, and I knew that the night was lying in wait, pursuing the stranger, trying to allay his suspicion by the silence and the fragrance. I saw phosphorescent flowers on the river bank, their beauty burned itself to death, occasionally I saw them, six feet tall burning in the darkness on a tree or in the middle of a bush, burning flowers of death beneath which the leopards waited.

What trick was there in my acquittal, why had they let me go, for whom had they branded themselves with the marks of wrath? Were they so sure of themselves?

I made good progress, I would, if things went on this way, be able to make a good three miles this night. I would reach Fanny and the girl earlier than they expected. I thought of Fanny, saw her sitting on the wooden veranda, listening into the darkness, the old army revolver lying on the balustrade; by now I should long have been home, perhaps she had sensed across the distance that something had happened to me. She had a good instinct, her instinct had sharpened the more solitary we two had become, this country of sleep and decay had shown us that man is by nature a solitary creature, a lost, lonely hunter on the trail of his own self, and we soon began to go our separate ways, soon after Sheila was born. Sometimes we both believed that we could do without each other, we worked silently and alone, each doing his share, we kept out of each other's way as soon as life tried to lead us together. True, Fanny and I were going in the same direction, our goal and our misery were the same, but we went towards that goal with a great distance between us. We had said everything to each other, we had confided in each other without reserve, and the time had come when we understood each other without speech, when we sometimes did not speak to each other for days, and things went on in their proper way nonetheless. I had often observed her secretly when she walked through the corn or clambered down the ravine to the river. I had observed her and noticed that her movements had changed, that they had altered since the early days. She moved more softly, like an animal; her movements flowed, she felt secure.

The river became shallower, a few boulders stuck out of its surface, and I jumped, whenever possible, from stone to stone and hardly had to touch the water. The water had become colder, the air had became colder, I began to feel cold. I remained standing on a stone and massaged my body and my legs. My shirt was torn over my chest, the tatters dangled in my face when I bent, they smelled sweetish and musty. I carefully covered my skin with the rags, I tried to pull the shirt down to make it longer and to push it under my belt, for I began to feel colder and colder, and I longed for the warm mud, and for the part of the river where they had dismissed me from their circle. I drank a little of the bitter water and was about to go on when I saw him: He stood close to the bank in a small bay of the river, only a few yards from me. Around him the bamboo had been trodden flat so that I could see his full size. He had obviously just noticed me, too. He had rolled up his trunk and stood motionless before me, I saw the matt gleam of his tusks, the small, blank eyes, and his slowly fanning ears: It was a large elephant. He stood and looked across at me, and I was so confounded by his look that I did not think of flight, I did not move and watched the large, solitary beast, and I suddenly felt the wonderful nearness of the wilderness. After a while he turned his head, unrolled his trunk, and drank. I heard a sucking noise, heard how his trunk moved aside a few small stones, which jingled together, and then he unexpectedly turned and vanished into the bamboo. I heard him break through the wood and, as if he had stopped, everything was suddenly still again.

Slowly I continued on my way. I had found a bamboo cane in the water and used it as a support when I jumped from stone to stone. The cane had been cut by a single diagonal blow, it had a point, and I would, if necessary, be able to use it as a weapon.

I thought of Luke, my gentle servant for fourteen years. I imagined that by now he would be sitting by another fire, that other men squatted before him to choke down the dough of hate that he had rolled into balls and pushed into their mouths; I believed I could see how their shoulders stretched forward, craving the heavy Panga knife, how their faces gleamed with heat and greed to receive the marks. I imagined that Luke went through the whole country, and I saw that wherever his foot flattened the grass, fire sprang up, the fire followed him constantly, changed direction with him, died down when he ordered it—Luke, Lord of the fire. I thought of the day I had seen him for the first time: He had fled north like the others of his tribe, the rinderpest had almost completely destroyed their herds and they had taken refuge in the north with their last cattle. And while they were in the north we came in and took their land, we did not know when they would return, whether they would return at all, we took the fallow land and began to sow.

But after we had sowed and had already harvested, they came. Back from the north, I saw their silent procession coming up the long valley, the women in front, then the cattle, and behind the cattle the men. We told them that they had lost the land by their absence and they were silent; we offered them money; they took the money, hid it calmly in their clothes and were silent, they were silent because they felt themselves to be the owners of this land, for a Kikuyu considers the sale of land legal only when it has been consummated by a religious ceremony. Our giving them money was of no significance, we had staked out the land without a religious ceremony and therefore it could never belong to us. I remembered how Luke came up the long valley in one of the processions. He walked at the end of the procession. I noticed him at once. His old, gentle face struck me, a face that seemed to have had no youth, and this face remained calm when I said that I would not give up the land. It was Luke's land that I had taken.

He was silent when he heard this, and when the procession began to move, when it went on in its silent search for the lost land, Luke went with it, and I saw him tread gently across the grassy plain, and I could not bring myself to let him go. I called Luke back and asked him if he would like to stay with me, I asked him if he were willing to work the land with me, and he nodded silently and did his work in such a natural way that seemed as if he had left it for only a short time and had now returned to finish it.

He worked silently and patiently, I never had to say much to him. I tried to teach him this and that, I endeavored to make his work easier, he listened politely, waited until I dismissed him, and before very long he had forgotten my advice. What ruse was there behind my acquittal, in those fourteen years what had Luke, the wonderful, gentle servant, thought up?

I went upriver until morning, The nights are long in this country and I had gained about four miles, more than I had hoped for. I examined the sky, the oblong rectangle of sky above the river. It looked like it would storm. The sky was covered by a single gray cloud, which stood above me and the river. Its edges were dark. Straight through the gray ran a vermilion trail, a trail of fire, and I thought that this might be Luke's track. I wondered whether, under such conditions, it was worth trying to cross the bamboo wood, then I thought of Fanny, of the girl, and of the term set for my return, and I decided to cross the bamboo forest come what may. For the first time I felt hunger, I drank of the bitter water of the river, and with the help of my bamboo pole, swung myself onto the bank. When I reached the bank I realized how exhausted I was, it had taken all my strength to jump from stone to stone, and my attention and skill had been so concentrated that I had had no opportunity to notice the degree of my exhaustion. Now that I was able to relax, I noticed it, I felt how unsteady my legs were, I saw how my hands trembled, and I felt the veil before my eyes, a certain sign of exhaustion. I could not allow myself to stand still, I had to go on, I had to will myself to be carried to the farm on the impetus, as it were, of the effort I had made. I knew myself well enough to know that I would do it.

Bent over forward I climbed some high ground. After each step I grasped bamboo canes and roots and pulled myself forward. I had to pull myself along carefully, for sometimes I took hold of the roots of a dead cane, one that had died and still stood upright because there was no room for it to fall, and when I tried to pull myself up by the upright, dead pole, it gave, the roots broke, and the bamboo pole fell towards me. Sometimes the pole would fall on other poles and I heard the roots being torn up and threw myself down, covering my head with my hands. From time to time I sank into the soft ground up to my knees, but not as often as in the night when I had first tried to cross the bamboo forest, for now I could see the deeper holes in the ground and avoid them.

The cold from which I had suffered in the early hours did not bother me anymore, the exertion made me sweat, my shirt stuck to my back, and when I was face down on the ground, my breath rebounded from the leaves and struck my hot face. I felt the sweat run down my cheeks and tasted it, thin and sour, when I licked my lips. I decided to rest a while in the corn, I would neither lie down nor sit, the risk would be too great; I would stand to rest so that exhaustion would not overcome me, I wanted to stand still for a few moments and break off a cob. I was already getting near, I could already taste the sweet mealiness of the kernels—it was a good thing to think about.

I approached a black cedar, I took hold of a cluster of creepers; they felt slippery and leathery, like snakes. I grasped them and pulled myself towards the tree, and when I stood on a root I saw a clearing. I saw it through the veil of my exhaustion, and when I went closer I noticed a number of large, heavy birds congregated around an object. They hopped about noiselessly, lazily and with limp wingbeats they circled the object. Some sat on it and tried to push off new arrivals. The birds were black. I was unable to drive them away. I could get so near that I was able to touch them with my bamboo staff, and this I tried, but they simply hopped awkwardly aside and remained there. The object around which they crowded was a tree stump; they obviously just wanted to sit on it, and since there were too many of them, there was the silent battle.

I went close to the stump and leaned against it, and I finally succumbed to the temptation to sit down. I sat down in the middle and drove off the birds with my bamboo staff, I could not make them leave for good. They jumped to the ground, lazy and reluctant; they hopped clumsily about my legs and looked up at me with their heads on one side. After a time one bird tried to fly up onto the tree stump. I ducked, thinking he was flying at me, but when I saw that all he wanted was to sit beside me, I let him sit there and took no notice. I leaned far back and examined the sky and saw that the cloud with the vermilion trail stood farther in the west: There would be no thunderstorm, I was confident of my way. I got up slowly and walked between the big birds through the clearing. They did not move, they squatted on the ground and looked after me.

I thought of Luke's eyes, of his look full of gentle sorrow, I thought of it while I battled with the bamboo, and I began to understand Luke. To understand him and all the others who carried the stigmata of hate. I believed I understood why they crowded to receive the marks. We had taken too much from them, but we had also brought them too much.

What trick had Luke devised? Why had he let me go, I who also was to blame that he had lost everything? I had to be at the farm before sunset, I thought of Fanny and of the girl, I saw them still sitting on the wooden veranda, the old army revolver nearby, I knew that they would not have slept last night.

When the bamboo forest was behind me, I was so exhausted I thought I could not go on, my body demanded rest, drew me towards the ground. I stood still in the middle of the elephant grass and shut my eyes, I would have given at the knees and sunk down if I had not leaned on my bamboo stick, I was so weakened that a deep indifference came over me, I ceased to care about Fanny's fate, and I appeased my conscience by telling myself that she could shoot well and could defend the house as well as I could myself. And I would have lain down, if it had not been for the hunger: Hunger made me open my eyes, and I lifted the bamboo staff, thrust it into the ground, and went on. I went through the waist-high elephant grass, my lips burned, the blood hummed in my fingers. I never once looked across the plain, my glance shrank from the horizon, I did not have the strength to lift my eyes.

Toward noon I stood before the cornfield. I threw away the bamboo staff, now it had served its time. I threw it from me in a great arc and tore off several corn cobs. I sat on the ground. I laid the cobs down on my lap, I tore the yellowish dry husk from one cob and bit into it, I did not take the time to thumb off the kernels but drove my teeth along the cob. The kernels tasted of sweet flour.

After I had eaten, I crawled between the corn stalks. I felt the coolness and shade, felt a strange sense of security: here, in the corn, I imagined myself safe. I crawled through the whole field. I imagined, while I crawled, that I was collecting new strength. I felt myself gaining strength and I lifted my eyes and looked ahead. And through the corn stalks I saw the farm. It stood on a hill, the large house with a veranda, and the corrugated iron sheds at right angle to the house. The farm lay there, deserted. McCormick had four dogs, and I had always seen one of them when I had passed by; one of the dogs had always lain in the dust in front of the veranda, but now I could not discover any of them. I wanted to leave the cornfield and go across, I had already stood up, when they came out of the farm. There were six men, lean Kikuyus with Panga knives. They walked slowly down the veranda steps, slowly, with calm feet. They did not seem to be in a hurry. For a moment they disappeared behind the corrugated iron sheds, then I could see them again, six lean men. They crossed the yard and passed a group of trees, they walked upright across a patch of grass in the direction from which I had come. Their way led them to the bamboo forest, to the river. I could not see whether Luke was among them, they were too far away. I could only sense whether he was among them—my senses confirmed that he was. I looked after them until they vanished beyond the grass patch, I knew that it was useless to go to the farm and ask McCormick for his car, I would never again be able to ask him for anything. I was sorry for him, for he had been there only six years. He had come directly after the war, a friendly, red-haired man who liked to talk, and who vanished for a month each year, went to Nairobi, it was said, where he disappeared mysteriously for a month.

I could see no one on his farm, and I pushed myself back into the cornfield and promised myself to come back, once I had settled everything at home. If I had had my automatic or even my old army revolver, I would have gone across to the farm, but without a weapon, and exhausted as I was, it would have been foolish.

They might have left one of themselves behind, they might all six return, it was no use.

I crawled in the direction of the small path that bordered the cornfield on one side, the path that led to my farm. The hardest part of the journey was behind me, I had rested and eaten, I had overcome indifference and thirst, I did not doubt that I would reach my farm in time. The nearer I came, the greater became my fear of their cunning and my suspicion concerning my release. Why had Luke allowed me to go, Luke, gentle servant and sorcerer, what trick had he devised for me? Fear made me stand up among the corn stalks. I pushed forward with my hands and began to run as best I could. I ran through the field, stood still, listened, heard my heart beating, and ran on again. I felt how my thighs became cramped, turned stiff and without feeling. On my chest I noticed the marks of thorns, small, blood-encrusted scratches. My arms trembled. My mouth was open, the upper part of my body was bent far forward: Thus I ran on through the corn, and when I reached the end of the field I did not allow myself any rest, I ran to the road, I believed I was still running, I heard my steps pounding against the ground and I thought I was running, but if I had been running I would have reached my goal much more quickly. I staggered forward, beaten down by fear and heat. I could hardly control my steps.

Then I reached another field of corn, long before sunset, and this was my own corn. Behind it lay the farm. One last effort and I would reach it. Already I imagined seeing it before me, though the corn still hid it from sight, my farm, Luke's farm. I turned from the path and ran through the corn, the stalks seemed stronger and higher, the cobs larger than those in McCormick's field—I ran to a furrow. Perhaps Luke, perhaps I had torn it in the soil? I had underestimated my strength, now I felt how much I still had at my disposal.

I saw the stalks grow sparser, this was the end of the field. I stepped out of the cornfield. I pressed my hands against my chest. I lifted my head and looked across towards the breadfruit trees. The farm was gone. It was long before sunset. I went toward the breadfruit trees and saw the ashes. I kneeled down and felt them with both hands. The ashes were cold.

Translated by Kathrine Talbot

Reinhard Lettau

Manig

ENTER MANIG

A gentleman in full regalia enters the room. He lifts his hat and already he has changed considerably. He peels off his gloves: first he tugs with the still-clad right hand at the fingertips of the left, rapidly, five times, now the same on the other side. The gloves slap the floor, the gentleman raises his hands: another movement in a different direction. He takes a small step forward, quickly slips the coat off his shoulders, tents it over his head, temporarily pulls it closed in front. Now a single eye peeks into the room: a spy in the parlor, in the thicket, at the iron fence, outside, in front of the villa, in the bushes, in any case once more a different gentleman. He abandons the coat: this new aspect comes as a shock. The sun enters the room, and the gentleman makes use of it: He lights up. The window squares the rays into a bright spotlight beam. Two-dimensionally the gentleman bounds to the window, a paper cut-out, ready to be folded. Now he could be quickly caught, pasted on cardboard, framed, hung over the mantelpiece. But the sun disappears and the gentleman rounds himself out again in the room, gains depth, he could be pinched now, once more he is convincing. Now he pulls out a flute, settles himself, legs crossed, into a corner, sends forth tunes with dancing fingers, he is an utterly different gentleman. Manig sits before us.

ACTIONS OF MANIG (I)

Manig is asked to remove the encumbering objects, the choice, then, is his. First he steps up to a lamp, raises the swooping shade, holds it over the bulb in a gesture of adieu, folds it a first time, it crackles. He lifts the brittle form, folds it horizontally with lightning-quick palms, and now vertically with his fingertips, once more horizontally, and the waxy cube flies to the floor. Glaring light fills the room. He shoves the armchair to the door; it springs open; the armchair roars down the corridor, we hear it rumble. He stomps the wastebasket, begins to roll up the carpet, pushing and kicking the recalcitrant bulk toward the middle of the room with violent movements of arms and legs from all sides at once. There he lets it bounce and overlap itself, catch itself within itself. Rigid ends stand up, obstinate corners rise in vain, are wrestled down. Dust whirls about the scene. Outside, the defeated carpet collapses. Was that a table? Envelope-size it leaves the room. Manig takes a decisive step backwards, doubles over, skips into the fireplace, where he stands straight, now visible only to the knees, not much to look at.

ACTIONS OF MANIG (II)

"I'm inviting you for this very evening," says Manig. And leaves the house. In the doorway he hesitates. Has he changed his mind? He is back in the room.

"I'm not inviting you after all," he says.

"All right, then don't," says the neighbor. Manig leaves once more. At the door he turns. He looks back into the room. The neighbor is sitting on a chair.

"Now what?" asks the neighbor.

"Let's make it tonight."

"Tonight then," says the neighbor. Once more Manig is outside. He walks a few tentative steps around the house. The low window shows him the neighbor, his guest. His guest?

Once more Manig is back in the room.

"Better not," he says. The door bangs shut.

Already Manig is knocking at the window.

"Coming," calls the neighbor.

Quickly he gets up and readies himself. He goes out to the street where Manig is standing and shaking his head violently. The neighbor turns, notices his friend's invitingly outstretched hands. He about-faces, walks toward Manig, whose hands sink to his sides, who hurries off, vanishes immediately. But a second later he is again standing in the light of a distant street lamp, hunching his shoulders, waving the neighbor over to him with a fanning hand.

ACTIONS OF MANIG (III)

Mr. Manig walks down the street. It is a narrow street. In passing he examines the shop windows, but the sun slants down at such a steep angle from the other side of the street that Manig does not see the window displays, he sees only the ghostly, sparsely colored reflections of the street, of passing traffic, people, himself. His image runs bluish across the glass wall, jumps, a shadow, the distance between two shops, now wanders hunched over the arched window of another shop, shrivels to a thread on a brass nameplate. A man is approaching from the opposite direction. Manig is already able to pinpoint the spot, somewhere on the rapidly decreasing as yet unused stretch between them, which the man will claim with his legs and whole body if he stays on course, and indeed he is heading toward it. Does the other man notice? Manig veers slightly to the left, they scarcely brush against one another. A deviation so slight, Manig can be sure he has not offended the other man, making him think for instance that Manig had wanted to hint that, in his opinion, the other man would never have given way, had not looked like a man who would ever concede even a small movement, let alone the somewhat tardy improvised sidestep, in which case they would have collided on the furiously decreasing stretch, in which case Manig's glasses would have described a wide arc onto the tracks of the just-then approaching streetcar that would have ground them to powder. Thus Manig.

ACTIONS OF MANIG (IV)

Manig is asked to go to see the neighbor. Immediately he turns, opens the door, exits and reenters in the same movement. He has been to see the neighbor.

Now he is asked to carry a helmet into town. Immediately he turns, the shining helmet in his left hand. One-handed he leaves the room, but his receding steps are already approaching steps, one can still see him leave and there he comes hurrying back, enters two-handed, helmetless, a rapid friend. Overconfidently he is asked to go to the seashore. The image of his exit is still on the retina, and already he is back, with a companion in oilcloth as proof. He takes leave of his companion, drawing him close with both arms, kissing him, letting him go, calling after him a promise to return. Turns to the door, pulls it open, rushes out, and back. Again the two say hello and goodbye, tears, reassurances. Again he enters, this time there are twenty of him, many Manigs fill the room with oval faces, wink twenty times, cry "hello" twenty times, twenty pairs of boots, all stamping. At that he is sent up to the roof. "Don't come back now," is called after him. One can hear them thumping about up there, slow sure steps, up one side along the gable and down the other, straight across the roof. One rushes out. The company is standing in front of the house, staring up to the roof.

ACTIONS OF MANIG (V)

Step in front of the mirror at night, with closed eyes. Prepare for the sight. Quickly open the eyes.

But how does one get there? One waits beside the mirror from late afternoon, rehearsing the darkening room in one's mind. Then it takes only an about-face. Or else take up position at a slightly greater distance, along the same wall. Stay closely pressed to the wall, decrease the distance at the proper time, until the smooth wooden mirror frame can be felt against the face. Or focus on the mirror from a wide angle, or from the side, until one sees the frame but not the glass. Or, should the glass be visible, then only as it reflects the opposite wall. Now it takes only a few blind steps. One can't miss the mirror. Or else from the more distant door by which one can enter the room, cleverly measure the required steps with eyes cast down. Memorize exactly how the room curves in the center. Then close your eyes and risk it. Or else look in from the other side of the door, from out in the hall. Memorize the exact height of the doorsill, the position of the doorknob. Perhaps it would be best to walk carefully backward, to remember the precise number of steps it takes to cross the hall. But then—with head held high along the hall and through the perhaps left-open door and into the room. Or else study the curvature of the staircase, remember the front door, start the whole thing from the street, cover the distance from the next block in a beeline. Or else retreat as far as the main square and start from there. Or skip to the gates of the town, cast a long look down over the canyons of the streets. Skipping shrinks the town's image. Instinctively avoid the pond. From here one gets off to a terrific start.

ACTIONS OF MANIG (VI)

The gentleman is standing in the room. Someone puts a hat on the gentleman's head. Its wide brim places the gentleman's face in shadow. His shaggy beard is in the dark. A sound comes out of the darkness, the gentleman is saying something. One replies that the gentleman should first please hold the glass. The gentleman is standing in the room with the glass, the partners in the conversation have departed. The gentleman speaks loudly into the empty room. He says, among other things: "I am standing here in this room, under a hat, in camouflage. I can't use my hands, because I'm holding the glass. But I can walk forward and backward in any direction." At one point a voice calls: "That's the spirit" from the next room. Then the partners sing in the next room. The gentleman calls something and they come back and say: "No, that's not worth the trouble either. It might come to your having to leave at once, the way you are, just as we had hoped. Incidentally, where is your beard?" The gentleman moves his beard, his partners see it. "We appreciate that," they call. Later they come back into the room. The gentleman is goose-stepping, the glass resting on his hands stretched way out in front of him. They tap him on the shoulder.

ACTIONS OF MANIG (VII)

The following may be described as: Manig standing in a park, someone stepping up to him, asking him to step right over into the bushes; just as he is about to comply, someone asks him from the other side to stand at the same time beside the pond, he replies to both sides that he will try to combine their requests. First, he walks toward the bushes, halts, turns, then walks to the pond, halts, returns to the bushes, turns, but finally, after several attempts, he stops halfway between both places, stretches, makes himself as thin as he can, even raises both arms straight up, and utters almost without breath that, this way, he won't deprive anyone of air.

ACTIONS OF MANIG (VIII)

Manig paces outside the gates of the town. He stands by the road-side and watches the people who are leaving the town. "So you are leaving town," he says to a gentleman who waves and keeps walking. Later he changes roadsides and watches the people who are entering the town. "So you are going into town," he calls to a group of gentlemen who are walking past him. Then Manig goes to the yellow railroad station. A train arrives from the town; Manig stands on tiptoe and peeks into the windows to count the number of travelers. Later he does the same with a train from the opposite direction. Then Manig stands on the bridge that leads to the coun-try and watches closely. In the evening he reports that the number of people leaving the town every day roughly corresponds to the number of people entering it. "Daily the town is entered and left by roughly the same number of people," he says. "In other words, it stays the same." He adds that the people who were entering the town walked faster than those who were leaving it. Those entering had been surer of themselves; they knew where they were going. Besides, they had also reached their destination.

ENTRANCE

Enters a gentleman.
  "It is I," he says.
  "Try again," we shout.
  Again he enters.
  "Here I am," he says.
  "Not much better," we shout.

Again he enters the room.

"It's me," he says.

"A poor beginning" we shout.

He enters once more.

"Hello," he calls; and waves.

"Please, not that," we say.

He tries again.

"Me again," he calls.

"Almost," we shout.

He enters once more.

"The long awaited," he says.

"Encore!" we shout, but we've hesitated too long, he stays outside, he won't come back, he skips away, we can't see him anymore, even if we open the front door and quickly look down the street, to the left, to the right.

A BRIEF VISIT

Manig finds the street, he reaches the house. The windows are lit, he sees the party. Two gentlemen are standing in bright illumination. One of the gentlemen speaks, then the other speaks, then both speak together, then both stop speaking, then one of the gentlemen laughs, nods, shakes his head, then the other, then both, then one points in one direction, then the other in the same direction, then both point in the opposite direction, then both point at one another, one of the gentlemen takes a step forward, the other a step backward, both step forward, both backward, one shows his hand to the other, the other shows both hands. Manig knows it all, he prefers to go home—so much for the party.

WELCOME, DEAR MANIG

My dear friend Manig stands in front of the house, near a bush on the evenly cut lawn. He's probably coming to see me. Should I wave to him? No, it's probably not necessary. Perhaps he hasn't seen me sitting on the porch, dark-green and shadowy, in the wicker chair, white-varnished, glass in hand. Well, dear Manig, come closer. Well, come on up, dear friend. Up the few more steps and we're in each other's arms. Is the bush increasing, is the bush spreading, or is it Manig who is shrinking? Why this hesitation? As always it is cool on the terrace. Manig would be welcome. Does he seriously expect me to get up, push back the chair, open my arms and call to him: Welcome, dear Manig? Could he, before coming, expect that I'd see him first? Maybe I'm mistaken. Manig skips back, bouncing from tiptoe to tiptoe. I look into the glass and I look toward the bush. Bush, garden, chair, glass, house, perhaps we are growing and only Manig remains the same? Or perhaps I am expanding? Does one hear cracking? Manig is moving away, backward. He shrinks into the distance. Now he is the size of a pencil. He has reached the neighbor's fence. The distance makes his retreat seem nimbler and nimbler. No difference between leaping and standing. He has reached the edge of the field. There his figure becomes a black line that touches a glass globe over which he wanders. When he has shrunk to comma size, I finally get up, but sit down again immediately, because he has disappeared altogether.

Translated by Ursula Molinaro and E. Sutton

Angelika Mechtel

The Cuckoo's Mate

I love Amanda.

Her warm, soft skin, almost wrinkle-free.

Amanda is interested in culture.

She purrs when I touch her, my motherly friend.

Her husband is another matter.

As a respected specialist in circulatory ailments, he holds office hours by appointment only; he fills enough beds in the private ward of the municipal hospital to be able to afford an unusual hobby.

Roland collects scalps. American friends bring them to him from abroad.

The first time I visited Amanda, I saw them hanging on the wall in the dining room.

The two of them have decorated the dining room full Renaissance style.

An impressive collection. Roland loves his scalps more than he does Amanda. He's working on his own procedure for the preparation of European scalps, he says; and he has friends in neurology. In his spare time he sketches, measures, and works out chemical formulas.

I understand something of that myself, otherwise my husband would not have died so quickly; the sudden death of a man in his late forties, who was actually still quite healthy, strong, and muscular.

For his friends, he expired unexpectedly. I had counted on that and published a death notice.

Twenty years of marriage are a long time. At the funeral I thought back on his life. First work, then play, he'd say. I clung to that when I poisoned him.

Shortly before the cremation, Roland received his scalp, under the counter, of course. We burned my husband with a wig.

With this trifle, I finally managed to win Roland over.

He hadn't liked to see me touch Amanda. I was a thorn in his side, one that I'd now withdrawn. And everything remained peaceful in the friendly city.

Here, no one questions anyone else, but everyone would like to have the answers. My husband did not suffer. After all, I'm a human being.

. . . Then play, he said, and I've taken that to heart; I've worked toward it systematically, so that I can now enjoy myself.

I don't dance on his grave, but I feel good. Just turned forty, and I'm beginning to put my life in order. It's fun.

I'm confident of success. What went well once, I tell myself, will go better a second time. That's why I have never turned my back on the needs of married men in their changing years. As a woman, I tell myself, it's your duty to stand by those whom a coronary— the result of worrying about a career, appearances, and status symbols—will soon call home. These men need help. You can make a start here.

For that, our city is a gift from the gods.

Johnny studied in Austin, Texas, and wrote poetry besides. That brought him to Amanda, who arranges cultural events.

He had already seen the rose gardens and altar paintings in the city, and now told us that American women are thinking about doing away with men.

I said: Not bad.

Johnny choked on his tea.

Don't be afraid, I soothed him, you're not a man yet.

Because he believed he would be a man someday, I promised him I would limit myself to our city.

Johnny wrote one more poem for me and traveled on.

My capable husband was still alive back then.

I made friends with the pharmacist. It was very easy.

Amanda says: Art arises from know-how. She ought to know. So, I drilled myself in my new art and my self-confidence grew.

I did some laboratory work and had success on the first stroke. He got a nice funeral. I didn't say anything about my hobby.

I was seized with a zealousness, a productive zealousness. That's why I undertook not only to nail men to the cross, but to lay them in the grave as well.

I had always been a loving woman.

Amanda didn't suspect a thing.

Slowly, but surely, I became a master of my craft.

I did not proceed indiscriminately. When the only son of the local champagne winery owner met with his incurable illness on the same day that he took over his father's business, I'd reached the pinnacle of success.

Today the procelain works are bankrupt, the chocolate factory orphaned.

There were a number of splendid burials.

Amanda and I take part in every interment.

Kindly, Amanda cares for the widows, women her own age, who blossom visibly as soon as the formalities of the burial are over. Amanda invites them to her home and thus widens the circle of the friends of culture.

I let her do as she likes. I'm happy that she is happy, and I procure new widows for her. Especially pleased, she took possession of the wife of the cultural attaché, whom Amanda had never exactly treasured.

I like Amanda.

She has the reputation of being a respectable woman. She likes to hear that said. She raised her children in a proper fashion, and always stood politely in her husband's shadow. Being interested in culture was a hobby her husband could only approve.

Because girl friends should help each other, I'm now going to start taking care of Roland.

From the beginning, it was a case for me.

Since he has been busy making it to the top, he's overdue. But because he appeals to me, he doesn't make it easy.

He's still going strong.

When I'm with Roland, I even forget about Amanda.

Sometimes she complains about him, and that brings me to my senses. Then I'd like to be finished with him.

Amanda will blossom like the others.

Because she suspects nothing of her good fortune, my relationship with Roland doesn't disturb her. On the contrary sometimes she takes me in her arms tenderly and sighs. In return, I gladly help her with arrangements for cultural events.

A violin concert ends the season.

Amanda is expecting a young woman artist. Roland took the day off and, because Amanda asked me to, I came early, at breakfast.

The three of us are sitting on the terrace. It's warm out. We crack open soft-boiled eggs.

Amanda is wearing a string of pearls close around her neck. She went to the hairdresser yesterday.

While spreading raspberry jam on my breakfast roll, I notice the direction of Roland's stare: his eyes are glued to Amanda's neck. I have trouble swallowing.

Amanda is looking forward to tonight. She still has a lot to get ready.

Roland slurps egg yolk from his spoon.

Eggs increase potency, he says. Amanda blushes, Roland laughs, and with his index finger he tenderly traces her scalp line. Amanda lets herself be soothed.

I don't like rolls with raspberry jam.

This man is no longer tolerable for Amanda.

Before she leaves the house, she kisses first me and then Roland.

I hear her back the car out of the garage, because she has some things to take care of in town, and I walk into the living room.

Roland offers me a drink, and while he's sipping his first martini, I imagine his corpse.

Practice makes perfect.

Because I'm thinking of Amanda, it's easy, even when he's standing right in front of me, a distinguished man, tanned, sporty, and not without a certain intelligence. I feel good around him. A vital man, one of the better sort. And yet so useless.

Afterwards he talks about his scalps; he gets excited.

There should be some law, he says, that makes the scalps of sex criminals legally fair game.

He talks about the lack of available material. Too bad, he says, that the death sentence has been abolished.

And because I'm always soft and yielding afterwards, I get careless.

Maybe I could help you? I suggest.

How? he asks: Do you have access to heads?

You might call it that.

Roland smiles and reminds me of the jam roll by making choking noises.

Amanda has a good hairdresser, I say.

For a valuable head, Roland answers, I'll pay somewhat more.

But I get hold of myself again, return to my principles, think of Amanda, and decide to keep being considerate of the pharmacist.

Live and let live. Everything at its proper time.

As usual, I feel the blessed pounding of my heart in anticipation of a job well done, and I close Roland in my arms once again.

Amanda wants to eat in town, to be on time at the train station when the young artist arrives. So we have a little more time left. Roland feeds me steak tartare and onions in the dining room beneath his scalps.

That strengthens a woman and increases her readiness, he says.

Because I can see his end is near, I remain friendly. I don't want to alarm Roland unnecessarily, that's only human.

Amanda gets back around six, the violinist with her. Amanda is happy. Now I'm glad I had that martini. I reach for Amanda's hand—it's warm and soft.

Amanda talks on and on. The girl that she's brought along seems to please her. She is dark. A madonna type. Amanda beams. I don't like this madonna. Amanda lays her arm around her shoulders, it doesn't seem to disturb Roland.

He offers the young woman some tartare, because I'm already strong enough.

You don't mind onions, do you? he asks.

You must eat something before you play, Amanda adds.

Roland is glad to give the madonna a helping hand.

Next year he could be fifty-nine.

He hand-feeds the violinist beneath the scalps.

A young thing, I say to Amanda, what is this anyway?

This is art, Amanda reminds me.

It will be a nice evening.

She lays her hand on my bare arm, then I change the subject, talk about deaths, and report that I had a martini with Roland. But she doesn't seem to understand.

The first guests arrive at eight. It's a tight circle that has gathered around Amanda over the years; a nice little fellowship, widows and academicians, educated people; even an officer belongs, and of course my pharmacist.

That afternoon Roland and I had set up the chairs in six straight rows. The madonna will play in front of the fireplace. Ever since the guests arrived, Amanda hasn't deigned to give me even a glance, and that makes me restless. Irritated. I turn to Roland. He is standing in back next to the door. From there he has a good view of the audience and the fireplace.

Look at Amanda, he says: She's all fired up. With bright red hair and swelling bosom, Amanda begins to introduce the young artist.

Then she sits down in the front row.

As the violinist begins with a tender stroke, Roland grabs me by the hair: Such a mass of hair, he says, as if he'd only just noticed, and he takes an even tighter hold.

Don't do that, I say. And try to get loose from him. What the girl in front is playing sounds like a lament.

Roland asks quietly: Do you like Amanda's hair?

I feel nervous and nod obediently.

Roland won't let up. The people in the last row turn around toward us: When I discovered my fascination for scalps, I also discovered Amanda's hair.

I'm cold, although I know that downstairs in the cellar the boiler for the central heating is going full blast.

Aren't I a good husband? Roland inquires.

Above all a man, I answer.

Roland begins to giggle, as if he knew. He's disturbing the music, and that embarrasses me.

Then he's quiet for a moment, and I listen to this Mater Dolorosa stroke her violin.

Nothing like this has ever happened to me before.

I think about the martini this morning and regret having given Roland an extension. I should have started earlier to get him out of the way. This sort of thing takes time, so that no one gets suspicious: terminal illness for four weeks.

Suddenly he's at my ear again, saying in a friendly way: But my dear, who is about to get panicky?

I want to scream, but that would be rude; besides, she just took the violin from her chin.

Amanda fetches the girl from the fireplace and pats her solicitously on the arm. She offers the guests refreshments in the dining room. She doesn't seem to notice that her Roland is harassing me.

That's the last straw.

I start to go to her, want to show her who's the woman in this house, but Roland has me in his hands. He's making me furious.

Because he's still got me by the nape of the neck, I have to walk alongside him into the dining room, whether I want to or not.

Most of the guests are already familiar with his scalp collection, yet again today there are some who stand in front of these hairy objects, perplexed, wondering about some new trend in art.

Roland, who won't let me go, likes to introduce newcomers to his hobby; he gladly explains the preparation of scalps to interested parties.

When asked if he merely collects scalps, or also prepares them himself, he answers: Someone willed his scalp to me. At the same time he strokes my neck with two fingers.

Scalping? The widows giggle. Amanda, who is standing next to her young guest, looks astonished, as if she'd only just now noticed us.

I try to free myself from Roland, and I say: I have to help Amanda. He doesn't listen, and my helpful friend, the pharmacist, mentions in passing how nice the young violinist's scalp would look on the wall: Wouldn't you have trouble with the long hair?

A good joke, Roland laughs: I have a different one in mind.

An enchanting evening, don't you think? Amanda says.

The best always comes last, Roland answers.

Thinking about it, I begin to doubt whether art arises from know-how. I'm afraid of backlashes.

When the guests have gone, the artist says she is also tired. Amanda takes her up to the guest room.

It's already past midnight. I stand in the living room and look out over the terrace and down the mountainside at the city.

Amanda comes back downstairs. Now she's busy in the kitchen. Roland is with her. I can hear his voice distinctly. Amanda grows quiet as he speaks.

The city below has also grown quiet. Only rarely now does a car drive along the river bank. Now and again I see the small dots of headlights.

A moment ago there was a strange noise in the kitchen, but now it's quiet.

I forget the madonna in the guest room, walk to the bar, and mix a drink for the three of us, push Amanda's and my glasses aside, and prepare Roland's whiskey; while doing that I think about living in this house with Amanda. Roland's death has become a real concern for me.

I'll spend wonderful days with Amanda. In the record cabinet I look for some piano music and put it on.

Roland comes back out of the kitchen.

You've mixed us a drink? he asks. I push his glass toward him.

He shakes his head and takes Amanda's martini.

Let's drink, he says, to a successful evening.

I'm freezing again.

Are you cold? he asks.

I nod.

You're not getting sick? His concern sounds almost believable. Or did you drink from the wrong glass? he inquires.

He's confusing me. And because I'm frightened, I keep quiet.

Let's go out on the terrace, he suggests. His hand surrounds the back of my neck, and he smiles, as if this were some new form of tenderness.

Do you know what I'd like to call you? he asks as he points out my place on the terrace. The cuckoo's mate.

You've stolen into the wrong nest, he explains.

He lights a cigarette and tells me: An unusual woman, that excites a man, you ought to know.

I wasn't born yesterday, but still I keep my mouth shut.

He counts off funerals, speaks of honorable people, of irreproachable citizens, and of my pharmacist.

He delights in my horror.

We should work together, my dear. First work, then play.

I bristle, tell him about Johnny, and then that men should be done away with.

Sympathetically, he takes his hand from my neck and lays it companionably on my forearm. But surely one must remain, for the propagation of the species.

A man with qualities, he adds.

I've finally seen through you, he asserts.

Roland is a distinguished man, not without a certain intelligence, and he is the first backlash of my career, because he doesn't want to let himself be killed.

What is Amanda going to say? I ask him and try to dodge him.

Amanda? He smiles and looks peacefully down over the city and its towers.

In the house all is quiet.

It's one o'clock, and the church bells begin to ring.

Roland says: Amanda was a good woman. Her long hair will enrich my collection.

I imagine how Amanda's round and soft body is slowly cooling down. I could never grieve before. But this time I understand it and decide to have my hair cut.

I want to wear it centimeter-short.

And for this man, too, I'll find a way.

Translated by Claudia M. Johnson

Christoph Meckel

In the Land of the Umbramauts

*—The most highly praised places on
earth are tiresome and lack enchantment
when one comes to them without hope—*

—Sainte-Beuve

The first part of the treatise contains accounts of the most prominent geographical features of the land as well as general descriptions and insight into the physical peculiarities of the Umbramaut
territory and the nature of the social system. The second part
introduces a selection of Umbramaut celebrities and eccentrics, in
addition to some altogether unimportant but typical inhabitants.
Finally, the third part permits glimpses into the everyday life of
the Umbramauts—its events, festivities, and particularities. The
chapters taken together should afford the reader an almost complete picture of the country.

PART 1

1

The land of the Umbramauts is a world power of twilight, located
between the land of day and the land of night. It darkens somewhat
toward the borders of the land of night and grows lighter near the
land of day. This viscid, never intermitted twilight lies in the mighty
shadow of no one, and all life in the region lives in it.

Trying to draw a map of the land would present all but insurmountable problems. The attempt has been universally abandoned. Even though boundaries can be defined approximately, the vast interior of the country offers no fixed landmarks that could be plotted with certainty on a map. Assuredly, there are mountains, lakes, forests, and rock formations, but whenever an observer had marked an entry, he would soon be compelled to change its location. Everything in the land moves on its own volition, and the laws of this perpetual random motion have never been deciphered.

Instead of a map, imagine something like one's traveling bag, filled to a mere twentieth of its capacity with various odds and ends. Imagine then taking this bag along on an extended journey, so that it is thrown now on its side and then on its top, scrambling its contents again and again. En route, open the bag occasionally. A new arrangement of the contents will be apparent at each examination.

In the land of the Umbramauts the loose pieces undertake the changes themselves. The ground surface lies immobile and animates them in no way. The mountains float in whatever direction they are inscrutably impelled to wander, and the lakes shift locations arbitrarily. Questions inevitably arise: Are there no villages, cities, fountains? Where are the avenues, parks, rivers, and bridges? Where are the institutions one can depend on?

Geographical study of the land of the Umbramauts requires some indulgence. For example, there is a city, but it has a particular kind of architecture, about which one might legitimately ask: Is it architecture at all? Nevertheless, there are meeting places where the Umbramauts congregate. However, forests and mountains are already different matters. There is no proper link between them and the Umbramaut terra firma. The ground is vacant, with an emptiness that stupefies the sight, unless one notices the few rocks lying scattered about. Yet they do not constitute meaningful variation, for they are swallowed up by the expanse. There seems to be no binding adhesive in this land.

Beyond this?

Not very much: Two half-shriveled, rarely blossoming belladonna gardens, which likewise wander; a couple of forlorn railroad cars. Sometimes, for a fleeting moment, a wandering mountain will turn up behind a wandering forest, or a hill appears as the far shore of a lake rolling by; but these are quickly withdrawn scenes, which occupy an Umbramaut's mind no further.

Emptiness. Vague expanses. Half-lit chasms. The Umbramauts keep their lanterns lit to counteract the twilight, and they live in the circles of light. Even their meeting places constantly move.

And then—who dared mention it till now—those sticky, billowy wads scooting low over the ground, so that Umbramauts have to fall flat when they see them, unless they prefer to be knocked over. Darkness and heavy masses of wet waft over the Umbramauts' heads. Moisture romps precipitously and puts the lanterns out, if they're not hastily covered up . . .

Clouds—wasn't that the name for them?

Move along, the stranger is told, move along.

2

A solemnly bored, bedizened rabble with medals and gewgaws hanging up to the ears has gathered here for a meeting. Peers of the shadows with composure, they lead other heavily laden Umbramauts on rope lines. Their beards are curled and braided, and their hats worn on their large, unsteady heads (some wear battered pails and broken vases), and their bodies are decked out in a gaudy collection of patchwork rags. All in all they represent the gentry of the Umbramautical population: celebrities and personalities, dukes, knights, and captains—deputies deputized by no one—dignitaries and unproven heroes, princes without principalities, and title-holders without retinues.

Their porters are behind them. Heavily overburdened with their masters' property, they stand there panting and yawning, waiting for a sign, a light tug on the line that tells them to sit down. Miscellany, an inexplicable hodgepodge of trifles, junk, flecks of dirt, and ludicrous refuse dangles from head to haunches on each of them: rags and pennants, quivers and rusty sword hilts, spoons and chips of porcelain, pump handles, canes, feathers, pot covers, bits of twine.

However, the chieftains are proud of it. They sport a tiny flag stuck in the hat or a metal choker around the neck. These are the marks of their station. They curry their forelocks with a nail, and wear a key, a feather, or an old ring wound in their beards. One who cannot attest to the possession of a certain quantity of these objects may never allow himself to be glimpsed in the circles of the ruling proprietors.

Many of their possessions can easily be distinguished, too easily in fact, as the former possessions of their slaves and porters. This is, however, of no importance. The proprietors must be certain of preserving their proprietorship. The loss of their possessions would mean also the loss of their honor and the shameful renunciation of every titular appurtenance. Many of them have indeed suffered loss of their estates and had to slink wretchedly away, never again to be included in the ranks of the mighty, much less in the company of those whose head they trod on in their halcyon days.

At a measured distance around the important persons and Umbramautical dignitaries there hovers a swarm of the sort that is dazzled by great wealth. At a whistle they stand at the service of their idols, eager to carry out each and every command. Bring us stuff! say the mighty, and in an instant the bootlickers swarm out, kick a few of their own kind in the belly, wrest away their little suitcases, and rush back to the masters, but not without laying aside some little knickknack or other for themselves. Indeed, they too hope soon to be counted among the mighty. They dream already of sauntering down the boulevards reserved in the Umbramautical metropolis for the Great Ones and of affording a few coolies themselves: promenaders, who have thoroughly done with the past.

Hop to it, you vermin, on your feet! order their Umbramaut highnesses when they have concluded their meeting. The common carriers awkwardly wrench themselves up, gasp for breath, and grasp their lanterns between their teeth. Then the secret princes and potentates jump up and settle onto the backs of their bearers, and the stooped and hunched-over bearers shuffle into motion. Swaying like ships and camels, noses sooty, poorly booted, tightly reined, and eaten up with grief, they are led away to the undiscoverable seats of the Umbramaut majesties.

3

Other things might be mentioned, were it one's intention to injure or to offend. It is not, however. Rather it is more a case of not being able to neglect disclosing certain other insights into the Umbramautical milieu. Insights that might indeed be better avoided.

Groveling in a far lower existence than the dignitaries, other Umbramauts have joined together to give one another a small sense of security. They flock around their lamps in the desolation and sit on their decrepit crates, battered suitcases, and ragpicker's bags filled with tinsel and scroungings. Little creatures with large eyes, shadow creatures, creatures of melancholy. Out of caution some of them have tied themselves to their baggage.

In banding together they made a wise choice, for who indeed would dare shut himself off from the safety of the group and try to scrape along in the wasteland, in this wasteland so full of danger and isolation? All things considered, these errantly Ahasverlike camps always ready to break are quite livable. Sentinels keep track of every movement in the wasteland. If something stirs, the creatures blow out their lights and imitate the Umbramaut twilight. 0, they know well how to play dead and keep their heads down. When the creatures sleep, their inner selves are not so soundly in slumber as it may appear. Their heartbeat works independently, forming a constant background rhythm, just as a small coterie of stokers maintains the fire in the furnace while the passengers of the ship slumber indifferently in their bunks.

Yet even among them, property and embellishment can be met with. They too have hats on their heads and bits of ornamentation for their beards, boots, and tattered raiments. While their possessions are much less presentable and can actually be counted on the fingers of one hand, they are nevertheless possessions. This is an important factor, for it sets some of them off from others, and puts them in a relatively favorable position.

This insight has surprisingly given many of them a feeling of arrogance, although more toward the still poorer Umbramauts than the richer, so some heads are carried a trifle too high. Kicks are dealt out to those who must bear their kicks without grumbling. To be sure, there are hordes of worthless, false brethren.

It is next to impossible to say with certainty what they do. One thing is certain, however: Each of their occupations is built upon the firm ground of inexhaustible boredom and bafflement. The things they undertake out of pure perplexity! They light their lanterns and blow them out again, light them again and swing them around until they go out, light them again and set them on their heads, first on their own and then on another's. They hide each other's lamps and ceremoniously go off on wild-goose chases (mustn't find the lamps too soon . . !). They play with fire and giggle and run after one another with their lanterns. Anyone not caught after a while has the right to spit in others' shoes.

What a splendid splendid feeling it is to be out of breath! How richly occupied they seem to themselves then. They tweak at their rags to tidy them up, shift their headwear back into place, and shake the dust from their boots, seeking the slightest ways to prolong their precious breathlessness. How complete they feel in that moment of rest. And with flushed faces they sink back into boredom disguised as recuperation.

4

The beings have their own paths and meeting places. They look to the creatures as behavior models, except to those creatures who kick them and tell them they ought to go back where they came from. Compared to the creatures, the beings have next to nothing on their bodies, and their possessions amount to the aftermath of a thorough ransacking. And they feel an even greater need than the creatures to stick together, for who among the weightier Umbramauts, what self-confident creature, would show any consideration for such a skinny wretch, such a puny glob of powerlessness, such an insignificant speck of displaced space? Alone a being would soon be trampled under boot heels.

So they band together to take up more space. A hundred of them cannot be ignored, at any rate, even if one or two lanterns is fully sufficient for the lot of them. When things become dangerous, they scatter into the twilight, and no one catches sight of them—isolated one by one. Names? There are no names here. Clothes? What would the beings wear, when they fill none but the paltriest rags?

They prefer to seek out the proximity of the creatures to ape them from close at hand. If a few beings see that a group of creatures is breaking camp and moving on, they get very restless. However, finally nothing can prevent them from also breaking camp and following those wandering ahead. If they see the creatures have developed a new pastime, they lose no time cultivating it themselves, not deviating in the least from what they have seen, not inventing or adding, for nothing enables them to deviate. They watch yearningly when a creature opens his little suitcase in the sphere of light around his lamp and inspects, feels, and counts his possessions (surely for the hundredth time), and a prodigal craving to own something too comes over them then. But they haven't the stature to own anything.

Once upon a time, they say, there was also wealth in their midst.

This is their only consolation: that there was once wealth among them, too.

5

Though Umbramaut dignitaries can be distinguished from one another by the composure with which they wear their stubs of crowns and headdresses, as well as by the number of their porters and kickable creatures, and though with effort it is also possible to count the creatures and recognize them by the lengths of their beards or by the holes in their rags, the beings are irretrievably forsaken as numberless and unidentifiable. But it is quite impossible to find a trace of the ever-turbulent dregs at the bottom of the Umbramaut hierarchy.

And what are we referring to here?

Teeming things, one would have to call them, innumerably abounding and super abounding phenomena that can be appraised as existent only in gigantic heaps; surging throngs that leave no tracks and emit no sounds, as numerous as raindrops and as impossible to individualize as the wind. Their masses, unsettled, lightless, and amorphous, like sponges soaked full of restlessness, move through the desolation without plan or direction. It is impossible to determine what keeps them moving.

There is some doubt whether one can classify them as Umbramauts at all. (The creatures shun the throngs altogether.) There have been attempts to capture them, but they can't be held, they slip through any net like effluent wind, like swirling droplets of vapor, like mutability and impulsiveness. These inscrutable presences show only through their movement that they are anything at all. Motionless, they quickly evaporate into obscurity, and one can walk through crowds of them without ever coming into contact with any of them. Their wild yearning for characteristics, distinctive features, and recognition drives them everywhere, moving just to keep moving, moving to escape the emptiness.

Now the reason for the great anxieties that cling in such a vise-like manner to the Umbramaut psyche can be mentioned: the dogs.

Huge canines, of uncertain number, lurking and ready to leap somewhere in the twilight, howling and barking so that the Umbramauts shake uncontrollably whenever the sounds carry to the meeting places. These hairy apparitions stand three creatures high, and two Umbramauts can snuggle into one of their paw tracks. Dogs prowling noiselessly through the twilight, their tails between their legs, their snouts stretched to the ground, following the scent of the creatures.

If a dog is sighted, if a bark is heard through the depths of the twilight, or if one of the sentries, ear pressed to the ground, reports a patter, or the dull scratching of a grubbing paw, fortunately still in the distance, emergency measures are taken: Lights out! Put the lamps away! Shoulder your packs!

The Umbramauts are quickly ready to flee, their eyes and ears fixed on the twilit expanses. Not that they're scared. They're just taking a few precautions to keep from being torn apart. How did they come to be afraid of these dogs, these filthy dogs? They jab the tips of their boots into the ground and look defiantly around. But beneath their rags, aren't there just a few little hearts palpitating?

And along comes one of those dogs—and the Umbramauts are nowhere to be seen. Footsteps flying in miniature seven-league boots, they set new flight speed records, ripping the rags on their thighs, clattering their baggage. Though undaunted, they still manage to raise a lot of dust.

Dug in between their bags and baggage, the fugitives lie scattered in little bunches. Flushed faces with round, nervous eyes pop up over the fortifications to check the vague vastness briefly. Later on, here and there the shimmering stars of their lanterns come out again.

Safe. The dogs slouch off grudgingly, far away.

Besides the dogs, the only other animals are the sloths. Fruits of untroubled sleep and lasting immobility resident in the forests, they seldom ripen to wakefulness and hence also seldom fall from the trees. Hanging in the forests, they travel around with the forests without ever coming to know that, or inform themselves why, they are traveling. The Umbramauts are barely aware of the sloths, as they rarely come near the sleeping colonies in the wandering forests, and the sloths rarely if ever come out onto the flats. A time will come when they will have forgotten each other completely, and the calm ignorance of their relationship will turn to horror, if they ever do meet after that.

6

It is a striking spectacle when the Umbramauts' only city, Kuaspitula, glides through the bleakness. Built at gargantuan heights on the granite cornices, upthrusts, and cliffheads, the great Umbramaut metropolis rides on the mountain of the same name. Secure citadel of the homeless, a fold for the creatures, and an absorbent of Umbramauts, the city offers squatter's rights to every Umbramaut, if, that is, he manages to squeeze into a slot between those city dwellers squatted there rag-to-rag. The mountain carries the great city along at a steady speed, and as all things except for rocks come into contact at one time or another in their travels, probably every Umbramaut has had a glimpse of wonderful Kuaspitula at least once. Kuaspitula itself has brushed up against all the wandering woods, mountain peaks, lakes, and puddles once and has seen them from afar.

Kuaspitula, nickering thousand-eyed city, wandering seraglio of light, capital of the twilight. To see her in motion from afar, one might take the city for the home of the legendary will-of-the-wisp princes, for the innumerable lamps swinging, swaying in the wind, rising and sinking, dazzle the gazer, and the speckled mountain draws him irresistibly toward it. He shoulders his bundle and wanders in the direction of Kuaspitula.

Having made his way through the swirls of dust that shroud the mountain and hide it from the bewitched Umbramaut's sight for a while, he must be quick to leap onto a stone outcropping or miss the mountain altogether. There, in the outermost outlying districts of Kuaspitula, he makes his way coughing through the dusty slums where the teeming things live, toward the heart of the city and the heights of the mountain. Before long he must lift his feet to climb over passive, squatting clumps of beings. Soon he sets foot in the higher part of the city where the creatures sit between bare walls and more bare walls and nothing but bare walls, eyeing the newcomer mistrustfully. Finally, it looks to him as if he's come to the hub of the city, for between walls and boulders and boulders and walls he spies the mighty and the magnificent, the lords and celebrities milling about with their burden bearers. A solid kick lets him know he's to be more humble, and a second kick sends him a good distance back to the lower-lying precinct among the creatures.

Here he has more of a chance to look about him. Here also his own kind sit squashed together. He jostles out a modest hole between them and nudges himself into it. So that's life in Kuaspitula! Walls, nothing but walls. Say, isn't there anything more and better than these walls? he asks. How is it that Kuaspitula is so famous, if it has nothing more to show for itself than walls, just plain walls? He is indignant.

You can leave, you know, if Kuaspitula doesn't suit you, someone tells him, adding that he should keep his mouth shut. But a neighbor leans over and gives him a friendlier look. When he came, he explains, he was kicked a few times, too, and he couldn't keep his mouth shut either. But now he knows enough to keep it shut, and now he knows it's the right thing to do besides. For the basic thing is that there are walls here. Actually, they are one of the comforts of living here. No one ever wants to leave Kuaspitula once he's discovered the joy of having walls and the comfort they afford. Kuaspitula is under no obligation to fulfill the expectations of everyone, the absolutely silly and vague expectations of every intruder. What sort of ideas did he have anyway?

Well, the lights ... the newcomer stammers, it was the lights that ...

No, no stick to the walls and nothing but the walls, he is advised further. Where else would he find hundreds of walls, which besides, as he can well see, are high walls at that, diagonally across from him. We should rather be doing everything, he says, to keep the walls, because who knows whether the walls are there for the Umbramauts or not? What we should be doing is stay between them, awaken in them an awareness of their absolute necessity, because, who knows, maybe they might secretly decide to collapse all of a sudden. And then we might as well be out squatting in the desert, because that would be it for Kuaspitula. Besides, he says, where else would you get the chance to see so many Umbramauts in one big pile? And where besides Kuaspitula is there such secure protection against the dogs?

Now he knows firsthand, he's been informed. He becomes calm and puts his little suitcase on his knee and begins to enjoy the presence of the walls that keep the desert away, really keep the desert away.

Soon he will see the uniqueness of the city of Kuaspitula. The Umbramaut market is open, someone shouts, and immediately almost all of the creatures surge up with their tightly packed possessions. He joins them, dragging his little suitcase in the direction that others are dragging their own bundles and boxes. He comes into a hurly-burly of Umbramauts, who are comparing and exchanging goods. He mingles in, barters a piece of broken mirror for a cork, then a little bottle for a key. Completely at peace with himself and with Kuaspitula, he goes off and finds a new place among new neighbors and feels the protection of the walls, and in the light of his lantern he examines his new possessions.

Long live Kuaspitula!

7

There can be no settled sense of security in the regions of the Umbramauts, for everything there is always wandering, except for the rocks. The woods move about, and their travel routes are uncertain. Bursting forth, they file past, rustling with a brushing sound. Stripling thickets and weak-rooted saplings remain drawn into their lightless cores, undulating pastures of shadow and dreary oases of foliage, in which many an Umbramaut believes lies the primordial lair of the dogs and the home of the legends of great times past. The sloths sleep in these thickets. There are a few serenity-seeking, rundown hermits, creatures that form small communities and run calmly along beside the woods, wholly indifferent to where they may turn. They cherish the hope that one day the forests will settle into a permanent rest. They carve little flutes and prayer wheels, with whose twittering music they worship the King of the Dogs.

But seldom do the wayfaring trees come to rest. If an autumn comes their way from some direction, they stop while their leaves wither and then wander on over the colorful mounds of fallen leaves, when they feel leafless and less weighty. This is the kind of autumn the woods are subject to. It returns at unreliably long or short intervals, often when the trees have barely turned green again. It comes without being noticed by the Umbramauts, for it brings no difference in temperature and affects only the woods. When an autumn has finished with a forest, creatures come running to gather up the fallen leaves and heap them into beds or stuff them into pillows. It is usually not very long before the stuffings are slept to bits, and the smithereens are blown off by the wind. The slowly reflourishing woods move on over the empty flats, always in search of a stationary water supply, which is impossible to find.

For the waters also wander and the mountains wander. A forest may happen to sail onto a lake, or the waters wander under the trees, which hurriedly absorb them. Then the forest and the lake separate without any harm coming to either. The water wanders on to collect itself occasionally in a basin. If it falls into place and succeeds in giving the impression of being a reliable, stationary body of water, several Umbramauts will no doubt come running with the intention of opening shipping routes on the spot. Surprising as this may sound, there are in fact four or five large boats in Umbramaut hands. Among these are two rather large canal barges, which like the other boats are carefully watched and maintained, for where would spare parts come from? Or a new ship, for that matter? There are no overhauls or ready-built deliveries for the Umbramauts—you could be deceived—and there never have been. What they possess through chance belongs to them, but enough of that. They must rely on themselves.

So a boat is launched. Hardly has it made its first dignified turn, when the water leaves the moments-before hopeful Umbramauts, and the barges so laboriously towed lie high and dry. Some fish are also left stranded, as well as a quantity of fishbones and shimmering fishtails. Sympathetic creatures hurry after the water, carrying the odd things. Certainly, there more often prevails a covert greed to take possession of the found objects, and most of the creatures can be seen hiding the strange, cool objects in their suitcases.

Fish, one may remark contentedly. So there are fish in the land of the Umbramauts after all.—No, there are no fish at all, strictly speaking. There are only dead fish that the water sloshes along out of habit, and scaly fishskins, fishbones, remnants of fishtails, muddy fins. Nominally, the water holds title to these things and usually keeps them concealed, unless it awkwardly leaves some behind when it withdraws from one of the basins. There aren't any fish. And the remains of fish that are discovered at such moments have neither value nor significance.

Really, there are no fish.

Not infrequently one can see Umbramauts traveling on the wandering mountains. In fact, there are mountains that have literally been taken over by Umbramauts. Travel-hungry mobs perch on the cornices and pinnacles and are satisfied, immoderately satisfied with the constant movement. The dogs will not trouble them here. Some jump off when a spot in the desolation particularly appeals to them, but most of them prefer the security of the wandering mountains.

One of the largest of the wandering mountains is caged Sympokul, the dreaded dog-carrier. When its swarthy summit appears on the horizon, nearby Umbramaut mountain-riders are gripped with unease. Which direction will it take? How will they avoid it?

The travelers wait in dismay to see which route their own mountain will take. Yet what joy and abandonment bursts out when two mountains with Umbramaut passengers float past, near or far, and the boisterous travelers shout tempestuous greetings to one another, waving their lanterns.

8

The Umbramaut population would have an easier time of it, admittedly, if there were no wind. When the wind begins to blow, they are all thrown into terrible confusion and panic. The wind is coming! they shout. Find some shelter! Save yourselves!

The creatures quickly gather up their belongings and fling them into boxes, bundles, or sacks. They stuff things into their coat pockets, provided they have coats and their coats have pockets, or they throw some dirt over precious knickknacks in some obscure nook in the wasteland, which they hurriedly commit to memory. From a distance comes the sound of the wind rampaging through the branches of the unconcerned wandering woods. Dogs' yelping drifts over from somewhere. They have to hurry.

A few creatures unpack grapnels—pothooks, barrel rungs, or scraps of wood—and tie them to their waists. Others tie stones to their hands, feet, and necks for anchors. Still other fasten themselves to large boulders lying around or squeeze themselves into holes hastily scratched out underneath. One or two screw their caps down tight over their curly mops of hair so that the wind will have nothing to catch hold of on them. Some clamp scissorholds around their suitcases with their legs. Everywhere Umbramauts are tying back their beards and throwing themselves prostrate on the ground. Let the wind come along then, it will find the creatures battened down and ready. The havoc it wreaks on them will be of the meagerest sort. If this is disappointing, the wind will somehow have to understand.

By now the wind has thrashed the wandering woods and is shooting in breaching gusts over the wasteland. Hearts thumping and knocking, the creatures lie wherever they could find safety. The beings dash head-over-heels to the leeward sides of the forests. The Umbramautical mighty are securely barricaded in bunkers and bulwarks made of their baggage and porters.

But what has become of the teeming things?

Destitute of any sort of protection, their swarms and hordes are seized up in the first onrushes and are now floundering in the wildly turbulent emptiness and tumbled and dragged along by each succeeding gust. The creatures, better prepared, flap back and forth against the rocks, think of the teeming things, and shudder. If one of them is torn loose, he can still throw out his grapnels. But what will become of the teeming things, picked up and swatted about like playing balls? For them, nothing can be predicted. The best that can be hoped for is the end of the tempest, raging now in its sharpest sounds and coldest surges.

When a lull finally sets in, they try to regain their bearings. Some are hanging to the borders of the woods, others find themselves lying in water. Some have been cast down into empty, unknown regions and rub the sand out of their eyes, groaning. One of them whines that he has lost a boot, and another one tossed aside nearby answers sullenly that he can't find his cap. Everyone seems to have lost something. Battered, weary, woebegone, and in many cases close to tears, the castaways set off toward the hiding places of their buried belongings and lost suitcases. And in the name of silence and hope, the teeming things and the beings fall back into their own desultory, amorphous mobility.

9

We probably can't avoid speaking again of the striking emptiness of the land of the Umbramauts. The ground there, as you know, is incapable of exhibiting anything stationary raised or arched, except for rocks. The wasteland stretches away without feature.

There were attempts to counteract this effect; they wanted to grow grass. The Umbramauts had the idea that grass would not fail to grow, provided a few water carriers could be found to fetch water from the traveling lakes and sprinkle it on the seeded spots until the grass sprouted. Quite confidently they also thought that trees would also take seed and grow up, willing to stay rooted in the same place. Other things as well, for which they had as yet no names.

The grass, however, did not meet their expectations. It could hang on only in sparse clumps where it had always hung on: beside the trees in the wandering woods. The Umbramauts gave up on the project and forgot about it.

Recently they again tried to bring in objects and spread them over the wasteland. They set up trees, hoping they would take root. From the land of day they received donations of all kinds of things called snails and ants, and many-colored stones, and delicate things called flowers. They took whatever they could get. They set the new items out on the ground. Masses of Umbramauts ran about every which way to see whether the novelties would adapt to Umbramaut conditions. The deserted regions were quickly transformed into spacious museums, reverentially toured by the Umbramauts, gawking hopefully this way and that to see what impressions the new things would make on eye and mind.

It looked promising in the beginning. Growing overconfident, some creatures soon babbled of splendiferous times to come. But then things all went quickly downhill. The snails dried up. The birds fed on rocks and sand (this was a bad sign) and could no longer get off the ground. They reeled and fluttered about erratically in circles and could not raise a wingbeat. The colorful stones lost their brightness. The trees fell over.

Disappointments. Renewed hopelessness. Yet at the same time personal property had been increased. Droves of creatures came running feverishly to snitch anything that could still be snitched. Not a stone remained in the desolation that had not been upturned a hundred times and was not still upturned again and again. Soon there was nothing lying loose, everything had found its thieves and new owners. Poking at the ground here and there with sticks and boot-tips, the Umbramauts wandered back to their meeting places. They did well to forget their recent endeavors, they did by far the best thing. In fact, their common forgetfulness was not long in offering them a brighter outlook. This came about inevitably when creatures carrying their suitcases realized that they had to switch hands more often than before.

Hadn't their suitcases grown a trifle heavier!

10

Now the Umbramauts have opened their umbrellas or spread out coverlets and cloth rags, for the first drops have fallen, and the rainy season can begin. The clouds—isn't that what they were called—have gone higher up, and a few isolated drops dare to take the plunge. Others demonstrate reckless bravado, ogle the dizzying blur below, and jump to join the first. More drops, thicker by now, follow into the wide-open, common grave of the twilight. The command is now out for the clouds to cast loose, and for raindrops to dive away. And soon the rain, rain, rain is off on its monsoon tour of the land of the Umbramauts.

An Umbramaut feels the first drop come down on him. Casually, but not slowly, he takes out his rain cover and pulls it over himself. Creatures with nothing to protect themselves from the rain, having perhaps misplaced their own paltry rags (which of the Umbramauts thought the rains would return once they had gone), are suddenly touched by a sentiment of neighborliness and nudge closer to those who have provided themselves with some form of shelter. All of them look after their belongings: One pulls his hat down over his ears; another puts his lamp in a dry spot. Thinking of their thirst, most Umbramauts set out jugs in front of their patches of shelter to profit from the rain, and those who have nothing concave set out their hats and boots in the rain, rain, rain.

The teeming things vanish into the wandering woods. Dogs run around dripping wet and howling, and finally slink into the wandering woods themselves. The Umbramauts breathe more easily and listen in peace to the rain, rain, rain.

The rains lull the Umbramauts into a deep, pleasurable languor that takes them close to sleep. Dread flows out of them, and if no wandering mountain comes into their path during their soporific state (the outposts would report it in time, they hope), their repose will be complete. Even the thieves have turned in, except as one or another of their number may be foraging about for an umbrella to remove from over a slumberer's head. Some have been taken by surprise on the open expanse. Now they plod and grope their way angrily through the puddles, but once they come upon an umbrella owner beside whom they can yield to their fatigue they relax. Out of the wet they lie down safe and satisfied, just listening to the rain, rain, rain.

Eventually, all the Umbramauts lie curled up and snoring under their umbrellas and indulge in reassuring rain-dreams, without exception playing the hero's role. Lying shoulder to shoulder they use one another as pillows and blankets. If one should awaken, yawning and wonder-struck, it only means he's stepped into a congenial clearing in his dream-jungle, where he won't stop for long. Many lanterns burn down and are not lighted again. Unabated over every sleeper's alcove and castle falls the rain, rain, rain.

PART 2

1

In the absence of wells and waterholes in Kuaspitula a thriving and well-regulated service has managed to grow. In fact, because of the unusual nature of the industry, those associated with the water business stand out from other Umbramauts. Now and then some of these creatures can be seen carrying pots, or patched-up casks, or any other receptacle, on their usual runs between Kuaspitula and the wandering lakes. These Umbramauts are in the transport end of the business, by far the most erratic part of it because the lakes are constantly moving from one low space to another. Disappointed water-carriers often arrive at dried-up hollows, believing the water would still be there. Creatures nearby, themselves often land-locked sailors toiling with stranded barges, show the water-carriers the direction taken by the departed water, and if finally the carriers do catch up with it, they fill their containers in straggling rivulets and errant pools.

They then carry their filled casks back to Kuaspitula, which itself must be sought out as well, for it has also moved on. When at last it is overtaken, the transporters bring the water into the districts occupied by the dignitaries, where they deliver it to water-vendors who are soon surrounded by crowds of title-holders, princes, and heroes needing water. They hold out their hats, jugs, and broken flowerpots, which are filled for them at varying prices. Payment is a crucial and delicate point in the transaction. They have every intention of having their vessels filled, but they have a harder time coming up with something to trade. The aristocratic Umbramaut spends a long time, an unseemly long time, groping deep into boxes before coming up with something from among his possessions.

Only after a difficult and painful decision does he take out the smallest trifle or the humblest shred of cloth. There have been those among the mighty who have punched out servants' teeth or taken their shoes to pay for water.

Meanwhile the creatures below queue up and wait for water that a second line of water-handlers picks up once the dignitaries have finished rinsing their beards, washing their rags, or cleaning their boots. For the creatures there is no fresh water in Kuaspitula, unless they get it themselves from the wandering lakes. But now they too are holding out their hats, boots, or potsherds. They dicker the same as the dignitaries, hemming and hawing when it comes time to pay. The difference is that the creatures are dealt with more impatiently. Fork it over or forget it, the vendors say, and the ladle hovers unpoured over the unfilled hat until a bargain is reached.

Get a move on, the vendors tell the creatures once they have gotten their water. And the creatures now drink and wash with great haste: scrubbing, rubbing, filling up one thing, pouring it out into something else, swishing it around, spilling it, wringing it, draining it, and emptying it back into the casks held ready by still another sales force. Let's go, let's go, don't make such a fuss, say the new vendors. The creatures really are forced to hurry to give back the water.

With the little that is left of the used and reused water, the vendors head for the outskirts of Kuaspitula, where the beings stand milling about, waiting in thirsty herds and columns. Let's see what you've got for it first, say the vendors. There isn't much of worth among the beings, and they stand helplessly before the tightly shut casks and look as impoverished as they can, hoping for a few drops to quench their thirst, just a few drops . . .

All right. The vendors take the lids off the casks for a few seconds.

In thirst-coiled handsprings, somersaults, flying leaps, and stumbling runs, the crowd tumbles in and presses around, wallowing and unwinding in the gooey liquid, slurping and lapping and gulping and splashing. Countless flittering limbs whip in a frenzy about the casks. Away with you! the vendors shout again, clamping the lids irrevocably back onto the casks.

Off then into the slums. The vendors now merely pour out the scummy dregs of thrice-used water down the mountain, and it flows into little rivulets and puddles around the teeming beings.

The same swarming and splashing in the declevities immediately begins again.

Elsewhere the watermongers gather to divide the day's receipts.

2

A lone creature has been captured.

His captors deal with him, none too gently. Boots and fists are thrust at him by way of interrogation, and his little suitcase is taken from him. He is about to protest and fumbles helplessly for his property, but a crunch comes down on his fingers. Watch yourself! someone advises.

They make him sit down just outside a ring of congregating dignitaries. The creature catches his breath for a second, and the lordly persons form a tribunal before which his case will be brought. We picked him up on patrol, reports the leader of the stool pigeons and bootlickers. He was alone, which was suspicious enough, and he ran away when he saw our patrol. We found this in his possession. The creature's little suitcase is brought forward.

And what is the name of this caitiff beggar, this insignificant shadow, this solitary specimen of the mob? demands an unmistakable member of the mighty.

Hey, tell him what your name is, a guard shouts, kicking the creature in the rear.

The shadow stutters that he has no name.

Is that so? queries the guard. And what do your upstanding brothers call you?

They say, Come join us, sit down, have you had anything to drink?

You don't say, rejoins the guard. And that suitcase you've got, huh? Isn't that where you've got it all hid? Huh? Everything that thievery would allow, anything your little mitts could pilfer just in passing . . . Huh?

No, no, says the speck of shadow, the suitcase belongs to me and the things inside it have always . . .

We thought so . . . Open it up, the command comes.

Giddy with anxiety, the creature looks on as his suitcase is broken open. The contents are thrown out: a few brightly colored feathers, a lantern, half a glove, a marble, some leaves, a fish fin, some other scraps.

Are his ears clean? comes another question. Instantly a pair of lackeys leap upon him and tear at his ears. But his ears are clean.

The word passes down the line: His ears are clean.

The mighty murmur to one another: His ears are clean. Hmmm. The suitcase stays here, comes the verdict, but he can go. The fish fin is chucked after him, and some leaves and scraps. He quickly snatches them up and runs away, helplessly shaking with unrelieved fear. He hardly goes two steps however, before the lackeys catch up with him again and bar his way.

Well, well, they say, you're free now. But, mind you, that makes no difference to us. What they say is none of our business, if you must know. Which is to say, we still have some things we have to settle with you. That is, there remain a few items that we feel we should discuss with you. Hasn't got a name. Has anyone heard of such a thing? No name, the fellow says, and he wants to slip away just like that, as if nothing had happened . . . You'll be staying here. For a start, you might show us what you've got in your pockets.

They grab hold of him.

Bam: a kick.

And another.

And another.

Let's give it to him, the freebooter, the coward. Give him something to remember us by. Let's hear him howl, make him crawl.

But suddenly there are bloody noses on the other side as well. He hopes they'll remember him too. They'll have something to remember him by. He too is now biting and punching, kicking them in the stomach or in whatever else falls within range. Finally he wriggles out between a pair of boots and runs away.

Later he lies bleeding and whimpering in the twilight, sobbing as openly and unrestrainedly as he can, so that he might sooner bring an end to his distress, his blind pain, his onerous, impotent hurt. Out with all the bitterness, so that he can stand up and laugh again soon. Indeed, he is a tested and true phoenix, about to rise from pain, anger, and exhaustion.

He is an Umbramaut!

3

Ho-o-o-ohhh hoo!

Bong-bong-bong-cha! Bong-bong-bong-cha!

Bong-bong-bong-cha! Bong-bong-bong-cha!

The brigades are on the move. Hassissi, sitting astride his riding creature, begins his review of the troops.

Ha-a-a-a-ats off!

Plucking the caps from their heads, the creatures cast bulging eyes in the direction of the commander.

Ha-a-a-a-ats on!

Shotlike, the caps are back on their heads. Hats on. Hats off. Hats on. Hats off. On. Off. On. Off. Bong-bong-bong-cha! Bong-bong-bong-cha! Bong-bong . . .

Content, Hassissi lets himself fall back on top his porters. Then the commander's eye lights with satisfaction on a row of suitcase drummers marching at the head of his army. He could use more of these suitcase- and trunk-beaters, he thinks.

Halt!

Hassissi gives his quadruped creature a thwack in the hindquarters and gallops to the front of the formation. He dismounts. Stepping in front of the host, he extinguishes his lamp and stamps his boots three times. This is the signal that maneuvers are over, and that the Umbramaut troops can disperse.

Hassissi is a mighty figure among the mighty in the land of the Umbramauts. He formed this army himself, built it up, and met with very apparent success, as was soon apparent. When his suitcase-drummer beats out a tattoo, Umbramauts stream in from everywhere and line up according to regulation. He in fact answered a hitherto latent yet universal desire by founding this private army. It allows the creatures of a military bent to stand apart from the nonmilitary. Although this army is mobilized against hardly anything but boredom, and although its military function is exhausted in mere maneuvers and more maneuvers, the maneuvers are engrossing experiences. Enthusiasm is the net result of all this rigorous idleness. The chief of maneuvers has repeatedly dared sallies and assaults with his reckless bands by capturing and occupying a wandering mountain. After thoroughly occupying the mountain, which was a complete success, along with the change in mode of travel, Hassissi returned in triumph to nowhere and dismissed his band of heroes.

Swi–i–i–i-ing lamps! sounds a command, which Hassissi has just thought up and now wants to test and drill into his troops.

Swi–i–i–i-ing lamps!

They take their lamps in their left hands and hold them out at arm's length. Then on command they raise them overhead and give them two vigorous shakes. They repeat the same on the right side. They put them out on command, light them up on command, and the riotously illuminated army disappears, hoo-ha!, swinging lamps into the twilight.

Bong-bong-bong-cha!
Bong-bong-bong-cha!

4

Throughout the wastes and expanses of the land of the Umbramauts resound the glory, repute, and renown of one of Don Quixote's greatest descendants. The traveling Oleander, a fearful and reproachable creature, has no need to learn the meaning of fear, for he long ago gained an absolute command of it and sallied forth to avoid adventures.

He takes indefinite paths through the Umbramaut twilight, leading a sloth on a rope. This has to be his most difficult feat, for who indeed could get a sloth to follow him everywhere? But, when Pesetembel, the sloth, can no longer muster the energy to put one paw in front of the other, what prevents Oleander from pausing as well for a long and restful break? How long a stretch the two of them have been indulging in this strenuous abstinence from activity cannot be accurately determined. Wandering woods returning to the place the second time, find the pair still sitting unchanged in the desolation, two sleeping blobs leaning against each other, of one mind regarding the avoidance of adventure, snoring tranquilly along as if to say "What do I care?" Oleander wears wads of rags under his beany, giving it the look of the stub-end of a magnificent crown on his large head. There is a sloth whip stuck in his boot, although he seldom uses it. Something like an umbrella is tied to his crescent-shaped traveling bag, which contains nothing, as the traveling Oleander can proudly demonstrate. Protracted inactivity gives him the right to carry no plunder.

It avails nothing to search him for weapons or similar death-dealing instruments. In their place one will find a large, slightly bowed piece of cardboard that he acquired in a trade, and which now serves him as a mattress, something to hide behind, or a roof for his sloth in case of rain. Leaning with composure against the inert Pesetembel, he murmurs to himself something one could better understand, if one heard: Am I not the handsome Oleander? Am I not the great Oleander? Am I not the glorious Oleander, who shuns all kinds of deeds?

Once again the time has come, it seems to Oleander, to avoid adventures elsewhere, now that he has already escaped countless acts of derring-do in this particular spot in the desolation. Tying the cardboard traveling bag to Pesetembell's back, he persuades his sloth to walk a few steps. Moseying along side by side, they are eager to avoid whatever may come unavoidably into their path. Since he encounters nothing, Oleander feels at the height of his career. The sloth carries Oleander's lantern in his jaws and lights the way for his unheroic lord and master.

They finally reach a wandering lake. At the edge of the just-converged body of water lies a barge, and passengers are crowding up the steep gangplank into it. Might one not avoid boarding this barge? wonders Oleander. Tugging his sloth behind him, Oleander quickly mingles in among the hurrying, scurrying, travel-ready creatures and dignitaries. Now, he calculates, everything depends on going up to the ship but not getting on. Oleander has not gotten his reputation as a maitre de plaisir of Umbramaut indolence for nothing, and it precedes him wherever he goes.

He throws himself into the melee of the shipward-crowding creatures and is soon caught in the general onrush. It presses him toward the gangplank. But this is not what he had in mind. He resists hand and foot, staving off the flow, hurling himself back against it. Nevertheless, he loses ground. Even now he stands on the gangway itself. But now the time has really come to avoid what can still be avoided.

With an expeditious leap sideways into the shallows, Oleander saves himself from the perilous gangplank.

Landing hard, he limps and scrambles over to his sloth which has waited patiently at the waterside. They quit the scene of the narrowly avoided adventure and walk off into the twilight. Later, they make camp. Oleander is sunk in gloom. How truly little there is to avoid, he thinks. How few opportunities are given me to elude adventure. One can't avoid melancholy, and one can't avoid either the thought of why the pursuit of avoidance is so much more adventurous than an unavoided and complete adventure.

My sitting here apparently can't be avoided, thinks Oleander. My sitting somewhere else can, of course, be avoided by sitting here. Yet there is no way to escape the fact that I could set out for somewhere else to avoid sitting here. Shaking his head, Oleander leans against his sleeping sloth and resigns himself to the avoidable.

And twilight envelops the imperfect hero.

5

Occasionally, a cluster of wandering creatures bursts into gleeful exultation at the sight far away high above them of a bobbing blue light advancing through the twilight, as if floating on air. Somba-Somba is coming, someone shouts, and they put aside their suitcases to greet him with open, welcoming hands. Over here, they call out to him as they signal with their lanterns, hoping to get him to stop.

There is an agreeing murmur from the direction of the lamp, and not long afterward Somba-Somba steps into the expectant crowd's circle of light. His lantern dangles on the end of a long stick laid across his shoulder: a famous lantern, a gem among lightgivers, carefully ornamented with buttons, fishbones, and fishtails. (My lantern is my guide, Somba-Somba supposedly once said, for it casts my shadow ahead of me, and I need only to follow it. Of course, my head gets in the way when I move my lantern stick from one shoulder to the other. But after all, nothing gets in the way but my head, which would get in the way far more, if it had to decide for itself which direction I should go.)

The stick is taken gently from his shoulders. His little suitcase is set on the ground. He is urged to have a seat. Relax, and get your strength back. Then tell us a story, the creatures tell him. For Somba-Somba is the storyteller of the Umbramauts. A perennial traveling salesman dealing wholesale and retail in trinkets of improbability, he brings with him a storehouse of reliable lies, factual reports, and precious truths, any of which he is always ready to trade for the bargain price of a willing ear and a friendly reception.

It is impossible to count the stories he has put into circulation. They have gotten so mixed into one another that Somba-Somba himself can no longer recognize them when he hears them. In the mouths of the Umbramauts his authentic facts have derived factual contradictions, and his dreams and fantasies have metamorphosed into historical accounts. Somewhat bewildered, the storyteller now and then has his listeners report them to him and then he recounts the tales anew, somewhat modified.

Do the Umbramauts believe him?

They believe him for the sake of unbelievability. Yet Somba-Somba does not demand that his stories simply be swallowed unquestioned. He has other things in mind. With his stories he tries to put a few things back into the empty heads of the Umbramauts. Early on he noticed deep pits of despondency and vapidness that had to be filled, hollow skulls that had to be refurbished with all kinds of glowing images. Deaf ears had to be made to hear again, and lackluster eyes needed transforming into balls of fire. Streams of thought had to get moving again with new and exhilarating ideas to brace them against the freezing encroachments of cold and exhaustion. These dreamless creatures have been weaned of enchantment; they need to be bolstered before they lose anything more, Somba-Somba thought.

The Umbramauts enjoy the bolstering. In the role of the master poet, Somba-Somba instructs them, and they eagerly attend his lessons. Soon most of them would be qualified to pass a proficiency exam in grasping and following unbelievable and extraordinary tales. He has told them the story of the runaway wind and the story of the intrepid Umbramaut who was able to tame the dogs, and he has explained to them the origin of the mixed-up smattering of possessions found in the land of the Umbramauts.

They are the lost wares of a cosmopolitan collector who went riding through the filled-up lands—he tells again and again—in long convoys of large wagons, taking what he could get, and loading his finds and his loot into the wagons. He went his robbing and collecting ways, intending to outfit a country elsewhere. He loaded mountains and scooped water into immense vats, which he rolled onto hundred-wheeled carts. He bundled up houses and trees, dug up springs, and his path led him through the parts that the Umbramauts live in today. The country was empty and nothing to look at. While he snatched up everything he could get in front of him and everything that fell beneath his glance, one of the planks in the last wagon broke, and a few things dropped out through the hole without his noticing. Several barrels of water rolled off and burst on the ground. A few stacks of forests and some mountains that had been thrown on top fell off. Walls and large crates filled with stuff like wheels, feathers, bottles, umbrellas, shoes, rags, hats, carpets, suitcases, ships, and a flurry of other hodgepodge that the collector would probably not have known what to do with anyway, fell off. The things were left where they were as the man went along. Soon a small horde of earth-dwellers, which fortunately had been overlooked, came along and settled where they found the lost things. Since then the mountains have wandered here and there in hopes of coming again to their old stamping grounds. The water has flowed around, and the woods have gone to and fro, with the same thing in mind. The settlers fell over one another to get at the things strewn there on the ground and took anything they could get hold of in the pell-mell pushing and shoving. They made bundles and tallied them up as marks of their worth and property.

Again and again Somba-Somba has had to retell this story, and wherever he goes, he is asked for it afresh.

Somba-Somba strokes his beard and pushes his little rag cap back from his forehead. Before he begins to narrate to the expectant group, he pulls off his boots, which have pinched his feet on his wanderings. He then tells them the story of the sloth who tasted and anticipated so much of death in sleep that he no longer needed to die. And he explains why creatures do not have to open their boxes when they die, because they are allowed to keep their possessions. But not the dignitaries, says Somba-Somba. They will have to share their belongings and stolen goods with the poorer Umbramauts.

There are a thousand questions, an enormous craving for knowledge among his listeners. While Somba-Somba again puts on his boots and shoulders his stick, he hears all kinds of surmises and assertions. The storyteller moves off without a sound. Behind him remains an animated and gesticulating camp full of Umbramauts, who can't and aren't about to swallow the new yarns without thinking them over. Again and again they voice their opinions in speech and whispers. Again and again they raise doubts and express convictions. As Somba-Somba turns to look back one last time, he sees them crouched around their lanterns, heavily armed with questions and answers, heavily armed with heads full of the stuff of dreams and eyes full of fire.

6

Peculiar noises are approaching through the twilight. They seem to be coming from the summit of a steep mountain, which right now is headed straight at a huddle of tremulous creatures, all about to dash for cover in every which direction. Larboard! a voice is heard, and there follows a string of gibberish curses.

The mountain darkens as it grows nearer and nearer, but a lantern is swinging on it. The creatures who have run aside with their lanterns hear several more shouts that they can't explain, and repeatedly they hear: Larboard!

It is Cabasbanzali, the captain of that sailing-ship mountain. Owning no ship he resorts to his imagination. His goods are loaded on the outcroppings, and his dream-built pilothouse is erected on the summit. The hold on the ledges is filled with heaps of mostly snoring creatures, his freight, crossing from nowhere to nowhere. Larboard! the voice shouts again. The lantern waves in another direction. Between the cries of Larboard! stones crackle down the mountain. Amazed, the creatures wait at a cautious distance, clutching their baggage, wait for the groaning, dust-churning, stone-smashing mass to grind by. Afterwards they sit together again around their lanterns with much to guess at and talk about.

Meanwhile Cabasbanzali, a genius among dreamers, dreams that he has run into foul weather. Lower the sails! he bellows. A squall is brewing in his imagination (how fortunate that it doesn't in reality). His Bramaut, as he calls his mountain ship, is rocking and diving. Quickly he lumps together his belongings and throws them down a stone hatchway. Imaginary rain is pouring down on his good, old steadfast Bramaut, whose foaming wake continues to swirl dust into the eyes of the Umbramauts behind. Cabasbanzali finds a spot away from the storm and winds a tattered end of cloth around his ears. He thinks he is being rocked by powerful adverse winds. Later, when his dream has run its course, Bramaut will roll serenely on the high seas again, having survived a Cabasbanzalian typhoon.

Umbramaut high society is able to report how in poorer times Cabasbanzali installed himself in an empty trunk. Evidently he had always gone in for shipdreaming, for he used his umbrella as a sail and rudder of the small trunk-boat, which he sailed on the spot, issuing commands in a loud voice. This form of dry high-seas voyage was his only means of navigation for quite a while, and it marked him with an aura of utter madness. He was scorned. The dignitaries and Umbramautical aristocrats left him to his odd adventures. When he moved up to his mountain ship, they soon forgot him.

But those who now scornfully forgot him cannot guess how soon they will encounter him again. Indeed, the wandering city of Kuaspitula and its legions of lanterns, its lair of aristocrats, has drifted close to the broad deck slabs and jagged stone prow of the mountain ship. Cabasbanzali watches awestruck as he draws toward the magnificent lighted cone of Kuaspitula Land! he roars, wildly swinging his lantern. Starboard! Starboard!

Full of excitement the Umbramaut Columbus paces around in his mountain-top pilothouse.

The gritty, dust-choked suburbs of the mountain city and the splintering bow of the mountain ship are both claiming right of way. An earthquake rumbles through the commandeered hulks, measuring their powers for a moment. Pandemonium breaks out in Kuaspitula, sparing not even the mighty. Suitcases roll all over and many a wall caves in. Cabasbanzali quickly rallies again. He dreams his ship is casting anchor in an exotic metropolitan port, but in the excitement he knocks over his lamp, which goes out at once. He fumbles helplessly with the wick, strikes two stones together furiously, and waits grimly for the spark to take, vexed at missing the city's splendrous welcome, which he had painted in his mind.

But by the time is lamp is relit, Kuaspitula has long since turned away and drifted into the twilight, and so has Cabasbanzali's mountain ship.

Now busily occupied with moving away from the lights of Kuaspitula, Cabasbanzali imagines he is the captain of an outgoing passenger ship. He counts his snoring passengers. Shouting out Larboard! Larboard! he comes around the last dreamed-up point of land. An ocean of twilight once again accepts him into its vastness.

7

An Umbramaut, wearing his cap down to his eyebrows and his beard in three braids, turns up in Kuaspitula. He walks straight for the district where the dignitaries live. He is known there already. Keggo, the lion of society, the Umbramaut model of the good-for-nothing gasbag. He carries a box in each hand with his fingers delicately splayed. His rags are elegantly wreathed about his middle, with a few, newly acquired feathers stuck into knots tied in the cloth.

Breathlessly he parks his boxes on the ground and pushes his cap back rakishly behind his ears.

Well well, he says, only a moment ago I made the acquaintance of an Umbramaut maiden, an unusually beautiful girl. Really, I couldn't believe my eyes—she had three suitcases, and told me she would give me a gift from one of them, if I should visit her again. Ah, what an exceptional girl she was! Of such a different sort from the wenches of Kuaspitula, and so charming, truly like nothing else you have ever seen. You ought to see her dainty boots and her hair, which she wore in long tresses and in curls wrapped around her head. Ydiyasala she called herself, ah yes. Keggo smiles to himself.

So you met an Umbramaut girl, his listeners say.

That he did. And how could he have forgotten to tell them that he had met with Hassissi and held a parade review of his troops? The general introduced him in front of the army, and he had doffed his hat as he was doing now. Keggo, he had said, and made a bow. Hassissi had gazed at him amicably and had the whole army halt and swing their lanterns for him. At the end he had been allowed to take a gallop on the field marshal's own riding creature. Hassissi had shaken his hand in farewell.

Of all things, say his onlookers, who have grown into something of a crowd. So you were Hassissi's guest.

Why, that I was, says Keggo, glancing around his audience.

And on his way home out there (he points in one direction), or maybe it was out there (he points in the other direction), anyhow, on his way home he was attacked by a swarm of clouds. He had thrown himself flat on the ground, but then he stood up again to see how long it would take for the clouds to really blow him over. But he hadn't been blown over. He was able to stay on his feet, and he stood that way until the clouds' incredible onslaught ended.

Yes, well, that was really . . .

But very likely you don't believe I stood up against the clouds, says Keggo, getting agitated as he notices the indifferent and mocking glances of the bystanders. You probably don't want to believe me! And you probably don't want to believe Hassissi shook my hand, or that I rode on his riding creature! Keggo's voice has grown shrill.

Sure, sure, say his onlookers, why not?

Vulgar riffraff! Keggo shouts at them, stamping his boots. You probably think I never ever even met Ydiyasala at all. Maybe you believe she didn't have three suitcases but just a little dented box like all the other raggle-taggle creatures, that's what you think, and you probably think she doesn't exist at all. Maybe you even believe I stole her suitcases and buried them on the way here!

In an obvious huff, he puts his cartons on his shoulder and stalks off, leaving his audience to snicker behind his back, doubting they should believe someone who has already lied to them so often.

And you probably don't believe—Keggo has turned around again and set down his cartons—I kissed her, either. He pounds a fist on his chest. I kissed her . . .

8

Old age has overtaken me, murmurs the sage of the Umbramauts, but it has left me with doubts about everything. The unknown looms over my head, taking back to itself all that I have lived through, making use of my forgetfulness. We both struggle for possession of what I still remember, but I have no doubt that it will be the victor. Before, he murmurs, the unknown was only ahead of me, but now I feel it at my back, too. I'm caught between the two unknowns, and my scope grows smaller all the time. When the two unknowns clash together, like two clouds, there will be a small thunderclap that will be my death. Yes, old age has come upon me, says the sage.

A small squad of creatures is gathered timidly around the hoary recluse. He bends fully bearded over his lantern and mumbles something to the gawkers. Several times they had to extinguish his beard when it caught fire in the flickering flame. He lives in an empty box, but everyone says he's buried all his possessions, the creatures whisper one to another.

You aren't bold enough, says the sage to those standing around him. You think it's enough to run away from barking dogs and strange yells, when what you should do is make such an uproar yourselves that you dazzle and drown out the noise. Then the world would have a notion of you and know that you are to be reckoned with.

But the Umbramauts merely shake their heads. They have other worries: Their possessions might be stolen while they sit listening to the old man. The dogs might come.

Don't be satisfied with anything, bellows the old man suddenly, I know you're afraid. But don't let your fear become a burden to you. (Cling to that one, little Umbramauts, cling to that!)

The sage stares around the circle; the creatures drop their heads and look at the ground.

Oh well, whines the old man. No need to be that bold. Flee from strange sounds and barking, so that you stay unrecognizable and so can escape the dogs. Take care that no one has a notion of you. Teach yourselves the ways of the stone. See to it that the world doesn't have to reckon with you. Yes, hold on to your fears, sighs the sage.

That's a lot more reasonable, the Umbramauts agree. Come with us, they suggest, and while we're guarding our belongings, tell us more. They arrange him in his suitcase and carry him to their meeting place, not forgetting his lantern.

Old age has overtaken me, whispers the sage, rocked back and forth by his bearers. But how can anyone not be afraid and still be wise? When I was only afraid and nothing but afraid, I was wise, for my fear told me how to protect myself. Since I began meditating on fear and its causes, I don't know where to turn.

Yes, go on being afraid, he murmurs wearily, then you'll know what you have to do. Give me a drink, he murmurs.

This they do understand. They set him down and run off to bring him what water they can find in their shards. Later they gently rearrange him in his box. Go to sleep now, old one, they tell him. Just go to sleep . . .

9

What's that clown doing over there?

He's practicing. Balancing a balloon on a comb tooth—or is it a pin?—, he walks back and forth proudly holding the gray orb high in the air, bending and writhing to keep it up. This is an impressive sight for the others, beings or creatures, who, crouched in troughs of dust, baggage holes, and caves, are craning their necks and watching. Where did he get that round thing? they ask each other.

Giving it his best effort, the little clown is nevertheless contemplating a timely exit. He is puffing laboriously. The first timid acclamations and dim cheers that come out of the darkness give him a bit of encouragement. If he was not aware he was watched here and there with such fascination, he would not be undertaking the whole thing. No, he would be huddling in some hole like the others, blinking, dozing, perhaps even dreaming a little, or yawning and feeling cold.

But now that he's acting out his idea, it seems to him positively sensational. He holds the pin steady during his wild capers and does not take his eyes off the balloon.

A short bang, a tumult of sound, cries of fear. The performer throws himself on the ground and burrows into the sand. A stone presses into his stomach. Dust sticks his eyes shut. His audience has fled and waits in hiding for what will follow, having extinguished their lanterns. The entertainer, too, quickly comes to his senses, for he has heard the snuffling of the wild dogs, which have been attracted by the sudden commotion. He grabs the comb tooth, trips, rolls over the ground, steels his nerve, and leaps behind a rock, where he curls into a ball and shivers all over. His wrap, his showman's cape, his mirage of a threadbare mantle, is now more torn than ever. His hat fell off and rolled away, but what's the loss of that against his breathlessly achieved safety? Now he peers cautiously out of the soothingly dark nook of his rock and tries to figure out why and from where this unusual thing befell him.

But there is nothing to be seen, nothing but emptiness everywhere and the careful movements of creatures behind obscure rocks: expansive views over the gathering places of the vague. A few leaves, sand clouds, and splinters of wood and a murmur and rustle of leaves, sand clouds, and splinters of wood. They hear the echoing barks of a few dogs that come closer on thumping paws and suddenly stalk into visibility through the twilight. The dogs stop and sniff. The sight of them shocks the creatures to the core. Just not be discovered. Just not have to cough all of a sudden.

As the Umbramauts watch, all the dogs trot over to a spot where there seems to be something lying on the ground. They sniff and snuff at it for a minute, then lift their scenting snouts to the sky. The Umbramauts gaze upward also, but they see nothing unusual there either. The dogs then go slinking off irresolutely, and the dispersed creatures venture out again and assemble at the spot the dogs were sniffing at. There on the ground lies a moist little heap: the tangled, shredded husk of a balloon. The juggler, running up, skewers it on his comb tooth and casts it aside.

This premier performance of the individualistic brother-Umbramaut does not pass without consequence. The idea catches on. Balancing artists begin making their debuts everywhere. Since there are no balloons left, they balance any object they can come up with on the tips of umbrellas, canes, comb teeth, fork-prongs, even on heads and fingertips. And they no longer become so senselessly alarmed when the teetering pieces and weights fall down. They carry suitcases on their heads or hold up boots on two fingers. They rummage through their bags and send aloft one after another of their treasures. Who knows? Soon they may even hold championships.

Meanwhile, boredom sits by and waits.

10

Why pout so, little Umbramaut? What's come over him? What's changed him so quickly?

He no longer talks to the other creatures as he used to, just sits mulling over vague schemes. With his two cartons placed in front of him he sits shining his lantern into their dark cluttered depths. He digs and rummages, takes out a scrap of dried fish and holds it to the light, selects a feather and strokes it across his fingertips, ferrets out a crumpled bell stuffed with leaves from the bottommost, tightest corner, pinches away the crisp, brown flakes, and swings it back and forth before his eyes. He seems to have decided on this, for he puts the other things back in his cases and plops the lids down on them. Then he runs off with the bell.

If only he had seven-league boots. The reason is that he just saw a pretty girl walk past, enticingly concealed in the twilight, wearing small boots and carrying a half-veiled green lantern. She's worth finding again. Absorbed in these thoughts, he sets one foot in front of the other, looking out for her in a twilight sprinkled with the lights of near and distant lanterns. And all at once his search seems to have met with success, for he suddenly stops and directs unflinching eyes on a green light placed on the ground not far from him. He walks a bit closer to it, kicks around a few stones, and lets his bell tinkle cautiously a few times. A winsome face with round, black eyes and an open mouth turns around toward him. Impetuously, he runs up to his find and holds out the bell to her. When she does not reach for it immediately, but merely gives him and the bell a cautious once-over, he drops it into her lap. And before she, puzzled, beautiful, can say a word, he whisks himself away.

From a safe distance, he then watches how in the dim light she lets the bell ring again and again in her hands. She peers inside it and taps on the vibrating curves of the precious thing. This touches his eyes and heart with an unforgettable thrill, and as he walks home he gives himself over to all kinds of reveries. He will lay his whole Umbramaut world at her feet. He's already given her the bell.

Later as he crouches brooding beside his lantern, he hears the approaching tinkles of a bell that he recognizes. A creature, a very important creature, steps within his circle of light. A black braid falls over one shoulder, and a slender smock of a thousand rags reaches from her breast to below her knees. The bell is hanging around her neck.

What's your name? she asks, and takes a few steps toward him.

Pook, he answers. What's your name?

My name is Siedebell, she says. What's your lantern's name?

Flickership, he says, but also Fisheye.

Will you give it to me? she asks. She is now sitting next to him.

Sure, take it, he says. His heart quavers for a second, but the lantern also belongs to the world of things he wants to lay at her feet.

Oh, no, no, no, she says laughing, and her voice is the second bell in his life. I was just asking.

Now they look at each other. He touches her hair, and he touches her smock, beneath which her breast throbs ever so perceptibly, then runs to his boxes again and with a lunge pulls out a piece of broken glass (he had prepared for this), and puts it in her hand.

For me? she asks.

Yes, says Pook, it's for you.

I've got something for you, too, says Siedebell. Would you like to look for it?

Pook launches into the quest and only a good while later comes up with a mussel shell that he found between her breasts. Wouldn't you like to douse your Flickership? she asks.

They stuff the bell with leaves again and go off through the twilight, where they lie down beside each other with the doused Flickership. They have piled their boxes in a heap . . .

PART 3

1

The Umbramaut mighty have settled on a plan: to settle the hinterlands, the empty provinces where even the wandering woods seldom venture. The beings, they decide, are perfectly fit for the project. The mighty ones will deport them and settle them there.

But how, one asks, will they catch these continually stirring nomadic swarms, which just appear now and then, here and there, leaving behind no reliable tracks? Optimistic answers are blustered about: Even if they are scattered in all directions, they might as well accept it. We know what has to be done. We know where the beings are vulnerable ...

They begin the round-ups. In every part of the land creatures are lured into service with false promises and are loosed on the beings. They flush the beings out of every which place and drive them through dry lake beds, through moving water and into the dark impasses of the wandering woods, where they become tangled in the tree branches and high grass and are easily boxed in. Other creatures sit crouched in the dark with their lamps extinguished, on the alert to call out if any beings show themselves. Other pursuit gangs concealed in the darkness rush out in stomping boots to stop anything that comes their way.

Several knots of beings are sighted in the licked-out bed of a lake that has just drifted off (you can still hear the last waves dashing). Somehow these beings have been able to pass unnoticed through the lines. They fancy themselves safe, holding still in the dampness. The hunters are commanded to drive them to the gathering place. They creep up and encircle the fugitives, throw them into a panic, and drive them to the gathering place. The hunters shoulder their harrying pieces—spikes, clubs, torches, and suitcases to use as drums—and close in on the hollow where the fugitives hide in their inhospitable camp.

On command they unleash a riotous racket. They wave spears and throw stones into the darkness, where they hear them slap dully into the mud or raining down on the terrified beings, who jump to their feet and don't know what's going on.

Reinforcements arrive now to join the flushing lines. Thudding their boots and stomping up dust, the squads circle around and form sidelines to use as a channel to push the beings through into the open and drive them to the collecting place.

Flying and fluttering in breathless leaps and tangled knots, the clustered victims bounce and tumble down the clamorous, tight gauntlet.

Houyouhouyouhouyouyou, the coursers whoop.

Seeeeeeeyouuuuuuu, they howl.

Eeeeeeeeeoooooooooooooo, they yodel.

There is huffing and puffing, screams resound, fur flies. Mindless and helpless beings run, run, driven into the herding place and jammed in with their peers. Off with them to the provinces. And the creatures again take up the chase, this time towards deserted, unknown parts of the twilight. There the mob is left to itself.

Later, the harried mass calms down and its members swarm out over an expanse few Umbramauts have ever seen before. The unknown frightens and repels them with its unimagined stockpiles of horror. The land, for its part, looks determined to resist becoming arable in any fashion. The beings meanwhile do not relish in the least having to work to reclaim the land. What should be reclaimed anyway? And how? The beings have no idea what to do with or in this place. So, happily agreeing with the unknown to leave it as it is, they sneak away again and filter back into the more habitable part of the twilight.

When the delegates of the mighty authors of the hunt—traveling officials, organizers and overseers, dignitaries and creatures alike— step out over the wide, barren panorama to view the progress they expected, they notice their subjugated advance-workers are gone. The twilight stretches before them impenetrably and impassively.

The officials curse, stamp their boots, erupt in fury. Feeling cheated, they make their way home.

2

As reported, the shipping traffic on the great Umbramaut lakes, the wandering ponds, and homeless pools is in jeopardy. What moved Umbramaut chieftains and their peers to protest? Those who know the background of the protests may indeed shake their heads and admit that Umbramaut boat service still in existence is brazenly exploited.

One of the five (or is it only four by now?) Umbramaut ships is beached on the shore of a body of water that has just settled into a low spot, no one knows for how long. Several passengers, who are naturally of the highest Umbramaut stratum (or at worst a couple of well-to-do creatures), are to be ferried across the large puddle. They have settled into their high-priced seats, and a gang of sailors—creatures who find diversity and kicks in the pants here—are running up to push the barge into the water. The captain signals other creatures standing by on deck to draw in the gangplank. But before they can put their hands to it, a numberless swarm of beings surges helter-skelter up the gangway into the barge, butts the collectors roughly aside, spreads out, and vanishes into the cracks of the frail and rotten boat. They want to make a sea trip, too.

The captain is notified of the incident.

These pump-handles, these vermin, these miserable whatchamacallits, these so-an-sos, these you-can't-see-ems-and-you-can't-grab-ems want to take a trip??? Flog them! shouts the captain. Thrash them, throw them into the water, massacre them! Get that raggle-taggle off my ship!

However, the sailors soon find out that they can't find much to grab and give a drubbing to, or to throw into the water, or to flog. Their steps tunk-tunk up and down the decks, and they grow more irate by the minute, finding nothing. Indeed, there are stirrings in places, even whispers and scooches and giggles, but the sailor-creatures can't sink their fists into anything. The stowaways, stunned with the urge to travel and the success of their boarding, are invisible and scattered all over the ship. Catching them is hopeless.

The sailors are nonetheless impatient to shove off, and the passengers are grumbling. The captain reluctantly blows the whistle to cast off. But on the shore steps forth a broad phalanx of creatures, not keeping it at all a secret that they too want to come aboard . . . without paying. All together they plunge into the water, thrash up to the boat, clamber up the side, and soon mass into the insides of the now lurching barge. The exasperated captain paces back and forth, crumpling his hat in his hands because his ship is transformed into a playground and fun fair for countless gangway crashers in spite of him and his now powerless mariners. Meanwhile, the beings and creatures cramming the decks and holds are getting their unpaid money's worth basking in the joys of travel and conquest. All the captain has is indignation.

Finally the captain can do nothing but give the order to shove off.

Before long all ships will have fallen into the hands of travel-crazed creatures and mischievous rabble, which occupy their evidence of success unchallenged and believe they can do without a captain all too well. Shoving off and traveling wherever they happen upon a body of water, they roll and pitch on the waves until they come to dry land again. Boisterous, singing flocks of passengers, waving their numberless rags, give their captain the sack. No need to pay if you want on board. Just know how to fight your way in and join in pushing the boat off now and then!

Even now only hulks and fragments, ravaged by perpetual play and the revelry of voyage, the barges have nothing more to do than keep the mobs above water until they fall apart, founder, and are forgotten.

3

Occasionally, when a lost car materializes, driving across the desolation with no particular destination, the availability of an Umbramaut railway is recalled to mind. Then the creatures who have glimpsed it run after and jump onto the vehicle, which rides on broken axles and three crooked wheels. When after a stretch they have the impression that they've come too far, they jump off again and wait there on the spot for an eventual return trip, torn with anxiety about their abandoned baggage and worried that they might not find their former meeting places again.

In rare cases a car happens by to take them back right away. Usually the creatures prepare to wait for some time to board another car and often settle for a wandering mountain that may also meander them home. In any case, they soon forget why they are hanging around and attempt to go on foot. An Umbramaut would never go home on foot as long as he remembered that a railroad car might come along. However, as soon as he forgets how he got where he is, he also forgets there is anything to do but walk. As long as he has no wandering mountain before him, no wandering mountain exists for him. Let one appear, and he believes there has always been a wandering mountain in the vicinity. But now he sees no mountain and no railroad car and thus remembers nothing. So the Umbramaut walks back, content with that.

If one were to put an Umbramaut into a barrel headfirst, he would nearly die of fright. Nevertheless, he would soon adapt to his situation, and once the lid was slapped shut he would feel quite at ease, if for no other reason than because after a while he would have forgotten he had ever been outside the barrel. Totally engrossed with standing on his head inside the barrel, he would be so caught up in his independence from any other state of being that he would see standing on his head as his only mission and sole destiny. In a short time he would be heard singing. But if anybody ever opened the cask again, pulled him out, and stood him on his feet, what consternation and terror would come over him then!

Engineless and unlighted, several passenger- and freight-cars shuttle over the Umbramaut wasteland. What pushes them may well be the same force that keeps the woods and mountains wandering. Train stations likewise do not stand still but drift vagrantly about with their loading platforms, waiting rooms, bells, and roundhouses. A station seldom comes upon a car, for there seem never to have been tracks, direction signals, or fixed rail lines. There is no direct connection between the railroad cars and the railway stations. The cars lurch past without using them.

Stations, we call them, but such stations!

A couple of walls, which with any luck meet at one or two corners to offer protection from the wind; piles of rocks, some rusted, clapperless bells lying on the ground, rattly and mangled metal disks hanging from bent poles here and there, loading platforms where a few flagstones lie close enough together that one can jump from one to the next in bounding leaps. Station halls, if two stumps of walls stand close enough together . . .

Creatures who think they have some function at these depots recall it when they see a car coming. They pound on the bells with knuckles and stones and make crude pealing noises. Without knowing why, they hurriedly hang up remnants of signals. The travelers between the waiting room walls, bereft of any desire to travel, passing time in forgetfulness, despite their forgetfulness have held out for nothing less than an Umbramaut railroad car and are shaken awake precipitously.

Now they are in a sudden hurry to be away, remembering the splendid plans they made for their travels. The entire staff of the station fans out to catch the car, which may only be passing on the horizon, and push it into the depot, where stones are set before the wheels, or fragments of wheels, to keep the car from moving during its whistleless stop. Then it's all aboard through doors, windows, and holes. Porters are pointless, for Umbramauts deem it wiser to drag in their own suitcases.

Let her go! The packed car is pushed from the almost indiscernible walled-in place, the hall and the railyard, out onto the plain and goes off full tilt, taking complete irresponsibility for its passengers. Some creatures, who the passengers fully believed were legitimately involved in some official capacity with the station, jump in at the last minute as well and leave the station to itself. Meanwhile, like the car, the station wanders on, roiling dust with its dilapidated walls and bell-ruins.

En route the Umbramauts have no doubt they have always been traveling. If someone were to hop on and ask what they had been doing a moment before, their answer would be:

Why, we were traveling, of course.

And if he asked, Where are you going? one of them would answer him:

Where are we going? What kind of question is that? We're just traveling, that's all. We've always been traveling and always will be.

If no one happens along to separate them from their cabooses and teetering boxcars, they will in fact always be traveling. Therefore, it is hoped for their sake that a marauding band of Umbramaut thieves will notice the lantern-filled car going by and decide to hold it up. By the time the car has been thoroughly ransacked and its passengers fleeced, each and every erstwhile traveler will sharply deny ever having been on a trip. Each one will aver he has always been sitting around on this spot doing nothing, in this and no other place in the wasteland. Even the forgetful thieves would disclaim all accusations that they had held up and looted a railroad car, if the stolen luggage and unlikely personal effects in their possession did not speak so plainly against them.

There will probably be a scuffle, during which the passengers will regain most of their suitcases, which by contrast they remember in every detail. There is no more talk of railroad cars, however, until another one turns up suddenly.

4

The two belladonna gardens are treasures in the land of the Umbramauts. Like everything else, they wander, mostly after the water. Large numbers of the Umbramaut mighty come galloping when a garden is sighted. From their riding creatures, they leap in between the bushes to gnaw on the berries, gobble down dreams and ecstasy, and behave quite as if the garden belonged to them alone. Their servants, who have come running up behind, stuff the fruit into their mouths, and before long they fall into deep daydreams and bliss. When the mighty are sunk in dreams, their servants glut themselves on what nightshade berries they could snatch off the branches and sink down next to their dead-to-the-world kick-bestowers. They dream and sing or slump off talking to themselves. The more clever of the servants seize the opportunity to sneak away as soon as their masters lose sight of them in their drug-induced transports.

Right on the heels of the dignitaries and their servants come the creatures, who also want a taste of belladonna. The more adroit among them manage to make off with a few berries and go off and hide to eat them. Many, however, grow bold and jump into the wandering gardens without regard for protocol, ceremony, anyone or anything, stepping on the bellies of their dreamy-eyed highnesses.

The beings have followed the creatures, although at first they could not understand what all the rush was for. They generally depend on the fortuitousness of circumstance.

They profit in their own way. Since they do not dare jump into the gardens (they would be trampled ruthlessly by the stronger dope fiends), they snap up handfuls of the spat-out kernels and, raving with sobriety, stuff, stuff, stuff them into their minuscule mouths and suck off the remnants of the bitter fruit, their eyes shut. The ones that aren't fast enough to get their hands on anything look breathlessly on as other mouths water and the drug goes to other heads.

Who could have prevented hordes of hungry and thirsty teeming beings from swarming after the rest? They too now buzz and rave around the mutilated remains of the garden and take in the aroma that drifts out to them. They wrestle for the twice-chewed pits, which none of them can swallow because they have no mouths to speak of, and rub and wipe and scour and scratch themselves with them. Finally they crowd their way into the garden and plant themselves in the bushes. Their frenzied movement knocks down the last of the berries, which are crushed and torn apart and devoured by the creatures and beings still scurrying after the wandering garden.

Snoring, yawning, turning over in incoherent dreams and disordered raptures, the Umbramaut personages lie under the bare, ravaged, and utterly-disheveled shrubs and sleep it off. Their servants have long been completely incapacitated to do anything for their safety or comfort. Thus the dignitaries lie with swollen heads and tattered clothes alongside the no less rumpled creatures. All are snoring or babbling in their sleep; their dreams are mixed with the droning, ominous muddle of impotent rapture. No one notices the squashed hats and slit rags, and the pillaged garden patiently and dustily wanders on, carrying its drugged cargo toward a later awakening.

Skulls aching, faces moaning, how will they face each other when they awaken? What awaits them when sobriety again sets in and the mighty insist that each of their bruises and each rip in their clothing must have its retribution on the spot. And how did all these creatures get here anyway?

Woe to the creature who has not awakened and stolen away before the mighty awaken!

5

Beyond the wastes, the image of Umbramaut vastness, beyond the wandering woods dangling on the horizon like great clumps of shadow, and beyond the last Umbramaut lantern an enormous phantasm has arisen, spreading fingers of illumination into the dusk. A creature sitting and patching his rags is the first to glimpse the fata morgana. With a shout he jumps up and points toward the distant, persistently gleaming shape. Others also spring to their feet and can hardly believe their eyes. In the black haze of the twilight stands a place bright as lightning. High-masted ships in full sail cruise in and out of the windows: colorful and exotic things, totally inexplicable and mystifying to the Umbramauts. Two wandering woods file past beneath the glorious mirage, while it presides high above the horizon.

Not hesitating long, some of the curious and surprisingly undaunted creatures set out in its direction to come closer to it. Nothing of its kind has ever been seen anywhere in the land of the Umbramauts. Running toward the glittering, inconceivably profuse squanderer of light, they somehow do not seem to get nearer. They go on running, but eventually they give up and turn back, for farther on they still come to nothing but empty plains, and the image remains as far off as before.

Rumors, intimations, divinations by the thousands. Some speak of the King of the Dogs ascending. Others claim it must be the vanguard of Umbramaut Paradise. Others say it must be a revelation of the source of the wind, so often mentioned by Somba-Somba. Many prefer to say nothing and to stay close to their suitcases. Some pull their caps down over their ears. In the distance they hear the dogs barking at the enigma, hailing it perhaps. Really, curiosity is out of place now.

Lying behind rocks and heaps of dust the Umbramauts watch the apparition intently. But constant observation of the wayward fata morgana finally tires them out. Gradually they reach a common conclusion. They yawn. Some fall asleep. Others stand up, and since nothing happens to them, others follow their example. They begin to comb the knots out of their beards. They slap the dust off themselves. As the soundless, wondrously luminous figment fades away, the Umbramauts lose sight and fear of it.

Occasionally, afterward, apparitions recur. Other palaces appear, drifting off from unseen islands or cities, whose origin not even Somba-Somba has yet explained. But whatever new chimeras materialize, the Umbramauts are no longer frightened. They soon grow used to the unusual, and since it in no way changes anything, they find it quite normal. They hardly bother to turn their heads anymore when a vision of light gleams out of the twilight and hovers there. The unknown no longer beguiles them. Those who still express wonder are told to make sure they have enough to drink or to mend their boots.

6

The large nomadic population and the all-enshrouding twilight of the land of the Umbramauts foster the growth of sundry gangs of thieves. Indistinguishable, they prowl through the wastes, neither identifying themselves nor letting themselves be seen, sniffing out anything that might be worth having, then taking it. Idleness, boredom, and certainly a great hunger for the kind of repute that comes from accumulating property seduce quite a few creatures and even some of the mighty (who, of course, generally dispatch their servants to steal for them). They make their camps in remote places and rove about with unlit lanterns.

Scouts sneak close to the gathering places of their erstwhile brothers. They send back messengers to the rest of the gang, napping at the hide-out, gathering strength for the job ahead.

A runner reports a promising haul to his lazing partners, who leap up, put out their lamps, pull off their boots, reach for their handy sacks, boxes, and crates—which they hope to carry back full—and wend their way silently, led by the messenger, to the ambush. There they see a few unsuspecting creatures, sleeping and snoring around a couple of fizzling lanterns; some are curled up on top of their possessions, and others are tied to theirs. It is well known that many Umbramauts keep their most prized possessions hidden in the hollow tree trunks of wandering woods, in crevices in the mountains, or in other secret places. Still, these rascals hope to get rich here.

They walk in among the sleepers, unobserved. Their leader shouts a signal, and they quickly put out their victims' lanterns, knocking them over, stomping out the lights. In the tumult that follows, the thieves snatch up anything they can get their hands on. They stuff things into their sacks and clutch up little boxes under their arms; they grab up rags and caps and boots and bottles, any other junk and all kinds of plunder. One by one, when they think they have enough, the thieves untangle themselves from a melee of assailants and completely surprised defenders and flee across the wastes as fast as their creatures' legs can carry them, leaving their whimpering victims in exhaustion.

After their heroic foray, the thieves recongregate at their hideout, where one of their party has kept a fire burning and guarded their boots. Treasures, spoils, wares, and bags of hodgepodge are piled together for distribution. Speculative glances full of longing remain fixed on the booty.

And suddenly the silent, secret fireside is transformed into a frenzied thieves' bazaar. Goods are auctioned or simply seized. Wide-open mouths clamor, eyes show anxious resentment, rags are torn to shreds, bottles thrown and shattered, crates smashed into smithereens, and hair ripped out. The leader of the gang composedly surveys the confusion and pulls on his boots, chuckling to himself. Unbeknownst to the others, he has already stashed his own selection in a safe place.

Just go right on with your shouting, he thinks to himself, looking around to see if the twilight behind him is unoccupied. Just go right on with your shouting! Then the dogs will show up, too. He slips silently away and runs to save his skin, for the present; later he will retire to a secretly established and secure old age.

Just go on shouting. Just go on shouting.

7

It's time the dogs got some of their own medicine.

That's what the creatures have decided. They scrape together and screw up their courage, chipping in thousands of hesitant pittances of mettle and brashness, donating small offerings of intrepidity and larger amounts of anxiety, and making huge contributions of good intentions and simple encouragement. They've had enough of being dominated by dogs. They've finally had enough.

Volunteer commissions, dog-combating committees, and battle forces recruited from among the creatures and the dignitaries set to work making traps for the dogs. Giant pits are excavated, while sentries walk around as usual to watch for the unexpected. Hassissi's troops also have been assigned to join in the work. All together, the diggers scrape and scoop, pile out dirt and sand, roll away stones. Then the pits are laboriously covered and disguised. The pit bottoms are garnished with jagged rocks and sharp-pointed branches as a surprise welcome for dog bellies.

Those damned dogs!

The Umbramauts, incensed by preparations for revenge and extermination, now pitch in to build noisemakers. A ten-Umbramaut kettledrum is fashioned out of a vat. Caterwaulers quietly test their voices at every pitch. Even the beings join in and scrounge up a few barrel halves. By bunching themselves up and running against them, they manage to make a thud. Anything to lure the dogs in.

Signaled by a shout the Umbramauts strike up their audacious cacophony from the far side of the pits. The kettle drummers beat with bottles, stones, clubs, sticks, staves. The beings make running leaps and unleash rumbles of thunder. Caterwaulers trill and bellow. Individual suitcase-thumpers do their part with flailing arms and beet-red faces. All squint sideways to see if the dogs are on their way.

Sure enough, before long the music-makers hear the all-too-familiar barking fast approaching out of the twilight. Ayee! Courage cools quickly. Wouldn't it have been better to have left well enough alone? They can't keep their hands from trembling as they drum and shout, squeal and bop, and they dart fleeting looks around. Just don't be left behind when everyone clears out at the last minute!

Here come the dogs, and suddenly the dogcatchers are nowhere to be seen, their instruments are cast aside, and . . . ???????

. . . A scuffling and thumping, panting, snuffling as the dogs thrash and howl in fury in the pits, dug so deep they can't jump out. Their courage returning, the creatures, filled with curiosity, poke long sticks down over the edge into the jaws, fur, and paws of the dogs expiring in the pits with wild looks in their eyes. Sand on them. Rocks on them: a rolling and trickling, scraping and groaning, and final barks. The dull thud of sand in the bottom of the dog-graves.

Then a triumphant march back to the meeting places. Laughter and songs and lantern parades and glowing stories. The dog-vanquishers show off their callused hands, their dusty feet, and their husky voices. Narrators' heads and tongues grow dizzy with glory in renditions of fearlessness and gallantry, while all the other, still-living dogs are forgotten.

Later the heroes fall asleep on rags and paddings chosen carefully for the occasion. The Umbramaut twilight grows calm. Hassissi's army marches away, its lanterns swinging drunkenly.

8

Sometimes it's not enough that the dogs strike fear into them; they have to strike fear into each other as well.

Several creatures, seeking amusement, have grabbed hold of one of their peers and thrown him into a mud hole. They stand and watch on the dry edge, clutching their sides with laughter as he tries to get up and walk and fails, and water gurgles into his boots, and he is soon up to his belly in the uncomfortable black mud. He is sinking visibly and looks helplessly around. But the creatures, standing above the bog, lift not a finger to help and merely watch his futile efforts to stay on top of the mire. However, he's not as stupid as his enemies think, for he knows they will have to pull him out when his collar gets damp. So, to awaken the impressions of great danger, he lets himself founder right before their eyes, gives a few timorous calls for help, and swallows some of the cold ooze. This has an effect on his observers, they become uneasy. Just as the poor devil gets ready to sink away melodramatically, his tormentors stretch out hands to him from all sides and pull him out. They lay him down, feigning unconsciousness, and clean him off, and pinch him a few times, too. Never, never would they have thought of killing him, unless he asked for it.

His enemies become palpably embarrassed when they find their victim has lost a boot in the mud. No one had expected that. What can they do but go in and fish it out themselves?

This pleases the owner of the boot. Chilled, but eminently satisfied with the unexpected turn of events, he sits crouched on dry ground and has the pleasure of watching while a couple of his enemies sink ever deeper into the gurgling black bog and run their hands around inside it, breathing heavily. They've got to find that boot.

Finally one of the searchers holds it up. The slime is dumped out and someone hands it by his fingertips to its owner. Amicably he accepts the wet hull and, in his bare feet (the boot has yet to dry out), follows his fellow creatures back to the meeting place, where they are looked at with astonishment.

New games of terror, new ways of having fun at others' expense:

A pouch, his treasure chest, his one-and-all-and-that's-all-he-has, is stealthily taken away from a sleeping creature. Then one of the thieves wakes him up and asks him where his pouch is. Half-asleep, he looks around and fumbles through his things and holds up his lamp to see: no pouch.

Give me my pouch! he shouts, jumping to his feet. Hand it over, you scoundrels, or you'll see what happens. Some of the other creatures laugh, but a few check quietly to make sure their own belongings are secure and look sympathetically at their comrade, the butt of the joke. Blubbering and gulping, distraught, he runs first one way and then the other, shoving his neighbors from their places and rummaging through their suitcases in a flurry. Several of the onlookers can no longer bear to watch this. With clenched fists, they spring on the pouch-thieves and their accomplices, who give themselves away by their malicious simpering.

Rags fly, boots thwack, hats are dashed off heads, and the spiteful creatures' ears are boxed.

Hand over that pouch!

Hand over that pouch! the vigilantes order, in rhythm to their punches. Some of the thieves sneak off and bring back the purse they had buried in the sand. The owner grabs it and looks to see if anything's been taken from him. Now the petty thieves have their chance to squirm. Their captors have a tight hold on them.

Nothing missing. They can go.

But don't show your faces around here again too soon, the creatures shout after them. Having snatched up their things, the violators are now camped in the dark, far outside of the meeting place. Some are scornful, others more repentant. When the dogs come, the Umbramauts say later as they relax in the security of their gathering place and talk it over, those rascals will be the first to run.

When the anger of the group has smoldered out, the thieves will be able to return. But woe to any of them who are seen before that!

9

In the Umbramaut back country, where the twilight seems to collect and condense into impenetrable black walls of shadow, a flashing, flaring, spark-spewing fire sweeps convulsively into view. All the sleepers are shaken and startled awake. They are about to complain about the disturbance when they see the heap of sparks and flames approaching. Their sleepiness vanishes, and an old, timeless fear renews itself in them, particularly because the dogs in the distance begin to howl at the blazing spectacle.

Awakened and startled everywhere, they see the hot glow of myriad flames cruising slowly past in the darkness. Shouts are heard, out of whose mouths it's hard to tell. Dark and light flakes of ash drift in twisting, uneven streams across the wastes. Soundless cloud bursts of cinder puff out over the baffled, flame-bewitched Umbramauts, heightening their perplexity. What has happened?

When the fire lets up, with nothing left of it but thick, hanging smoke roiling darkly over Umbramaut heads, some of the creatures venture to approach. There, instead of a wandering wood, they find only bare, glowing twigs, smoldering stumps, and logs floating along amidst clouds of black ashes. Scorched sloth skins lie littered among the ash heaps. A wide trail of sooty blackness leaves a long reminder of the wandering path of the ruined forest.

How could that have happened? the Umbramauts ask one another in consternation. Angry suspicions are voiced. They can't be sure of what they're capable of doing, if they get their hands on the filthy pyromaniac. One pounds his fist angrily on his suitcase. Another rips off his hat and throws it on the ground, then picks it up and throws it on the ground again. What an idea, that instead of a forest an ashen waste will be wandering around.

Just you wait, says the hat-stomper. Just you wait. You're going to be sorry, Umbramaut, that you threw your lamp into that forest. You'll be sorry, all right.

Later some of them come across an Umbramaut without a lantern.

What've you done with your lantern, eh? they ask. Where is your lantern? Is this by any chance your lantern? And they hold up the charred husk of a lantern found in the ashes of the forest.

I just don't know, the little fellow moans, grabbed by ten fists. Really, I don't even have one . . . really, I'm not the . . . oh, please, no no no . . .

They lynch him. He whimpers, but they laugh. 0, you rotten firebug. String him up. String him up.

Then they say: Just leave him lying there. However, the avengers fail to fade so neatly from the scene. They can't abandon this strangled, trampled, scrambled little heap of rags and blood, dust and bones. He had bitten himself in the arm. A boot lies here, a tuft of hair there, and he lies here, inscrutable, appalling stillness.

Horror chills the avengers inside. What if he was the wrong one? What if he really didn't own a lantern? The best thing to do, they decide, is just to bury him, just get him away. Away. Hastily they scratch a hole out of the ground. In he goes. There is still his suitcase. They stand in a circle around it, unresolved.

To whom will it go, to them or to the corpse? Their unresolve won't quit, until finally somebody throws it on the body in the grave.

Let no one dare return secretly and dig the suitcase up.

Now they can no longer conceal their worry and embarrassment. And something else, still stranger, stranger still: tears. At first they fall surreptitiously into rag folds, but then they are sobbed unrestrained, loudly and unchanging: Tears, tears, tears, and the crying is not about to stop.

10

Whereas the suffering and visitations of boredom are all too frequent in the land of the Umbramauts, the Umbramauts themselves have become masters in the art of dispelling the doldrums, for they have been through the hard school of idleness and have some notion about what to do with themselves. At least half of the boredom that comes over them can be rendered harmless.

Somebody is always trying to do something, and successful attempts always give encouragement to other attempts, new trials and new test runs. Of course, there are many who prefer to sit around and gaze off with melancholy as their fellows keep busy. Scorning calls to arms in the battle against monotony, they claim they've already done all that. However, they have never been seen taking part in any activities with other Umbramauts.

Do they know what to do with themselves? In truth, they really have little idea. But, for an engrossing and anesthetic while, they give themselves over to games, projects, and pastimes and come out of them renewed and strengthened. They have to think it all up themselves. That makes the trouble worthwhile.

Their need for any kind of merriment has led the creatures to hold a celebration. Dignitaries and princes, mighty lords and heroes are too busy trying to impress themselves and each other with their possessions and porters ever to think of cheering themselves up, but not the creatures. They tidy up their suitcases and comb their beards. The Umbramaut women put up their long hair and tresses, scrub their lantern frames, and arrange their rags in new fashions around their necks and breasts. One Umbramaut can be heard singing as he dusts off his hat with a rag.

Then they rise up and mingle. They look each other copiously up and down and bow. They stroll sedately down elegant avenues, constructed ahead of them in their imaginations. They lift their caps and hats, and those who have nothing and their heads wave with their lanterns. They show off their boots and necklaces, take note of one another's draped and hanging valuables, and silently admire one another.

Later the lanterns are set up in a row and foot races begin. Whoever can run and grab his or somebody else's lantern first and wave it in the air is raised on shoulders and carried in a circle.

Hey, look out! comes a sudden cry.

Dark mists come scudding in over the ground, bringing cold and driving moisture before them. Some of the festival participants are blown right over. Full of terror the scattered and scurrying Umbramauts cling to the ground. Lights are blown out. Rags skid, hair falls out of place. Hats roll away:

The clouds have come.

Afterward the Umbramauts get up again.

Exhausted, exasperated, knees black and blue and faces caked with dust, none of them lets on he notices. The Umbramauts shoulder their belongings and set off in search of another place to continue their interrupted celebrations. Each takes up his lantern, his shimmering, glimmering mark of HERE I AM, and the indefatigable throng fades off into the mighty shadow cast by no one.

Translated by Jay Dean and Kenneth Oliver

Sten Nadolny

The Man Who Got Stuck

On January 23, 1965, he came out of *Lawrence of Arabia* at approximately six P.M. and, on the level of the old laundry, walked toward the bridge across the Inn. He blinked because of the snow flurry and thought about the reasons why he couldn't do so many things, not just talk. That talking was necessary to achieve anything in the world had been proven once more by the movie. Nobody would ever say approvingly to him, "Thy mother mated with a scorpion," as Anthony Quinn says to Peter O'Toole. Certainly he could cross the Nefud Desert, but he would have to do it all alone.

He didn't find his way to speech, and if, on occasion, he succeeded, an accident was imminent. Even before he opened his mouth, a bright confusedness, a flickering of thoughts, which raced up and down in all directions. Every word seemed wrong, every encouragement made him sick. Somehow gifted.

Now he was on the bridge across the Inn, staring at the old railroad viaduct on the other side. "I have to investigate the reasons," he thought, "why one kind of people finds the right words, another kind of people doesn't." He looked down at the river that was gray as dough. "A natural sequence—how can it be achieved?"

The river didn't answer. Gazes, questions, and the thickest snow flakes drowned in it as though they had never existed. It was simply there, had always been there; it didn't need to become anything, didn't need to be able to do anything. A mountain river with three letters, untouched and flowing in a completely natural manner. But why talk? Power, for instance, is very taciturn. "Maybe," Alexander said to himself, "I'm someone who is silent and active." A

Hemingway—short sentences, steady hand. He still wasn't altogether happy with this idea. Hemingway had killed himself.

Now Alexander stood on the castle hill above the bridge across the Inn, looking down on the city of Rosenheim and wondering if he had anything to tell it.

Through the snow flurry he saw some lights, churches, and smokestacks of the factories. To say a few proven words, that would be it; and nothing else would be necessary. If all human beings were simultaneously smart, curious, and meaningful—a horrible idea. Suddenly he knew: Babbittry was an ingenious institution to check all overly complicated thoughts and to keep the number of really smart people down. There had to be enough people in this world who would forget the important issues and talk about the unimportant ones. People who felt at ease in spite of all dangers and who kept on going as long as they had bought life insurance. Now he even admired Wolfi Trieb, his schoolmate from the local prep school, who was able to explain for an hour and a half during the entire climb to the Hochries why he took along for skiing a backpack with wax for the skis, sandwiches, an extra pair of socks, and a roll of toilet paper. "Away with prejudices!" Alexander admonished himself. His esteem for Rosenheim had been so low only because it used to be the big world for him just ten years ago. After that, he considered only lungs with dumplings and beer in the Cellar of the Schmid Brewery and a blue faltboat with an inflatable rim as Rosenheim's greatest creations.

He tapped the snow off his windbreaker and decided to go back down. In Rosenheim there lived beer brewers, cattle breeders, rope makers, woodcutters, and wood researchers, refugees, and brush makers. They and their wives, who were not only experts in pork roasts and stuffed geese, lived in houses that were adorned with bays and had arbors and balconies. In general, the front elevation would be horizontal: Italian influence. One man once had had a vision in this small market town with giantism: Thomas Gillitzer, hotel owner, planter, and fish breeder, above all an important developer at the end of the nineteenth century. Whatever Gillitzer built would have made a good impression in Rome or Berlin, too.

"I prefer to be number one in Rosenheim rather than to be number two in Rome!" Caesar. If necessary the mark "Ro" could be reinterpreted. Just once to deliver a great speech in the overcrowded rococo room of Gillitzer's "German Emperor Hotel"!

This room, in which even actors from Munich had performed, was undoubtedly the center of intellectual Rosenheim and, still, the wide world.

But he wasn't even from Rosenheim. Just a school boy who for nine years had to commute from Degerndorf on the Inn, a "wandering scholar." Wandering performers. He wasn't even from Bavaria but a descendent of Salzburg Protestants who had settled in East Prussia. Thus he came from Austria on a detour of more than two hundred years. A refugee's child raised to the power of two. Not good qualifications to give a speech here.

He wondered if he should go on to Simser Filz but it was too dark for him, and in the military he had to spend enough time outdoors anyway.

What was he able to do? He was able to see and to feel many things simultaneously. This way a vision and some sort of courage emerged. Yet the simultaneity had a devastating effect on his sentences. All he had to do was to bring forward three sentences, and nobody understood the meaning of his contribution anymore. One of the painters in Degerndorf had told him, "It's as though you're working on a panorama," and the German teacher, meaning the same, "Just think beforehand what your point is! Like intellect, like speech!" He was the one who also taught French and who liked to talk about "esprit," a patronizing droner, a fat, jolly foghorn, and behind all of it was nothing but pedantic mischief in grading.

Of all people, he met that German teacher on the bridge across the Inn on his way back. What business did he have here in such weather? Maybe suicide, Alexander thought, and I prevented it! The teacher stopped, eyed his former student as though he were a prodigal son, and was certainly about to say something concerning the weather or Winston Churchill; either was possible. His hand was already reaching for the fur collar to open it for a conversation. Alexander slowed down his pace, did without a greeting, and waited with suspicion for his teacher's words. His situation wasn't hopeless, for he had already graduated. And still it felt uncomfortable, since his father used to be in the same party as the foghorn.

"Alexander in Rosenheim, in this kind of weather! Well, how's it going?"

Going? How was what going? Now he had to somehow manage to say "good' and maybe that would take care of it.

"Good."—Hopefully there wouldn't follow any memories of his father, not from that person.

"You see. Military service isn't that bad.—Do you know how it will go on?"

He's certainly going to tell me about it, Alexander thought, but first I have to answer. How it will go on. Go on, that would be nice. He hated small talk. This guy here, he would have liked to reproach him, but he couldn't think of any word, except Mickey Mouse. Ice floes in his mind, aggressive fragmentation. His teacher's hand was still resting on his fur collar, his face had by now assumed a very disgustingly sympathetic slanted position. Altered pigmentation on the back of his hand, so-called age spots. After graduation you saw everything more clearly but it didn't make you feel more forgiving. How it did go on? Good-bye, Mickey Mouse, old fart, like intellect, like speech, Heil Hitler! Until '45 school principal in Franconia. Prevented the worst.

"You can't decide everything at once," the teacher said.

"Well," Alexander went.

"Hold your head up."

The guy wanted to be friendly. But again, with the speed of lightning, Alexander had several ideas that all knocked each other down. "Head"—Klaus Störtebeker appeared, running in Hamburg on the Grabrook past twelve of his loyal friends without his head. And Hermann Göring, for some time Rosenheim's really famous "great son," in Nuremberg on trial with headphones.

"Well, then . . .," the teacher said.

"Yes," Alexander answered, "same to you."

He hastily crossed over to the other side of the bridge, as if someone were about to throw himself off the railing there, in the end he himself.

A defeat. If you are able to talk, then even in snow flurries with such a—well, what was he? "An idiot," Alexander said. With single words he was on target.

He plodded through the snowy town and wondered which answers Hemingway would have formulated for that teacher, and how Peter O'Toole would have delivered them. At last he now also knew why he wanted to learn how to talk: He wanted to intimidate, to hurt, to chase away all those benevolent toads together with their voracious smiles, to silence the jolly gossipers.

He noticed that he had missed the train to Brannenburg. Now he would hitchhike to Degerndorf, but he had to walk very far until a car came. And it didn't stop. He thought about Lawrence in the desert, furthermore about Churchill's aversion to declaring himself defeated. "I have nothing to offer but blood, sweat, and tears," he said to himself. With a stoic face he saw the taillights of the car disappear. The sound was important, the rhythm. "I have nothing to offer to you but—" that was an introduction like a ski jump, and something chiseled followed: short, short, long. Such a sentence set people into motion, even without meaning. He began to practice, ". . .nothing to offer but fury, hate, and hyenas, enemas, enemies," "but liberty, equality, and fraternity." You should have a platform, the words would come automatically.

Churchill lay dying, the news on the radio all began with communiqués from his personal physician.

Until he reached the intersection at Happing, Alexander was thinking about "fraternity." It was not that he expected a lot from it. It was something for hitchhikers and people who want to borrow money—reality was not fraternal. However, a Mercedes from Kufstein did give him a ride, well-heated and with American music coming from the car stereo. In the light of the headlights the snow flurry looked like a dissipating chrysanthemum. One day I will talk, he thought, and in all fraternity slap the truth in the others' faces. Maybe that's a way to get a Mercedes.

He got tired. At home the house was already dark. He locked the door behind him and went to bed as quickly as possible.

In front of Alexander's eyes lay the world's largest arena, a gigantic building, with innumerable decks, one upon the other, built into the mountain, with wide areas full of people just as at a revolution, and there were always smaller groups sitting separately above or next to the others in niches and boxes. Just everyone was here. It did exist, then: one single space for the whole species.

Alexander was sitting in the last row below the mountain. It wasn't the best seat. The seats next to him had remained vacant for good reason: high above them doves, jackdaws, and swifts had built nests in the cracks of the rock. They let drop incredibly much on the last rows of the theatrum mundi; there was a continual ticking and splashing, and the seats were speckled brown and gray. He looked up to the mountain. Yes, there they sat, occasionally flying away, peering down from the cracks and nests with curiosity.

Below them, halfway up, other more clumsy creatures were hanging from the mountain. They were cows. They wanted to imitate the doves and swifts, and now they knew that they could neither fly nor climb. Quite broodingly, they were hanging from the mountain and didn't feel at ease, since they couldn't go either forward or backward. Alexander formed his hands into a funnel and shouted upward: "So much for 'esprit'! What now?"

He looked ahead again. A tall figure was strolling through the rows, noting down volunteers for the speakers' list—Wilhelmine Lübke, the wife of the president of the Federal Republic. She looked in an amiable and cunning manner like a cat, slowly walking in the sunshine.

At a short distance he saw a man who looked attentively toward him and gave him a nod. Probably his brother. Surprise, he wasn't dead after all. In any case, he didn't look stupid, a comforting thought. You can be quite taken in by brothers who died a long time ago. This one, he certainly wanted him to give a speech.

He remembered that there really was something to be told. From one moment to the next there was coherence. He remembered a film he had seen, the greatest in the world, an American one, of course; it contained everything that ever happened. Nobody could know it yet, since he had seen it only in a very small movie theater. The film narrated the long story of all the peoples and their miseries, and how indestructible and crazy humans were. They hoped, loved each other, didn't understand each other, hurt one another, repented terribly, hoped again. Thus it had gone for hundreds of generations, and people kept on dying all the time; nothing more was accomplished. The film had a title, and now he knew it again: "A Mickey Mouse for Little Jesus."

He had to talk about that. Power and love flowed through him. He felt relieved that the nightmare of silence and confusion would have an end now. Not to give a speech—only talk about the film lovingly—it was that easy!

He wanted to start with the doves on the rock and with the bad luck of the poor cattle who had climbed too high—that was the present, from it light was shed on everything. Alexander looked into the cat's eyes of Wilhelmine and said in a firm voice, "Okay."

It was his turn already; it went fast. He started on his way to the front of the railing, so that everyone could see him. For a moment he stood calmly and saw the human masses on the terraces of the mountain and in the gigantic, dusky stadium that disappeared into the distance and encompassed everything: cities and beaches, beach chairs, sand castles, everything, and also all other arenas of the earth. All he had to do now was to pass on his power and warmth. Would they suffice for so many people?

He didn't yet exactly know how to begin. Near him some people had already inclined their heads, out of interest or like people with bad hearing do, so they won't miss anything. Suddenly his brother was much higher in one of the rows on the side; he looked down with a brooding, moody expression.

"I am standing here in this place," Alexander began. He tried to bring his breathing under control.

"Oh, well. I do hope that everyone will hear me." What if they didn't?

"Please, raise your hand, if I am speaking too softly . . . Okay? In that case I'll stand in another place. All right. Okay."

He already noticed it now: danger was imminent. What was it that he wanted to say. In his brain only flurries. It had something to do with—it was about the world! Okay, okay. Now boldness was the only way to go.

"Anyway, I would like to begin with saying that I consider it quite a scandal, I mean, a stadium like this one here, it did cost several billions, and still you don't even know whether everyone hears you."

Disgustingly sparse applause by, at the most, ten people right in his vicinity. They probably felt pity for him. His brother was busy watching the people. The old trick: I'm on your side, I'll watch the people for you. Alexander listened in himself, heard twaddle, and didn't even bother to let it out. The pause was taking too long, time was running out. Indeed—there it was: The rococo clock above the stage? Stage? The arena shriveled up more and more; it was hardly bigger than the room in Gillitzer's "German Emperor Hotel," and the rock sprouted stucco ornaments as though it wanted to comfort him: "Things aren't that rocky here."

Still he didn't say anything. Yet he had a brilliant insight that he wanted to write down right away: The only thing you are guaranteed not to avoid by remaining silent is a pause. The rocky rococo theater was becoming restless, since nothing came, no power, no warmth. Alexander's eyes met those of Wilhelmine Lübke, who gave him an encouraging nod. At that moment it was completely over. A division of air masses ruled in his head: cold against warm, clear against overcast, a climate of confusion.

Alexander woke up, his pyjamas soaking wet with sweat, and turned loose of the blanket that like a lifebuoy had probably been supposed to prevent his sinking. His brain immediately remembered, with scornful reliability, "Mickey Mouse for Little Jesus." His pulse was slowing down.

If he had started in that stadium like this: "I have nothing to offer you but—," then everything would have gone fine, "but doves, jackdaws, and swifts. Of cattle we also have to talk. There"—gesture with his hand—"they hang from the mountain and are anything but jackdaws and doves." Then five/six more sentences, and the world would have been depicted convincingly. Or if he had said: "Speech is always the speech of the speechless," "Heaven is always the heaven of the strangers," "Freedom is always the freedom of the dissidents"—begin with tautologies, and then a really big surprise. "Brotherliness is always brotherliness towards sisters," "God is always the god who deserts us."—There were sentences like sand in an arena; and he could handle words. The problem was quite a different one: His fear was not constant. At first he was afraid of talking too little, then he was paralyzed by fear. A stupid condition, since he didn't even know whether he was too cowardly or too courageous.

At the age of seven he wrote on blotting paper:

ONE HAZ TO BE CORAGIOUS AND ALSO SMART.

Around the letters of the words CORAGIOUS and SMART he had continued to draw their contours in many parallel lines, as if they were bobbing in water and making waves. They covered each other with their echoes; the word SMART almost disappeared again.

Alexander got up and went to the garret window, from which he looked over the Inn Valley, which was shimmering white in the dawn. Today the weather was clear and freezing.

Theatrum mundi. Couldn't it be somewhat smaller, on a more modest scale? Why the entire Inn Valley, including Rosenheim, Kufstein and—? Erl on the Inn came to his mind, "the passion play town with three letters." Passion. Jesus. Had *he* been able to speak at any given moment? Why then did someone feed five thousand people with bread and fish?—He got stuck with his second Sermon on the Mount and needed time. And Demosthenes, Cicero,

Rosa Luxemburg, Churchill—didn't they ever have those flurries in their heads?

Downstairs in the house the tea kettle whistled and was turned off. Now the newscaster's voice joined in, for one moment roaring loud, then turned down quickly. Metallic poking sounded from the fireplace, an impatient and hasty noise—Mom was tending the fire. He got dressed. Today his job was to shovel the walk to the road; it had snowed all night long. "Home is always the home of problems"—he wondered whether that would be a good sentence for Gillitzer's room. He rejected it, although he thought it was true. He imagined too well the listeners who would applaud.

He tied his boots and got the shovel. The most important things always would happen here in the mornings, later only the usual things would happen.

As he stepped out of the door he contemplated the panorama again and compared it to that in the dream. Kranzhorn, Spitzstein, Heuberg, Hochries, and the Samer Mountains, and farther down, in the flatter land, Neubeuern Hill, which looked like a cat arching its back. All the way to the right towered Madron, with the big quarry in which Alexander had practiced—what else—speaking again and again, in front of lizards that listened attentively without motion and that didn't want to miss anything, not a stutter, not a slip of the tongue. Past the Nagelfluh barrier of the "Beavers" was Flintbach, where in 1948 his older brother had been seen alive for the last time, before the accident with the amunition he had found; that brother who was loved by everyone and who enchanted every human being with his speaking, a happy little boy, shedding light. As a dead body, he cast a huge shadow over the years.

Alexander shoveled his way through the hard-packed snow to the public road and, from there, looked at his accomplishment, panting. The most important things would happen here before breakfast, in his head as well as in the house.

Translated by Ingo Roland Stöhr

Christa Reinig

Three Ships

The day grew dark beneath the sun. The sun rained down upon us. We were dying of thirst and dread. Off in the distance a house dazzled us. We did not avert our eyes from it, even though our eyes turned blood-red. The house grew smaller and more distant. But we put our hope in this house, and just when we had given it up, we stood before the gate. We entered and demanded something to drink. The proprietor asked us what we wanted. We answered him, and he asked us once again. Then we noticed that human speech no longer came from our throats. We made signs, and he brought us something to drink. We drank, and the roof above us began to glow hotly. We drank all the more, and our shirts stuck fast to our sweat-drenched skin. Night fell. We lay down. Our shirts grew ice-cold and as stiff as a board, and the salt ate into our cracked flesh. We lay in contorted poses, and sometimes one of us cried out in his sleep. The next morning we hurried onward and blew on our fingers. We entered a swamp and soon became separated from one another. The packs on our backs weighted us down. Midges rose in swarms and pursued us. We wallowed on through the mire. A brushy slope rose up out of the swamp. We clung to the brush, and the thorns tore our hands. We dragged ourselves out of the swamp. Some fell into the thorns. They called out for us to kill them. But we left them there and climbed on into the mountains. The stone turned the flesh of our feet red. Yet it burned black and fell away from our bones when we stepped onto the ice. We tore brushwood out of the ground and ignited it. The wind blew out the fire and lacerated our faces. We pulled our feet from the ashes and climbed down to the sea. We put a cloth to our lips and licked the salt water. We put stones in our mouths, and I saw one person who went crazy and bit open his veins. Then we sighted the ship. We cried and embraced one another, and the ship took us on board.

We received as much to eat as we could gulp down, but only a handful of water. It ran through our fingers. We had to go down into the ship's hold. We listened to the noise of the cannons and to the cries above us. We lay in the dark for a long time. We were idle and insulted one another. The madman raved. We struck him and bound him tightly. He tore himself loose. We felt our way through the hold and searched everywhere for him in vain. We did not sleep anymore after that. We called one another by name and strained our ears. We did not find him. We became ill from the food and fouled the hold. We screamed and pounded on the hatch. We were set free. The light stunned us. The captain and the sailors chased us around the deck. We worked until we collapsed. At night we lay and rolled with the motion of the ship. Our hands could not hold us steady any longer.

Once I said something terrible. I said: God will surely save us. Everyone laughed at this joke and passed it on. The sailors came up and laughed. The captain approached. He was not laughing. He called me to his cabin and interrogated me. He listened, and I went away relieved. The next morning I was awakened early. Two sailors showed me an order from the captain and flogged me until I was unable to move.

A long time later, when the old bandages were torn away from my back, I said: I do not believe that God can be held responsible for this world. I went to work. One day I was called to the captain's cabin. You are to be commended because you are smart and capable, said the seaman. I hid. I was dragged from my hiding place. The captain said: You are one of us. You are to take the pirate flag over your shoulders and are to hang it from the mainmast. This is an honorable assignment, do not forget that. I grabbed hold of the rope and began to climb. The rope ladder swayed beneath my feet. I looked at the rung ahead of me and paid no attention to anything else. But I knew that emptiness surrounded me, and that twice each moment my torn hands released a thin rope that was stretched across the void. The flag over my shoulders became infinitely heavy. I turned back and took it down. The captain struck at my legs with the whip. The flag was torn from my shoulders, and I was chased back up by the blows of the whip. The sailors howled up at me. When my joints grew slack, I sank my teeth into the rope. I raised my head and opened my eyes. Then I trembled. I had only a single breath of courage left. With that I released the rope, ran the length of the spar, and dropped into the sea.

I found myself in the water and swam. After a day and a night, the image of a ship rose up before me. I believed in this image. I surged up and flung my arms high. I was sighted and pulled from the water. After I had slept, the captain called for me. His tricorne lay before him on the table. There were braids and gold buttons on his blue coat. He was called the Barbarian by his people. I was permitted to drink wine with him, and he said: It is a good thing to know whom one has before him. Not everyone is everyone else's friend. The world is wicked. I answered: There is much injustice, but the responsibility for everything that happens must be borne by all men. He said: Man is weak, that you will yet discover. He gave me his hand and invited me to the evening religious service. He preached, and his sailors cried. Some were called forward and commended. The Barbarian gave *me* the Bible to read from. I opened it and read: Lo, I am with you alway, even until the end of the world.

The ship came from Africa and was loaded with wild animals. Occasionally they roared in the ship's hold and dashed their bodies against the hull. Their chains could be heard clanking. One day a sailor came and reported: A good ten or so of them are dead. The captain swelled with rage. His eyes bulged out of his head. They suffocated, stammered the sailor. The Barbarian roared: Lead them up on deck. I will not have another one die on me. The sailors armed themselves with whips and clubs. The officers loaded their pistols. I took an iron rod for myself. I was pale and agitated and awaited the beasts. The hatch was thrown open. There was complete silence. Then a chain clattered, and a head appeared. A man crawled out onto the deck. He had an iron ring around his neck. When he tried to straighten up, he pitched back onto the deck, for he was chained to two others who dragged him back down. One after another they emerged. Their chains became tangled, and they staggered into one another. They were led in a long line across the deck. Between them they dragged the dead, who were still attached by their neck rings. I noticed that my lips were becoming cold. The captain wanted me to go to the cabin. No, I heard myself say. The Negroes slowly came to their senses. One bent down and picked up a piece of iron that was lying there. The sailors flogged the thief and struck the others as well. The Negroes scattered. Then they all turned toward the middle and closed in on us with their chains. The officers fired their pistols into the air. Just don't kill them, screamed the Barbarian. The Negroes choked the sailors, and the sailors bashed their heads in. I did as the sailors did. Suddenly it grew still. The Negroes ceased their raving. They stood around dull-wittedly or squatted down. The dead were removed from their neck rings, and the living were herded back down through the hatch. The deck was cleared for the religious service.

I left the ship. We lowered the boats and went to get drinking water from an island. I ran into the forest. They called and searched for me for a long time. Then I was alone. I had brought an ax along. I began to build. During the day the forest rustled above me, and at night I climbed endlessly over rope ladders and struck at Negroes. I dreamed of footprints, which I followed, of deserted campfires, from which I raked white human bones. I fell from this dream as from a reality. I awoke and searched for the footprints. I crept after them. I crept after my own footprints, until in the evening they led me back to my hut. I threw myself down and slept. I laughed out loud in my sleep and awoke. I took my ax and climbed up the highest tree on the island. I tied my shirt tightly to the treetop, and chopped off one branch after another as I descended. Then I waited. Each day I made a notch in the door post of my hut. A ship sighted the mast with its shirt-flag and took me on board.

The sailors rowed listlessly out to the ship. It was a strange ship. Long black sacks hung from the spars. Seen from a distance, they swung like hanged mutineers. I clambered aboard. Where is the captain? I asked the sailors. There is no captain here, they answered. I looked up at the spars. It occurred to me that my rowers had not brought a single barrel of water back from the island. The cabin was packed with people. Everyone lived in the cabin. A huge drunkard offered me a drink and slapped me on the back. A couple of bookshelves served as a partition. The books, dirty and well-thumbed, fell off the shelves, and a short, thin man bent down and put them back on the shelves. His hair hung down below his shoulders. He straightened up. He was made up like a whore. An old rug had been thrown over a sea chest. That was the divan. A man who had been standing at the helm came in and lay down on the divan. Three men should probably go up and set the sails, he said. After a while he asked me: Are you going up there with me? I am not a sailor, I answered. Nobody here cares who you are, the painted slut said and offered me a smoke. Someone clicked at his lighter. I shall examine your soul, said the whore: What is the significance of your wanting to give me a light and your lighter not working? They all laughed, but no one else dared to offer him a light. He spoke of Buddha, of death, and of bawdy things. Do you like it here? he asked me. I thumbed through a book. Suddenly I jumped up and climbed into the galley. The rats ran under my feet and were not frightened. I raised the light and shone it into the water barrels. They were almost empty. The water smelled rank. I lifted a small keg of rum onto my shoulder and carried it up the steps. The people howled, and the drunkard kissed me. They drank and retched and were miserable right down to their drinking songs. The whore never drank. He said that life and death were one and the same. The people quarreled among themselves. The drunkard wanted to go ashore for women, and the whore wanted to sail across the sea until we rotted. They challenged each other to a knife fight. The people cried for blood and laid wagers. The next day the drunkard did not get up. He was feverish and vomited. I know the cause of your seasickness, cried the whore, and threw a knife right past his head. Everyone jeered at the drunkard. In the evening all of the people left the cabin. Only the whore stayed on and placed cloths on the drunkard's forehead. The next morning he was dead. They did not dare to touch him. The whore dragged him out on deck and threw him overboard. The same day two more people became ill. The people hid from one another. I lay on the bridge and slept for several nights with my ax in my hand.

In the middle of the day it grew cold and the sun vanished from the sky. I pulled myself up. I climbed over a corpse. It turned over and lunged at me. I found no one. Only the whore lay on the divan, smoking. We must beach the ship, I said. We must die, he said. I walked to the stairs, and he followed me. He sat down on a step and held me tightly. His hands grew limp. Help me, he said, his teeth chattering. How can we justify what we have done?—I cannot, I said, I cannot even justify it to myself. I leaped out and slammed the door shut over his head. I tied the helm firmly. One of the hanged men had been blown loose by the wind. All of a sudden he was hanging right above me. I was terrified to see him so close. I wanted to take them all down. I took a knife and clambered up. The wind slung me about. Ice-cold rain slapped me in the face. I began to steam. Suddenly I could not take another step. I thought: I have carried the flag up to this point. I roared: God save me. I climbed from ladder to ladder and cut the sails loose. I descended and fastened myself with my belt tightly to the mast. The sea broke over the ship.

When I awoke, I was no longer alone. I saw a man who said: Set yourself free! I unfastened the belt from around the mast. He said: Jump! I jumped from the ship and touched bottom. I waded ashore. The stranger walked in front of me. His back was covered with scars like my own back. I looked at it as if I were standing with my back to a mirror and gazing over my shoulder. I ran after him. I wanted to see his face. When I caught up with him, he disappeared. I fell down and called upon the name of God. When I arose, everything was more difficult than before. The day darkened beneath the sun. The sun rained down. Perhaps it was all familiar to me. I passed over the dunes and entered the desert

Translated by Suzanne and Carl Clifton Toliver

Wolfdietrich Schnurre

The Burial

I'm standing on a chair in the kitchen. Someone knocks.

I get down, lay the hammer and nail aside. I open the door. Night.

Rain.

Hmmm . . . , I think to myself, didn't someone knock?

"Psss . . . " goes the gutter.

"Anyone there?" I ask.

Someone calls behind me: "Hello!"

I go back. A letter is lying on the table.

I pick it up.

The door slams downstairs. I lay the letter on the table and go back downstairs. I open the door. Nothing.

Funny, I think to myself.

I go back upstairs.

The letter is lying there. White, with a black border.

Someone must've died, I think to myself.

I look around.

"It smells like incense," my nose says.

"You're right," I say, "it wasn't there before. Strange."

I open the letter, sit down, and polish glasses. Let's see now. Right. An obituary notice. I go over the words very slowly:

LOVED BY NONE, HATED BY NONE, HE BORE HIS SORROWS WITH A HEAVENLY PATIENCE. TODAY, AFTER A LONG ILLNESS, GOD DIED.

In small letters below:

The burial will take place tonight, without ceremony, at St. Zebedee Cemetery.

Well, I think to myself, it looks like the Old Man has finally bit the dust.

Oh, well. I put my glasses in their case and stand up.

"Emma!" I yell. "Get me my coat."

"What for?" she groans from upstairs.

"Don't ask silly questions," I say, "I've got to go to a funeral."

"I know you," she whines, "you're going off to play cards."

"Don't start that," I say. "God died."

"So?" she says. "Why don't you buy Him a wreath?"

"No," I say, "but you can get me Franzl's top hat. You never know who'll be there."

"So," she says, "you think you're a real gentleman? Don't matter. It's so dark out that no one'll be able to tell you've got a top hat on."

All right, I think to myself, have it your way, you old bag.

I put my overcoat on, turn my collar up, and go down to the door.

Rain is pouring.

The umbrella, I think to myself. But Emma's got the umbrella.

"Good night," I say and close the door behind me.

Outside it's the same as always: slippery asphalt, dim street lights, a few cars, and a couple of pedestrians. The streetcar goes by.

I ask a man: "Did you hear? God died."

He says: "No, just today?"

The rain gets worse. A newsstand appears in front of me, lit by a carbide lamp.

Wait, I think to myself, let's have a look.

I bend over. I search through the pages.

TODAY: nothing. TOMORROW: nothing. NEW WORLD: nothing. THE FUTURE: Nothing. AFTER HOURS: Not a line. Not even under *News in Brief*.

"Is there anything else?" I ask.

"Ad supplement," says the newspaper man.

"Let's see it," I say.

I leaf through it. There, on the last page. Pure luck. Under *Miscellany*, teeny-tiny:

LOVED BY NONE, HATED BY NONE, HE BORE HIS SORROWS WITH A HEAVENLY PATIENCE. TODAY, AFTER A LONG ILLNESS, GOD DIED.

So. That's it.

I show the newspaperman. "Well . . . ?"

"Poor devil," he says, "it's no wonder."

On the square a policeman is standing in the fog.

"Any news on the radio?" I ask.

"The war," he says.

"I don't mean that," I say. "Anything else?"

"No," he says.

"No death bulletin? God's supposed to have died."

He shrugs his shoulders. "That's what He gets."

It turns darker. The street becomes narrower.

At the corner of Kadettenweg I bump into a man.

"Is this the way to St. Zebedee Cemetery?" he asks.

"Are you the priest?" I ask. "Are you going to the funeral?"

He nods.

"Whose is it?"

"A certain Clod or God or something like that," he says.

We walk together. Past a large block of apartment buildings with flaking firewalls. Gas lanterns flicker.

"Are you related to the deceased?" the priest asks.

"No," I say, "I just felt like going."

A window is thrown open behind us.

"Help!" screams a woman.

A flower pot smashes on the pavement. Across the street, shades fly open. Light falls on the street.

"Shut up!" someone roars.

"Much farther?" asks the priest.

"No, we're almost there," I say.

The rain is so heavy now that you can barely make out the streetlights.

I'm wet to the skin.

"Here," I say, "to the right."

Where Marshall Street runs into the coal dump, barbed wire is strung up all around. It is a quarantine area for returning soldiers.

They stand in the rain, waiting. To the left is the Zebedee Cemetery, a narrow area squeezed in at the back of Waldemar's Ballroom. On the right is a nitrogen plant. Its smudged windows are bright; you can hear that it's running full blast. Its smokestacks, lit from below, are lost in the heavy mist.

In front of the cemetery a wagon is pulled up with a box on it. Two men and a horse are standing nearby.

"Good evening," I say.

"Are you the priest?"

"No," I say, "he is."

"OK, let's move it."

The priest grabs hold without saying a word. They heave the box on their shoulders and stagger through the gate.

"Hurry it up!" yells the driver.

He has a blanket over his head and is leaning against the horse. He is smoking.

The gate creaks as I close it. I follow the men slowly.

Two of them have shovels. I know them: They are the gravediggers. The third man has on a pair of blue overalls (a streetcleaner or something). A soggy cigarette is stuck behind his ear. The two other men in filthy work shirts, wearing caps. More than likely they are soldiers from the camp.

The sixth man is the priest.

They fall out of step and the box tilts on their shoulders. It is because of the priest; he can't stand up straight. He groans, then yells: "Set it down!" He tries to duck out of the way.

It hits the ground.

The lid flies off. There's an ugly mess.

The priest is limping—the box fell on his foot. The dead man has rolled out. He lies there, pale. The acetylene lights from the camp fall on him: he is a scrawny little man in a gray shirt, with dried blood on his mouth and beard. He's smiling.

"Idiot!" yells the man in overalls.

They turn the box over and lift the body back in.

"Watch out," says one of the returned soldiers, "it's a real mess."

"All right," says the other one.

When the lid is back on they bend down again.

"Ready . . . lift!" the gravediggers yell.

"Let's go!"

The priest hobbles along.

A woman is waiting by a lumpy pile of dirt. I know her; she's the inspector. Her umbrella has such big holes in it that you can see the illuminated smokestacks. Her dress is sackcloth; you can read on it: MUNICIPAL NITROGEN PLANT.

"Over here!" she yells.

By the pile of dirt is a hole. Next to the hole is a rope. Next to it a tin cross with a number on it.

The men carrying the box wheel around.

"Ready . . . down!" the gravediggers command.

The box jolts to the ground. MR. GOD is written on it with a crayon. Under the name is a date. Already washed away though.

The priest clears his throat.

"Isn't this a sight?" says one of the soldiers and dabs his forehead.

The other soldier puts his foot on the box and stoops over. "Shitty weather," he says and wiggles the toes that stick out the end of his shoe.

"Get going, guys," says the inspector. "Let's get started."

One gravedigger measures the hole with his shovel handle. "Well, I'll be," he says.

"What is it?" asks the other one.

"It's not deep enough."

They start digging.

You can hear little splashes when pieces of dirt fall back into the hole—ground water.

"That'll do," says the man in the overalls.

The priest clears his throat. "Dear ones gathered," he says.

"Here," says one of the gravediggers, "take hold of this rope. Lift the thing on it."

They lift the box and set it on the rope; three ends stick out on the left and right sides.

"All right . . . all together!" yell the gravediggers. The box hovers over the hole.

The acetylene lamps make everything as bright as day. The tin crosses sticking up all around them are no higher than cabbage heads.

The rain keeps pouring down.

A piece of plaster from the moldy back wall of Waldermar's Ballroom falls off and knocks over two of the crosses.

"Let it down," says a gravedigger, "let it down real slow."

The box sinks into the hole.

"What did he die of?" I ask.

The inspector yawns. "How should I know?"

In the quarantine camp someone is playing a harmonica.

"At the count of three let it go," says one of the gravediggers. "One, two . . ." he counts.

"Just a moment," says the priest as he pulls his leg out of the hole.

"All right.

"Three!

A sound like a sack hitting water.

"What a mess!" says the man in the overalls and wipes his face.

The soldiers take off their caps. The priest folds his hands.

"Well, that's it," one of the gravediggers spits and winds up the rope.

"You could've dug it a little deeper," says the inspector.

The priest has finished his prayer. He picks up a lump of clay and throws it in the hole.

There is a dull thud. I bend down, too.

Thud.

The man in the overalls kicks in his piece with his foot.

For a moment all is still; the only sound is the rattle and clatter of the machines in the nitrogen plant. Then the music starts up again, only louder now. The soldiers have their caps back on and are gently swaying back and forth and humming to the music.

"Through?" asks the man in the overalls.

"Through," says the inspector. "Make sure the cross is in good and deep."

The priest wipes off his hands. "Dear ones gathered," he says.

"Hey!" yells the driver from the street.

"All right!" growls the man in the overalls. He tips his hat: "Good evening, everyone."

"Good evening," say the soldiers and leave, too.

The inspector follows them. She looks like a turnip with her aproned skirt.

The gravediggers start shoveling.

The dirt splatters on the box.

"Damned crap," says one of them and kicks the clay off his shovel with his heel.

"Is something playing tonight at the Odeon?" asks the other one.

The priest stares at the wags of Waldermar's Ballroom.

"I haven't checked yet," says the first gravedigger. "We can go by."

"Giddyap!" yells the driver on the street.

"Good evening," I say.

The priest doesn't move.

"Good evening," say the gravediggers.

The cemetery gate creaks as I shut it. A piece of paper is impaled nearby on the fence. I pull it off: It's a piece of newspaper. Advertising section, soggy from the rain. On the left the Patria Bar is looking for a waiter who can furnish his own uniform. On the right someone wants to trade a bedsheet for a frying pan. In between, with the black border, is the obituary notice:

LOVED BY NONE, HATED BY NONE, HE BORE
HIS SORROWS WITH A HEAVENLY PATIENCE. TODAY,
AFTER A LONG ILLNESS, GOD DIED.

I turn around.

One of the gravediggers has jumped in the hole and is trampling the earth down solid. The other one blows his nose and shakes the snot off the end of his finger.

In the nitrogen plant the machines are clattering. Its smokestacks are lit from below. Their tops are lost in the mist. Behind the barbed wire at the coal dump the soldiers that have just returned stand waiting. It is still raining. The acetylene lamps have made everything as bright as day; where they don't reach, it is night.

The harmonica strikes up again. Someone is singing along: "La paloma ohe!"

The cemetery gate creaks. It's the priest.

He hobbles by.

Translated by Gary Wilson

Gabriele Wohmann

An Irresistible Man

The whole thing has been over now for a year, and it is really sad that I have nothing better to do at Christmas than to put down on paper a story that is decidedly un-Christmaslike. But the Christmas holiday of an old maid who refuses to combat the advancing grayness of her hair with the cooperation of a capable hairdresser can perhaps not be more meaningfully occupied than by intensive submersion in a past that showed her in a very cruel way the wretchedness of her spinsterhood.

I can remember all too well that Christmas Eve a year ago, remember Allan's nervous right foot moving up and down, unceasingly, Brenda's stony face, and the fatalistic expression on the pale features of the small, untamed girl and her long fingers clenched together, with nails painted dark red. And between these three I sat; and I still know well that an uncomfortable feeling caused in me by my mere presence in this company was combined with intense pressure on my stomach and that, along with all the other sensations, I was aware of the urgent desire to open the zipper of my tight tweed skirt. I finally did this and with the tip of my black stole concealed the disgraceful place that was one of the characteristics of my age.

But I must begin at the beginning in order to make the chain of events intelligible that finally produced this fateful evening. It began with an invitation from Brenda to her California home, where I was to spend my summer vacation. I was at that time still new in America. I felt foreign and isolated in the small town in the Middle West. I seemed to myself to be a very little dot in an immense and boundless mystery: America. My colleagues at the college treated me with a certain aloofness, even though not without that naive imbecilically affectionate manner with which I was treated everywhere else here. At the time I was exhausted and a little enervated by everything: by the bad accents of my students, by the lively progressivism of my chairman, by the neo-baroque furniture in my tiny apartment, and by American cooking. And most of all I was suffering from loneliness. All the more pleasant, then, did Brenda's invitation strike me, and even though it was not without some doubt about what would await me that I set out, still I knew with a feeling of relief that my trip would at least bring a change and thus an interruption of my loneliness.

As a matter of fact, life at the Dennet's was excellent. To please me they cooked in the French manner; they took me everywhere where there was something to admire and wonder at; they showed me the tallest and oldest trees in the world, the most productive soil, the fattest seals, the deepest valley, and the highest mountain in this state of superlatives. And incidentally I fell in love with the most irresistible man I have ever met, Brenda's husband, the very busy architect Allan Dennet. The few hours during which I gazed upon him sufficed to reduce me to a state that, for my age, was not only ridiculous and disgraceful but also extraordinarily painful. What had not happened to me in thirty-nine years of the greatest endeavor came to pass here under the California sun effortlessly and without any doing of my own: I was ablaze, I suffered through all the phases of passion—of course, known only to me—and I pined away—unnoticed by the world around me, for outwardly I suffered not at all—in an old-fashioned and absurd amorous rapture for a man who was two years younger than I and whose wife is my best friend. At that time I kept to myself alone my private fiasco of having come too late, after I had been forced to recognize conclusively that Allan did not look at me in the way that love requires. With distressing familiarity he was accustomed to clap me on the shoulder and say "old friend," and his evident affection was expressed in a friendly, brotherly companionship that could not help but wound me that much more in my condition.

But I departed without resentment: I returned to my college in the expectation of a less acute solitude; for an entirely novel sphere completely unknown to me was opened for my consideration by this belated love. It surely would be nice to be able "to think about someone," when sitting with a group of colleagues; and it would be exciting when alone with one's books to get lost in dreams and memories. It would be a way out of the clutches of boredom. I finally had my "love," my "passion," even though it was undeniably what is called hopeless. I entertained no doubt at all about the impossibility of the fulfillment of my secret desires and about the absurdity of the fanciful ideas that I manufactured for myself on long autumn evenings in my little room and that I became absorbed in. I surrounded myself with a filigree of fancies and portraits of the future, which I continued to add to, on and on, with quiet satisfaction without being in any doubt about how very much I was reducing my self-respect, how profoundly my lovesick, daydreaming ego was being degraded before my observant, rational ego. I ignored all those things that made me seem ridiculous to myself: the offense against the chronological laws of love, the symptoms of teenage foolishness that I recognized in myself, the unproductiveness of this new, peculiar pastime. I was content that my thoughts were all absorbed by Allan and that consequently the melancholy spirit and the idleness of my spare time had come to an end.

To the world around me I remained unchanged: To my landlady I was, now as before, that somewhat whimsical Frenchwoman who threatened and disappointed her tourist-flavored notions about Paris and Parisians with deficient make-up and a modest wardrobe. Still, she was eventually satisfied with the comforting thought of the exception without which no rule can exist. To my colleagues I continued to be the intellectual friend of a few famous literary personages; I even enjoyed a sort of respect, a mixture of Latin Quarter romanticism and Sorbonne fame. And my students noticed no relaxation in my obvious disgust at every wrong sound and no diminishment of my verdict in the crime of using the indicative where only the subjunctive would do. I was experiencing springtime when everyone imagined me to be in the midst of autumn or at least in a cooled-down late summer.

To my disappointment Christmas passed without an invitation: The Dennets were traveling to Europe. I tried in vain to explain to them the disadvantages of such a trip in winter; they departed, and I did not see them again till summer.

Then, to be sure, it was marvelous. Allan outdid himself in the things he suggested: I swam in the Pacific again, I plunged again into the densest and tallest forests, and again I admired the national parks and indulged in flower extravaganzas. And again I enjoyed most of all the propinquity to a man whom intense application through a long year had brought so close to me that I often felt as if I were caught red-handed when his eye suddenly met mine as I was watching him. Yes, I was afraid he might recognize the fundamental knowledge of himself in my look, caught *in flagranti*. But he was unsuspecting and blind like all men. I was astonished how blind they are when they have no idea about the women who love them—they act stupid enough when it is a case of an *amour réciproque*.

One evening Brenda disclosed to me the reason for the exceptional cheerfulness I had noticed in her. Their trip to Europe had brought them the happy certainty that they could have a baby. Allan had wanted one for years, and I learned that her childlessness had been a threat to their marriage, something that might have escaped my notice from a simple lack of comprehension, even if I had really tried to make a play for Allan. Now Brenda was going to have a baby and she was happy.

I looked upon this blind wish to propagate with little understanding. It seemed to me quite foolish to make a pilgrimage from one specialist to another just because of a longing for progeny. I attempted to treat Allan with a certain contempt, which I actually felt, but I could not do it. From this I could judge the degree of my infatuation.

I was afraid that my age and the decidedly female existence I had led until the meeting with Allan made me especially sensitive to his intense, thoroughgoing masculinity. In him those things pleased me that would previously have repelled me in others. His most nonsensical contentions and demands smacked of male chauvinism. The way he dressed I would have rejected in any other man as obtrusively extravagant and even dandyish. But I enjoyed looking at Allan in his tight, snow-white pants and in the extremely soft sweaters, at the necks of which he was in the habit of wearing colorful scarves, and I cherished a real admiration for the elegant socks that encompassed his slim ankles and for the choice footwear that he always had on. He was a little vain, but it suited him well. Because to me it seemed the natural expression of what was obvious, his vanity meant nothing discreditable; it was not a diminution of his magnificence. I loved to see him radiant, to watch how he bathed in the glow of his own grandeur, how he walked and spoke and acted in the protection of an assurance that only the knowledge of one's own perfection bestows. Mademoiselle Cleremy's gymnastics course could never have made me so uninhibited and so self-confident as Allan's consciousness of his own competent masculinity made him.

Again I had to leave, and again I was laden with memories and new impressions that I carried with me to my quiet realm of a somewhat arduous scholarship. I returned to the four walls that conceal too much bad taste ever to be able to awaken in me any feeling of being at home. I was rather depressed after this holiday, and I didn't know what to do anymore with my unlimited supply of love. I came to the conclusion that I would return to reality and give up my Allan romance.

Then Brenda's letter arrived. It was the sort of letter I would never have expected from a person who had seemed to me the most content in the world when I left her a few weeks before. It was a cry for help, a plea for advice and for a little comfort, and it left me stunned, at first incredulous and then uncomprehending, without all understanding. Allan had been unfaithful to his wife. "He claims to love her; for the first time in his life he is experiencing true passion, he tells me," it said there. "He even brought her here with him, for a discussion, as he called it. She is very delicate, he instructed me, and I should be considerate of her. And he wanted everything to be settled favorably. But even though I am carrying his child, I know that I cannot compete with so much youth and effrontery." It went on like that for five pages. The youthful object of Allan's spontaneous and irresistible love Brenda introduced to me as a costume and stage designer, whose aspirations leaned toward the movies. Since Allan had no connection at all with the movies, it was unfortunately not possible to brush off the girl's feelings as the result of ambition and the desire for success, and Allan could not be seen as someone who was easily fooled or taken in. That made the problem more difficult.

On both sides there appeared the picture of a serious passion, serious above all because it was absurd and could not be justified and was unmotivated and because it had seized hold of someone like Allan. There was not a woman who could resist an Allan touched by passionate love, she would have to surrender and follow him wherever that might lead. Allan had so many instinctive qualifications and skills in the business of love that in return he had to be given the equivalent in absolute love and surrender. In addition Allan seemed to have found his counterpart, the feminine woman had met the masculine man, and their love would be not a mere farce but a true duel between equals.

Brenda called the girl uncultivated, not even pretty, much too thin ever to arouse the suspicion of any of those nice, ageless, and adroit wives of which Brenda was one. But she was very young and had an impudent lack of constraint toward the lawful owner of Allan, whom she "could never stop loving." Brenda's catastrophic situation was clear. Even if she kept Allan because he would not infringe upon the decency and respectability of a woman who was to bring his child into the world, she would lose him. And I knew suddenly that she had never really possessed him.

Of course, it requires an excess of conceit when an old maid like me attempts to be the judge of people who are acting on the basis of practical application. And therefore I also took care not to communicate these sentiments to Brenda, who would have gotten the feeling from them that I credited her herself, her, to whom this injustice was being done, with the principal fault. I did not want to make her angry. The genuine anger that I felt in regard to Allan who, after all, had betrayed not just Brenda but me also, me and my wonderful filigree of imagination, produced a letter full of more sympathy than friendly compassion would have made possible.

We exchanged letters of honest indignation; they were all little manifestos of disappointed and revolutionized femininity, directed at this prototype, "the male," at this unknown creature who was so similar to us that we had to doubt either his human nature or ours. If my letters, inquisitive as well as comforting, had an almost exploitative character, then Brenda's litanies did not lack a certain envy of my independent and peaceful single state, which I did not attempt to take away from her, deriving a malicious joy from being envied for once in my life for something, be it ever so worthless; but how much more I would have liked to suffer like Brenda than to remain in the barrenness of my college existence and observe life as through the lens of a telescope. Of course I must admit that one dwells quite calmly behind the palisades of a maidenhood that remains less rigorously defended than relatively unmolested; and as much as I often detest the monotony of my existence, I have little doubt, nevertheless, that I have gotten so used to it that I would miss it if I ever lost it. My letters of consolation to Brenda betrayed nothing of the many-layered quality of my feelings, no false note allowed a certain share of selfish curiosity to be inferred. They were the letters of two accomplices in a plot against that brutal power, "the male."

The Christmas holidays approached, and Brenda pleaded with me not to abandon her: I simply had to come. I let her beg me for a long time and consented only with reluctance: hateful tactics of deceit, but they seemed to me necessary. I did not want Brenda to recognize my penchant for the sensational, born of years of loneliness. That I came mainly for love of Allan she would not have believed, even if I had been stupid enough to inform her of it.

On the first two days at the Dennets I did not get to see Allan at all. And then came that Christmas Eve that was to end in such a theatrically fateful manner. Without the slightest effort it is possible for me to place myself back in the Dennets' splendid drawing room. Again I see the cloud of blue smoke rise from Allan's pipe and disperse in the light of the floor lamp. I believe I am conscious of the flavor of one of Allan's cocktails on my tongue, and my heart beats as at that time in the reconstructed presence of this man and the two women who laid claim to him. The outward appearance of a Christmas celebrated together in harmony and peace was deceptive. Following Brenda's wish, Allan was to decide this evening: He was to choose between the two women who sat in their chairs, apparently indifferent, enduring a confrontation they could justify only by their state of intense agitation. It was not difficult to decide which of the two had the best chance with Allan. His glance, that of a wounded animal, pierced the really fascinating Sally Whitebrook. In spite of her thinness and her rather wild getup, she was attractive and possessed an un-American individuality; she had a refreshing and beneficial effort on the elegant, somewhat dismal formality of the drawing room.

Brenda had lost her single advantage in the competition for her own husband: Sally, too, was expecting a baby. The affairs of the Dennets had reached a crisis since the summer in a way that had escaped me in Brenda's letters. I saw now that Brenda had kept much to herself. Allan had run away with Sally in the fall, and in some enchanted fisher's hut on the Canadian coast they had experienced an ecstatic two weeks of passion. After this manifestation of love Sally refused more decisively than before to relinquish

Allan. And besides that, the baby provided her with a certain right to him, almost the same right as that of his wife. The situation was precarious, tragic and comic at the same time, and it was clear to me that my role on this evening and throughout the whole holiday would be no purely passive one. The confirmation of my suspicions I learned from Allan himself.

When Brenda and her guest had gone upstairs and I was about to withdraw also, Allan held me fast by the arm and implored me to stay with him. He found he absolutely had to talk to me. I stayed, fluctuating between anger and joy. I did not possess his love; for him I would never be a woman in the sense I would have wished—so at least his confidence in the help I could be to him should have comforted me. But I showed him only the expression of the negative feelings that his request evoked in me, and with an indication of good-humored indignation I sat down in my chair again with a sigh. He paced back and forth in agitation.

I can still remember the sound of his voice exactly, as he then began to speak: It was different from before, almost pathetic, and yet bewildered and angry at its revealing lack of control. I always find it contemptible when men do not have the courage to acknowledge their feelings—a lack that they criticize most energetically in us women. But with Allan simply everything pleased me. I would probably have loved him still, even had he furnished worse proofs of cowardliness. I loved everything about him, even his insecurity and his weakness. I loved the way his larynx moved convulsively up and down, reminding me of the timid beating of the wings of a newborn bird. I loved the movement of his lower jaw, a sort of grinding motion—a certain sign of nervousness in Allan. I lost myself in such details, while his explanations and adjurations rushed past my ears; and I did not take in much more of them than the timbre, the sudden fluctuation of his voice, the modulation of tone. Allan was no orator and also not a good actor. He was honest down to the deepest layer of his unchanging potential, incapable of any dissimulation. In his love affair he had behaved, from the beginning, so ineptly only because he was so honorable, almost a little stupid, and because he was not burdened by an amorous past. Now in a self-incurred labyrinth he was groping along looking for an exit like a blind man, and I was supposed to serve him as Ariadne's thread.

"You are a Frenchwoman, Marcelle," he said. "You understand more about love. You have more aptitude for it. Tell me what your countrymen would do in my situation. I am convinced they would decide in favor of love." I swallowed his remark about my French talent for love—its absence may perhaps be the fault of a German ancestor—and said harshly:

"No. We are rationalists and not romantics. We always do what is pleasant as well as sensible."

"But what is pleasant is never sensible," Allen exclaimed.

"But for us it is," I maintained inflexibly.

Allan's difficulty, however, was that he did not know anymore where clear sailing was. The announcement of a second baby had torn the rudder completely out of his hands.

"You could adopt Sally's baby," I suggested. "It could grow up together with the other one."

"And not know who its mother really is? Never be truly loved?" Allan roared. "No, never!"

He seemed to me amateurishly pathetic and a little ridiculous. He settled opposite me on the stuffed arm of a chair and leaned over close to me. That was almost too much. I lit a cigarette and leaned far back.

"Another possibility would be to postpone the decision," said Allan slowly, suddenly calm. "We could wait for the birth of the babies. Since I very much want a girl, I would belong to the woman who gave birth to a girl."

I laughed out loud. A lottery with fetuses: a remarkable novelty. I reproached the young Don Juan, telling him that so much tension could perhaps be injurious to health during pregnancy, and above all that it was a little unfair to forsake the one who, not entirely without his own participation, was blessed only with a boy.

"You are being flippant," Allan maintained, "flippant like all the French."

He did not seem to notice how paradoxical this very assertion was after his strange suggestion. I enjoyed ridiculing him even more. Love never exists completely without the wish to offend and to injure, and unrequited love often borders on hate.

"And what would happen if they were both girls or both boys?" I asked. "The decision would have to be made dependent on other characteristics besides sex: hair color, sturdiness, intelligence. One would have to differentiate. . . . "

"Oh, be quiet," Allan interrupted and jumped up again. He lowered his voice and continued ceremoniously: "I thought you would help me. I believed you would take it upon yourself to talk to Brenda or to Sally, whichever one was to be left."

I fear nothing so much as sentimentality because it is so foreign to me that it affects me from sheer curiosity. I noticed that Allan had gone so far as to become hopelessly sentimental. I regarded him as he stood in the middle of the room, tall and slim, very handsome and very masculine, and I was on fire from the secret, bitter desire to be joined here with him in another kind of intimacy than this less than gratifying one that had been presented to me without my requesting it. His lips quivered, lips not made to shape rational words but seemingly to have as their only destiny the creation of confusion. His entire, masculine beauty was in this moment negative; its power to make someone happy had fallen victim to the power of destruction. There he stood like the accused, a criminal on account of his innocent vocation for passion. Not only the two women who loved him were his victims—and very incidentally I, too—he himself was a victim to a high degree. He was the victim of his own divine body, his masculine strength, with which he could not help winning effortlessly every contest over womanhood.

"You were clever, Marcelle," he said disconsolately, "one should not marry. In that one tiny moment, that second in which one utters that momentous 'I do,' one cannot answer for one's invulnerability to the temptations of a whole lifetime. It is idiocy, a presumption, an overestimation of one's own power of resistance, which one can simply not be responsible for."

I was silent. I would gladly have told him that I had not remained unmarried out of cleverness and that the idiocy was only in marrying someone whom one did not love enough. But since I would have had to explain to him how complicated the examination of one's own emotional power was, I remained silent, more from inertia than because of the certainty that he would still not understand.

"I must have Sally," I heard him say, suddenly stricken, completely changed, at last in a tone of honest, desperate certainty. I looked up and was alarmed. He had sat down at the desk, his elbows propped on the top, and buried his head in his hands. I saw only his smooth, chestnut-brown hair in an unfamiliar, extremely charming disorder.

This moment is perhaps the most distinct one in my memory; it will be unforgettable. An intense desire seized me to stand up, to go over to him, and to touch his hair, to offer myself to Allan as something that had lost its value anyway and that he should use, in that way making it valuable again; something he could handle as he pleased. I had the feeling that the moment of my deliverance had come, and perhaps even of his. Desire and hope easily create an excess of self-conceit. I saw myself next to him, I saw the glance with which he looked up at me, roused by my imaginary touch, still hesitating between surprised resistance and happy acceptance. I felt his mouth on my hot lips, which were insane and ardent and at most twenty years old, and to the contact of our heads I allowed that of our bodies to follow: I melted away.

But of course I remained sitting there without knowing if it was smart or stupid. I remained sitting there because I would have been ashamed to be rejected and because I would have been too inept in my amorous state to put the stroking of his hair on a basis of purely maternal sentiment when he looked up questioningly. He would have understood everything, and the disclosure even of an unrequited love is only desirable between the ages of fifteen and twenty-five. What business of Allan's was my bad luck, that during all of my years I had never once experienced an unhappy love? I had no desire for Allan to acknowledge my forty years, against whose dignity and precepts I would have been transgressing, had I followed my youthful feelings. And so I remained sitting there and busied myself with the role that he himself had assigned to me. I spoke with him, advised him well, asked questions and let him ask, and answered. Allan remained firm. His love for Sally was something elemental, irrational, and incorruptible—he had to follow it.

"Don't you love Brenda anymore at all?" I asked objectively. The more excessive his conduct became, the more it drove me to a prosaic, realistic, somewhat brutal inquiry.

"Oh, yes," he contradicted me warmly. "I have a good, affectionate feeling for her. A kindly feeling, you know, but nothing more of that feeling that creates the aura between a man and a woman."

I understood only too well. I knew about Allan's "aura," after all.

"But Sally intoxicates me. I desire her every minute. This is something that I did not know: passion."

His voice became very deep with the word that I had so often used in reference to him and me and that he used now for the first time in my presence. Unfortunately his precise meaning was in direct contradiction to my fantasies.

"I always felt that our marriage lacked something without being able to recognize what that something was. Now I have been forced to realize that Brenda and I are not compatible," he finished arrogantly; but he was absolutely right. I was lost in reflection about how in our world good, human feelings are inevitably overcome by passionate, intoxicating ones. Man's drive toward self-destruction spurs him on and never abandons him. He needs no pity.

I stood up. I dared to interrupt prematurely a meeting with the man I loved. I had the feeling of having failed, and I believed I was obligated to make a little joke in conclusion to save my honor. Though I deeply longed for the fervor of passion, I firmly declined it in regard to comforting advice in emotional questions, particularly with the object of my love. So I casually said, as I offered my hand in leaving:

"My only advice is to shoot yourself. I knew a Frenchman who did that in a similar case. And things were not even so complicated for him."

His disconcerted look, and the way he let my hand fall after he had clasped it in an agreeably firm manner, should have alerted me. But I was blind and considered only the biting effect of my words.

"That would be best for the two ladies," I continued. "Even with children it helps to avoid arguments and jealousy by simply eliminating the object of their desires, longed for too much, or by relinquishing it to a third, neutral person."

Here I stopped and observed him. Was it possible that he did not notice the insinuation? He had turned his face away, and I saw only his profile, hazily illuminated by the lamp, and the up and down and up again of the little bird imprisoned in his larynx. He swallowed a few times, and I might even have imagined that he was weeping. But he was not. Still turned away he asked:

"Do you mean that seriously?"

I can never slip back easily from a tone of playful mockery to one of gravity. So I nodded and said:

"Naturally. That way problems are eliminated and conflicts avoided. After a year of mourning, whether it is for your death or for your defection to a third party"—Allan made a contemptuous gesture that sobered me—"for whatever reason, after a year the enemies will have made their peace and two little new Allans, male or female, one a child of love and one a child of intent, will play peacefully with each other in your garden."

"But the newspapers, the acquaintances, the questions of the curious?"

Allan's compliance with my nonsense did not make me suspicious.

"There are enough excuses there," I said. "Have you by any chance had professional problems?"

Allan thought about it.

"Not enough to cause a suicide," he said.

I reflected a bit, with pretended gravity on my knitted brow.

"Never mind," I warded off all his doubts. "The uproar over your sensational death will have faded away when the children are big enough to investigate the death of their father. The world forgets quickly. Too much is happening for all that to be able to retain its importance."

I took leave of him and went to bed. I swallowed three sedatives, the same thing that Brenda and Sally had done two hours before, and did not have enough time left to bewail my difficult and unjust fate of being a woman unloved and thus alienated from all meaning and purpose.

The tragedy of Allan's death lies in its humor. None of us, put to sleep artificially, was awakened by the report of his pistol. The maid had the day off and did not come back until everything had already happened. Unsuspecting she went by the closed door of the drawing room. The silence of the house seemed warranted to her, not suspicious or alarming.

On the holiday morning we had our breakfast trays brought to our beds, but had given the maid instructions to make her appearance only upon our ringing. That Allan did not ring seemed surprising to no one. To Brenda it was customary that on Sundays he even occasionally slept through lunch. For that reason we did not "awaken" him either when we sat down in the breakfast room at meal time. Besides it turned out to be less complicated and less agitating without his presence.

I will never forget the cry Brenda emitted when after the meal she went searching for cigarettes in the drawing room. Stretched out on the rug lay Allan, dead in a tiny pool of blood. Over his forehead ran a dark-red, encrusted streak. I was astonished how little blood needed to be shed to kill a man like Allan. He was still completely himself; his body did not look dead, and still he would never again be restored to life. I do not know if Brenda and Sally cried as much as I.

The holidays in the company of a relentless and suspicious homicide squad was a severe nervous strain for the three of us. I was furious with Allan because he had forced us into this ridiculous, histrionic situation. I departed as soon as I was no longer needed. And along with a terrible guilty conscience I took more sorrow with me back to my college than Brenda could suspect. It made no difference to me whether she took my premature departure for indifference, lack of compassion, or a manifestation of selfishness. Naturally I had told her nothing about the frivolous end of my last conversation with Allan. Nor the police either. If they had known how much I loved him, how suspicious I would have looked, how easily they would have found an explanation for Allan's death. With the grief that I could conceal too poorly, I would betray my love. I had to get away.

Without suspecting it or wanting it, I had been right in my thoughtless prognosis: Brenda recovered more easily from Allan's death than from his unfaithfulness. I had to take cognizance of this incomprehensible phenomenon in the character of feminine emotion, whether I wanted to or not. Brenda's letters became more and more positive, and they even contained a certain subdued pleasure in the anticipation of the baby, whose existence proclaimed itself ever more clearly and in whom she—I could no longer doubt it—would find a sterling substitute for the man who had engendered it. The fate of the two women who, when he was still alive, would not have given him up under any circumstances, was just what I had prophesied in derision. Now and then Brenda mentioned Sally, who had found a good, if somewhat limited, young man who was prepared to take on the fatherhood of the product of Allan's love. Sally was without illusions with regard to the man, but full of confidence and joy in the expectation of a life with the child, with the incarnation of the memory of a love that she could now give up because she had to. I am certain Allan would have been disappointed at the peaceful reception that his death had found: From his death came life.

In April Aline Dennet saw the light of day; two months later Alice Turpin followed. Poor Allan, fortunate Allan! What new complications you avoided when you followed the impulse inspired by a half-crazed person who—this much I know for sure—loved you more than the two women who destroyed you. A year ago today, at this same hour, you were very close to me, and I almost kissed you. But I felt the weight of each single one of my years and especially the years that were more than yours, and I did not want to be laughed at. For that reason I took flight from the confusion of my emotions to my cherished supply of irony, and my rashness killed you just as much as the importunate love of Brenda and Sally. But I can surely take comfort that my frivolous proposals alone could not have decided you. Probably the pistol was prepared already and the decision already made, when I only strengthened it.

I present a pitiable picture when I attempt to justify myself in this way. Should I not be satisfied that in the life of the man who taught me to love and to feel, something I had not learned to do through years of boredom, I have at least one share: the guilt for his death?

Translated by Jeanne R. Willson

Biographies

ILSE AICHINGER (1921–   ), Austrian-born widow of famed poet and radio play author Günter Eich, is a celebrated poet, novelist, and short-prose author. In 1952, she received the Group 47 Prize for her remarkable story "Spiegelgeschichte" (Mirror story). The same year saw publication of a collection of stories, *Rede unter dem Galgen* (Speech under the gallows), which contains her most widely praised story "Der Gefesselte" (The bound man). Aichinger lives in southern Germany.

JUREK BECKER (1937–   ), former East German who lives in what used to be West Berlin, is a born storyteller, a distinguished novelist and essayist, who makes points in his novels with revealing, luminous anecdotes. "The End of the Line," first published in *Dimension*'s special issue of East German writing in 1973, captured the imagination and empathy of many readers, who could not forget the blue lamp. Becker is an author noted for extraordinary frankness. He is the author of *Jacob, the Liar* (also made into an unforgettable film) and other novels.

HANS BENDER (1919–   ) is probably Germany's best writer of short prose and the author of early novels. With Walter Höllerer, in 1954, he founded the premiere German literary magazine, *Akzente*, which he continued to edit after Höllerer's resignation as coeditor, and which in 1979 he turned over to the editorship of author/publisher Michael Krüger (the Hanser Verlag in Munich). Bender is an anthologist of note and an admired critic. His early novel *Wunschkost (The Mud Sled)* is a fictional account of his own travails as a Russian prisoner of war in World War II. The story "The Wolves Are Coming Back" is probably the most anthologized German short story of modern times, read by every German school child. Bender lives in Cologne.

PETER BICHSEL (1934–   ), a Swiss, made a name for himself with short prose while a school teacher, having received the Group 47

Prize in 1967. He is an experimentalist in part ("A Table Is a Table") and a satirist as well of Swiss and other mores. His literary forte, the short-prose form, is the instrument with which he practices his at times razor-sharp satire.

WOLFGANG BORCHERT (1921–47), famous for his radio play/drama *Draußen vor der Tür (The Man Outside)*, also wrote marvelously simple and laconic short stories. An unwilling and resistant soldier, repeatedly charged with antiwar activities, including telling political jokes, Borchert's punishment was imprisonment followed by front-line service, which resulted in the ruin of his health. He died in a Swiss hospital on the eve of the premiere of his famous play.

THOMAS BRASCH (1945–   ), son of an East German political functionary, was born in England but grew up in East Germany, where as a university student he got into trouble with the Communist authorities because of "political recidivism" and his protest in 1968 against the invasion of Czechoslovakia. After his first volume of stories, *Vor den Vätern sterben die Söhne* (Sons die before fathers), was rejected by East German publishers, he was permitted to move to West Berlin in 1976. He is a poet and dramatist as well as a writer of prose.

HANS CHRISTOPH BUCH (1944–   ), novelist, essayist, short story writer, and intrepid journalist, lives in Berlin. He is the author of a monumental fictional trilogy on the travails of the Haitian people, a wry combination of history and imagination. His audacious prose ruthlessly examines human flaws and foibles but is curiously palliative and positive, supremely empathetic and humanistic.

HANS J. FRÖHLICH (1932–86) was a radio play author, novelist, and short story writer. A combination of experimentalist and traditionalist, he made good use of surprise and fateful coincidence. His fascination with Franz Schubert, which resulted in a biography in 1978, brought his writing to maturity. The story here was written in 1985.

MARTIN GRIZMEK (1950–   ) is a novelist, literary critic (Walter Benjamin, Rolf Dieter Brinkmann) and short story author. His collection of stories *Stillstand des Herzens (Heartstop)* appeared in 1982 (translated into English by Breon Mitchell), followed by the novel *Die Beschattung* (Shadowing) in 1989. A second volume of stories appeared in 1995.

HANNAH JOHANSEN (1939–) is a Swiss novelist and short story author who lives near Zurich. Her novels include *Die Stehende Uhr* (The stopped clock), 1978, and *Die Analphabetin* (The illiterate woman), 1982. A collection of stories, *Über den Wunsch, sich wohl zu fühlen* (On the desire to feel good), appeared in 1985. She has translated works by American authors Donald Barthelme, Grace Paley, and Walker Percy.

MARIE LUISE KASCHNITZ (1902–74) was highly regarded as a poet as well as an author of fiction. Known in her later years primarily as a poet, her poetic voice lent a special musicality to her prose. She was the author of numerous novels, story collections, and volumes of poetry. "Long Shadows" is the title story from *Lange Schatten*, stories that were published in 1960.

BARBARA KÖNIG (1925–) lives near Munich and is the author of stories, novels, and radio plays. Her short novel *Der Beschenkte* (1980) appeared in English as *The Beneficiary* in 1994, in a translation by Roslyn Theobald. The entertaining humorous/earnest reflection on aging here is from a longer work, *Die Schule des Alterns* (The school of aging), which will appear with the Hanser Verlag.

GERHARD KÖPF (1948–) is a professor (University of Duisburg) as well as an author of note (twin callings that critics in Germany seem to frown upon). Undaunted, Köpf is a playwright, novelist, and storyteller. The story here is framed in his novel *Der Weg nach Eden* (The way to Eden) and has since experienced a new existence as a J. D. Salinger riddle in a retelling entitled "Ein besonderer Anlaß" (A special occasion). Köpf's novels *There Is No Borges* and *Papa's Suitcase* appeared in 1993 and 1995, respectively, with George Braziller in translations by A. Leslie Willson. His most recent novel is *Nurmi, oder die Reise zu den Forellen* (Nurmi; or, the trout trip), 1996. He lives in Munich.

GÜNTER KUNERT (1929–), a marvelous satirist and graphic artist, author of poetry, essays, short prose, radio plays, and novels, was for many years a thorn in the side of the East German state security forces, the Stasi. His semester at the University of Texas at Austin in the fall of 1972 produced a nonfiction account of America entitled *Der andere Planet* (The other planet). Kunert is noted for his imaginative prose, his uncompromising honesty, and the wry way he looks at the world. At first glance an uncompromising realist, he is always ready to jump into fantasy. He moved to West Germany in the summer of 1979 and lives with his wife Marianne and several cats in a remodeled schoolhouse near Hamburg.

SIEGFRIED LENZ (1926–) is one of Germany's best-known novelists, as well as the author of dramas and radio plays. A superb stylist, he has written notable stories as well. His novel *The German Lesson* was a best-seller in English translation. The story "A Helping Hand" is a very funny story about academia. The tale "The Blindfold" (also a two-act play) is a hair-raising story of the tyrannical subjugation of a people (in a village, where all children are blinded). He lives in Hamburg.

REINHARD LETTAU (1929–), a talented storyteller, became a political activist during the Vietnam era and was tormented by a schism between his artistic integrity as an author and his far-left political views. He finally stopped publishing fiction and settled down as a professor at the University of California at San Diego. His prose is distinguished by an astonishing and original spatial perspective.

ANGELIKA MECHTEL (1943–) was one of Germany's earliest modern-day feminists who for a time published books at a small press based in a spacious barn near Munich. A poet as well, she is best known for her unorthodox but thematically timely prose in stories and novels.

CHRISTOPH MECKEL (1935–), a unique author of poetry and short fiction, is also a fantastic graphic artist. His work is in many ways childlike, both in the features of his literary imagination and in his graphic work. Meckel's grandfather, a stonemason, inscribed his work with the Chinese character for "the doer, the maker, the creator," which contains the same idea as the Greek word for "the maker," from which the English word *poet* is derived. Meckel signs his graphic work with the same character, even involving it in his etchings (falling headfirst with bombs, for example). Many volumes by Meckel are illustrated with his own graphic work. He lives in Berlin and France.

STEN NADOLNY (1942–   ) taught history and was a cinematic camera director before publishing his first novel *Netzkarte* (Season ticket) after receiving the Ingeborg Bachmann Prize in 1980. He is the author of two other novels and a number of stories.

CHRISTA REINIG (1926–   ) is a poet and author of short prose and novels. She has a sharply honed lyric voice, a witty and ruthless imagination, and observes the world around her with a penetrating gaze. Her novel *Die Entmannung* (Emasculation), in which a man is bereft psychologically of his masculinity by a circle of women, takes feminism to its logical extreme. Reinig lives in Munich.

WOLFDIETRICH SCHNURRE (1920–89) was a poet and a prolific author of radio and television scripts as well as volumes of prose, novels, and stories. He read "The Burial" at the very first meeting of authors who formed the renowned Group 47, whose final meeting was held near Prague in 1990 (after an interval that extended from 1968 to 1990). The story—which was translated in the early 1980s by a gifted young student at the University of Arkansas (who died soon after from a terribly swift cancer)—is famous in Germany. It exemplifies the attempt by postwar German writers to come to terms with their German language, which had been despoiled by Nazi jargon, and to adopt the laconic style of writers like Ernest Hemingway.

GABRIELE WOHMANN (1932–   ) has written voluminously—poetry, stories, novels, and radio plays—mostly with a familial focus that examines relationships and society's impediments. Her modest and shy personality masks a disarmingly oblique prose style that, with the objectivity of a scalpel, reveals layers of social mores and distinguishes her fiction. Her short novel *Der Kirschbaum* was her first book in English translation, by Jeanne R. Willson, entitled *The Cherry Tree* (1994).

Acknowledgments

Every reasonable effort has been made to locate the owners of rights to previously published translations printed here. We gratefully acknowledge permission to reprint the following material:

"The Bound Man" by Ilse Aichinger. *Der Gefesselt.* © 1954 by S. Fischer Verlag, Frankfurt am Main.

"End of the Line" by Jurek Becker appeared in a special DDR issue of *Dimension*, 1973, and is reprinted with the kind permission of the author and of A. Leslie Willson.

"The Wolves are Coming Back" by Hans Bender. From Hans Bender, *Worte Bilder Menschen,* München: Carl Hanser Verlag, 1969.

"There Is No Such Place as America" by Peter Bichsel: from *Kindergeschichten.* © 1969, 1995 by Luchterhand Literaturverlag. The English translation by Michael Hamburger is reprinted with the kind permission of the translator.

"On that Tuesday," "The Bread," and "Rats Do Sleep at Night" by Wolfgang Borchert: from *The Man Outside.* Copyright © 1971 by New Directions Publishing Corporation. Reprinted by permission of New Directions. Published in Great Britain and Commonwealth by Marion Boyars Ltd., London.

"An Angel of Death" by Hans J. Fröhlich, "The Liar" by Martin Grzimek, and "The Man Who Got Stuck" by Sten Nadolny appeared in *Dimension* volume 18/2, and are reprinted with the kind permission of A. Leslie Willson.

"Long Shadows" by Marieluise Kaschnitz is reprinted with permission of Claassen Verlag, Düsseldorf.

The English translation by Christopher Middleton of "Fabulous Monologue" by Günter Kunert appeared in *Delos* number 4 and is reprinted with permission of the University of Texas at Austin.

"Luke, Gentle Servant" by Siegfried Lenz. From the collection *Jäger des Spotts. Geschichten aus dieser Zeit.* © Hoffmann und Campe Verlag, Hamburg 1958. the English translation by Kathrine Talbot is reprinted by permission of *London Magazine*, 30 Thurloe Place, London SW7.

"Manig" by Reinhard Lettau: From *Schwierigkeiten beim Häuserbauen. Auftritt Manigs* München: Carl Hanser Verlag, 1979.

"The Cuckoo's Mate" by Agelika Mechtel is reprinted with the kind permission of the author.

"In the Land of Umnbramauts" by Christoph Meckel is reprinted with the kind permission of the author.

"Three Ships" by Christa Reinig: *Drei Schiffe.* Düsseldorf 1978, © by Verlag Eremiten-Presse.

"The Funeral" by Wolfdietrich Schnurre, from *Erzählungen 1945–1965* © Paul List Verlag KG, München.

"The Irresistible Man" by Gabriele Wohmann is reprinted with the kind permission of the author.

"The Bottles of Venice" by Gerhard Köpf from the novel *Der Weg nach Eden* © 1994, Piper Verlag München.

"Fritzleben, for Example" by Hans Christoph Buch, "Virginia" by Hannah Johansen, "Waiting for Wisdom" by Barbara König, and "The Bottles of Venice" by Gerhard Köpf from *Dimension*, volume 20. Courtesy A. Leslie Willson.

THE GERMAN LIBRARY
in 100 Volumes

Friedrich Schiller
Wallenstein and Mary Stuart
Edited by Walter Hinderer

Friedrich Schiller
Essays
Edited by Walter Hinderer

Johann Wolfgang von Goethe
*The Sufferings of Young Werther
and Elective Affinities*
Edited by Victor Lange
Forewords by Thomas Mann

German Romantic Criticism
Edited by A. Leslie Willson
Foreword by Ernst Behler

Friedrich Hölderlin
Hyperion and Selected Poems
Edited by Eric L. Santner

Philosophy of German Idealism
Edited by Ernst Behler

G. W. F. Hegel
*Encyclopedia of the Philosophical Sciences in Outline and
Critical Writings*
Edited by Ernst Behler

Heinrich von Kleist
Plays
Edited by Walter Hinderer
Foreword by E. L. Doctorow

E. T. A. Hoffmann
Tales
Edited by Victor Lange

Georg Büchner
Complete Works and Letters
Edited by Walter Hinderer and Henry J. Schmidt

German Fairy Tales
Edited by Helmut Brackert and
Volkmar Sander
Foreword by Bruno Bettelheim

German Literary Fairy Tales
Edited by Frank G. Ryder and
Robert M. Browning
Introduction by Gordon Birrell
Foreword by John Gardner

F. Grillparzer, J. H. Nestroy,
F. Hebbel
Nineteenth Century German Plays
Edited by Egon Schwarz in collaboration with
Hannelore M. Spence

Heinrich Heine
Poetry and Prose
Edited by Jost Hermand and Robert C. Holub
Foreword by Alfred Kazin

Heinrich Heine
The Romantic School and Other Essays
Edited by Jost Hermand and Robert C. Holub

Heinrich von Kleist and Jean Paul
German Romantic Novellas
Edited by Frank G. Ryder and Robert M. Browning
Foreword by John Simon

German Romantic Stories
Edited by Frank Ryder
Introduction by Gordon Birrell

German Opera Libretti
Edited by James Steakley

German Songs
Edited by Inke Pinkert-Sältzer

German Poetry from 1750 to 1900
Edited by Robert M. Browning
Foreword by Michael Hamburger

Karl Marx, Friedrich Engels, August Bebel, and Others
German Essays on Socialism in the Nineteenth Century
Edited by Frank Mecklenburg and Manfred Stassen

Gottfried Keller
Stories
Edited by Frank G. Ryder
Foreword by Max Frisch

Wilhelm Raabe
Novels
Edited by Volkmar Sander
Foreword by Joel Agee

Theodor Fontane
Short Novels and Other Writings
Edited by Peter Demetz
Foreword by Peter Gay

Theodor Fontane
Delusions, Confusions and The Poggenpuhl Family
Edited by Peter Demitz
Foreword by J. P. Stern
Introduction by William L. Zwiebel

Friedrich Nietzsche
Philosophical Writings
Edited by Reinhold Grimm
and Caroline Molina y Vedia

Hans Magnus Enzensberger
Critical Essays
Edited by Reinhold Grimm and
Bruce Armstrong
Foreword by John Simon

All volumes available in hardcover and paperback editions at your bookstore or from the publisher. For more information on The German Library write to: The Continuum Publishing Company, 370 Lexington Avenue, New York, NY 10017.